The

Empirical

Stance

Other volumes in the Terry Lecture Series available from Yale University Press

The
Empirical
Stance

Bas C. van Fraassen

Yale University Press   *New Haven & London*

Published with assistance from the Ernst Cassirer Publication Fund.

Set in Minion Roman types by Keystone Typesetting, Inc.

Printed in the United States of America.

The Library of Congress has cataloged the hardcover edition as follows:

Van Fraassen, Bas C., 1941–

The empirical stance / Bas C. van Fraassen.

p. cm. — (The Terry lectures)

Includes bibliographical references and index.

ISBN 0-300-08874-4 (cloth : alk. paper)

1. Empiricism. I. Title. II. Series.

B816 .V36 2001

146'.44—dc21

2001046649

ISBN 0-300-10306-9 (pbk. : alk. paper)

A catalogue record for this book is available from the British Library.

The paper in this book meets the guidelines for permanence and durability of the Committee on Production Guidelines for Book Longevity of the Council on Library Resources.

10 9 8 7 6 5 4 3 2

The Dwight Harrington Terry Foundation Lectures on Religion in the Light of Science and Philosophy

The deed of gift declares that "the object of this foundation is not the promotion of scientific investigation and discovery, but rather the assimilation and interpretation of that which has been or shall be hereafter discovered, and its application to human welfare, especially by the building of the truths of science and philosophy into the structure of a broadened and purified religion. The founder believes that such a religion will greatly stimulate intelligent effort for the improvment of human conditions and the advancement of the race in strength and excellence of character. To this end it is desired that a series of lectures be given by men eminent in their respective departments, on ethics, the history of civilization and religion, biblical research, all sciences and branches of knowledge which have an important bearing on the subject, all the great laws of nature, especially of evolution . . . also such interpretations of literature and sociology as are in accord with the spirit of this foundation, to the end that the Christian spirit may be nurtured in the fullest light of the world's knowledge and that mankind may be helped to attain its highest possible welfare and happiness upon this earth." The present work constitutes the latest volume published on this foundation.

voor mijne bonne amie

Contents

Lecture 2. *What Is Empiricism and What Could It Be?*

Lecture 3. *Scientific Revolution/Conversion as a Philosophical Problem* 64

Preface

What is empiricism, and what could it be? All the philosophers we count as empiricist rejected the positions of their predecessors, even while acknowledging them as their philosophical heroes. For each of them, the question what empiricism could be or could become was more important than regret over past failures. So it has been for me as well. In an earlier book, *The Scientific Image,* I tried to define what empirical science is according to an empiricist today. That does not answer the question of what it is to be an empiricist.[1]

The Dwight H. Terry Lectures at Yale University gave me the opportunity to confront this question and to present a range of related, subsidiary questions that an aspirant empiricist must face along the way. I reject not only most of the answers but many of the questions concerning knowledge and belief that have historically been associated with empiricism. But I join the traditional empiricists' revolts against metaphysics. Their main epistemological concerns appear very saliently in philosophical problems about scientific and conceptual revolutions. They appear also in the not unrelated ruptures between different ways of seeing or conceiving of ourselves, in that perilous place where future waves break on the shores of tradition. Accordingly, the first and second lectures present a general empiricist philosophical stance, and the third, fourth and fifth focus on those two areas of concern.[2]

When Dean Richard Woods invited me to give the Terry Lectures I was surprised as well as honored, for my work has been mainly in the philosophy of science and not of religion. I do not engage in philosophical theology, and I stay far from the "science and religion" debates. But Dean Woods assured me that I had a free hand; and on reflection I had to admit to myself that my work has touched on myth and religion.[3] The Terry Lectures also challenged me to express my views to a general audience.

Yale gave me my first opportunity to teach philosophy, at a time that I shall always remember with some nostalgia. Colleagues there whose thought continued to influence me in all the intervening years included Richmond Thomason, Robert Stalnaker, Henry Margenau, Norwood Russell Hanson, Robert Fogelin, Frederick Fitch, and Charles Daniels. I want to thank Dean Woods and Robert Adams as well as Keith DeRose, Laurie Paul, Dianne Witte, Nicholas Wolterstorff, and many others at Yale University for making me welcome again and engaging me intellectually in such a hospitable context.

My debts in this book are numerous; most I can only indicate in the notes. Special thanks go to Paul Teller, both for his extensive commentary and suggestions for revision of the manuscript as well as for his stimulating recent contributions to closely related topics. Anja Jauernig commented helpfully and critically on almost every page. I received valuable comments on versions of this material also from Arnold Burms, Michel Ghins, Beatrice Longuenesse, Bradley Monton, Jerold Neu, Richard Otte, Alvin Plantinga, Gideon Rosen, Sherri Roush, Eleonore Stump, and Steven Tainer. I have a very special debt to my late colleague David Lewis, whose views and audacious stance in philosophy have helped me so much to define my own. The sprinkling of references to his work do not reflect adequately how much I have learned from his very different ideas as well as from his personal engagement in philosophy. Catherine Chevalley made me very conscious of how my work relates to certain themes in Continental philosophy.[4] To all these colleagues I am sincerely grateful. I also want to thank Princeton University, Yale University, the University of Louvain-la-Neuve (where I presented part of this material in the Chaire Cardinal Mercier), the Infinity Foundation, and the National Endowment for the Humanities, for financial support to provide me with research and writing time. Along the way I accrued also some special debts as I struggled with those empiricist wishes. Paul Benacerraf precepted for me in a philosophy of science course where he did his best to keep me on a straight and narrow path with respect to realism and scientific revolutions, and was tremendously supportive in other ways. Hilary Putnam, in conference encounters from Taxco to Thessaloniki, kept me convinced that reason cannot be naturalized. Jill Sigman I thank not only for her support and severe philosophical critique but also for her work of astonishing transformations that never allow philosophy to sever itself from art.

Introduction

When Sophocles depicts Oedipus in conflict with Tiresias the prophet, he shows us the tensions between science and religion in embryo. The king whose intellect had saved the city, the puzzle solver, represents the increasingly secular progressive forces against blind tradition. Or so at least it seems to the king himself. But this king is blind to his own condition and ends the play blinded entirely by his self-inflicted wounds. The situation is not without its irony or its tragedy. Nor is it a historical accident of ancient Greece, of course. We have found ourselves in this tension in every century since then.

I do not intend to try for either a head-on confrontation or an attempted reconciliation. For I see this tension as part of a larger problem, the perennial problem of philosophy. In every century we must reinterpret ourselves to ourselves. We do not come into our century with a tabula rasa. We must interpret what we find ourselves to be, with an eye to what we have been and to what we could be and can be. That is the perennial, ever-recurring task, ever new. What we find includes both science and religion, the secular and the spiritual—and what we transform in our reinterpretation includes contrasts and boundaries between the two.

In these lectures I present a personal response to philosophy as I found it, try to interpret what it was and is, and be quite frankly partisan about what it could and can be. I mean to offer an empiricist view. But no empiricism today can be empiricism as it has been. The empiricist tradition, like any tradition, cannot live unless it renews itself. The empiricism we need now, if it is to be viable at all, must be as different from the various empiricisms of Cambridge, Vienna, and Berlin as theirs were from Locke's or Hume's. I realize that I can only do a very little toward bringing this about. The little I can do now has three major parts.

First of all I present the empiricist recurrent rebellion against metaphysics. As I see it, analytic philosophy—which is the strand to which I belong—began with a revolution that was subverted by reactionary forces. I am speaking here of reversion to a seventeenth-century style of metaphysics. I do not reject all metaphysics, but this reversion I see as disastrous. Paradoxically, this disaster seems to be worst in two areas that scarcely relate to each other at all. I mean, on one hand, the area loosely characterized as "science and religion" studies and, on the other, academic analytic philosophy. Both suffer from unacknowledged as well as explicit metaphysics. A shoemaker does well to stick to his last, so I will concentrate on philosophy. The largest question there is precisely what a philosophy is and can be other than a metaphysical theory. Indeed, as I try to show, such paradigmatic examples of metaphysics as materialism or physicalism are not what they purport to be. The problem of appearance and reality affects first of all philosophy itself. I argue for a view of philosophy as stance, as existential.

Empiricist philosophers have always concentrated on epistemology, the study of knowledge, belief, and opinion, with a distinct tendency to advocate the importance of opinion. In the third and fourth lectures I attempt to confront the problem of knowledge as we now face it, by focusing on the intelligibility of scientific revolutions. Revolutionary developments show us a very different face, depending on whether we approach them from the past or from the future. From the pre-revolutionary perspective, the change in view is inconceivable, absurd, unratifiable; postrevolution, it can be justified, ratified, rationalized. Since we do in fact endorse some of the radical conversions in our collective and individual past, our epistemology must make room for such changes, and make room for them not only in our past but even in our own possible epistemic futures. Is science preserved in truth when it passes through such a radical transformation? If so, how, and how can we reasonably think so? More generally, are we preserved in truth—we, in our dealings with science, with our reality, with ourselves? In the last analysis, I argue, the highly theoretical, epistemological problem is not an academic but existential question.

Science moves forward by discarding past images and forgetting the agonies of those fratricidal, matricidal conceptual wars. But Oedipus and Tiresias keep facing each other in every successive generation, perplexed and anguished by how the other sees the world and how the other's vision is transforming that shared world. In the final lecture I have tried to reflect on that tension as it exists now. This king and the prophet, as often as not, face each other not simply in society but as protagonists in our own minds. Taking sides is not the way out when we play both roles or are simultaneously drawn to both sides. Nor is mutual respect enough; each is most diminishing and condescending when honoring the other in its own terms. For the final lecture I tried to spell out what it is to be secular, in a way that is intelligible to both secular and religious. I failed, but the partial, imperfect approximation I found myself with may perhaps still point to some sense of mutual understanding.

Against Analytic Metaphysics

'Tis mean Ambition to define / A single World:
To many I aspire . . .
This busy, vast, enquiring Soul / Brooks no Controul:
'Tis very curious too.
—THOMAS TRAHERNE, "Insatiableness"

Let us begin with a statement that I am sure you must have heard before:

God is dead.

You are right if you take it that I am serious about this. But what do I mean? When Pascal died, a scrap of paper was found in the lining of his coat. On it was written "The God of Abraham, Isaac and Jacob, not the God of the philosophers." Pascal was a contemporary of Descartes in the seventeenth century, and the God who appears in Descartes' *Meditations on First Philosophy* was the paradigmatic philosophers' God. He is of course omniscient, omnipotent, and omnibenevolent, and he is designed precisely so as to guarantee that everything that Descartes says is true. So Pascal had a very good example near at hand. Here is what I mean when I say that God is dead:

The God of the philosophers is dead.

This God is dead because he is a creature of metaphysics—that type of metaphysics—and metaphysics is dead.

1. LIVING WITH A DEAD METAPHYSICS

You realize that this point is not exactly new: it was precisely Kant's message about the metaphysics of his time. But even Kant's monumental work was not unambiguous in its impact. The truly critical part of his First Critique was the Transcendental Dialectic. There Kant exposed the Illusions of Reason, the way in which reason overreaches itself in traditional metaphysics, and the limits of what can be achieved within the limits of reason alone. Here the unacknowledged presuppositions behind traditional metaphysics were brought to light through antinomies and paradoxes that this metaphysics was powerless to resolve. Given this work, it should never have been necessary again to go about demolishing the metaphysical enterprise. But on one hand Kant's arguments were not faultless, and on the other there was a positive part to Kant's project that, in his successors, engendered a new metaphysics. About a century later the widespread rebellions against the Idealist tradition expressed the complaint that Reason had returned to its cherished Illusions, if perhaps in different ways.

There was more to Kant's message. Somehow, in between the critical part and the part that engendered a new metaphysics, so to speak, Kant directed us to a practical question for philosophy. If Reason has after all such distinctive limits, is it not all the more important to look into what else there is to our existence, besides reason? We are right today to see the nineteenth century Idealists as prey once again to illusions of Reason, but it is also true that they listened to that additional challenge. That accounts, I think, for a sense of loss still felt when we look back to the (in other respects) necessary demise of idealism. What we lost was precisely the way idealism was after all not just a return to that discredited form of metaphysics.[1]

Since a good deal of philosophical and theological activity today is clearly within precisely *that* type of metaphysics, you may not believe in its demise. You may not wish it, either. You may have reacted instinctively with: But to reject metaphysics is automatically to say that God does not exist, that the divine is a fiction or mere myth. That was certainly one reaction to Kant. It has also its secular parallels: But to reject metaphysics, is that not also to reject the very concept of a person, a conscious being, and to settle for the spiritually anemic tastes of scientism? I do not believe so.

I reject metaphysics, and still I'll say that you exist and that you are a person, a conscious being. Of course, what it is to be a person, and what consciousness is, are both topics in metaphysics and have metaphysical theories written about them. So am I at once inconsistent? Only if these assertions about your existence can't be true unless some metaphysical theory about them is true, some metaphysical underpinning, as one says. But I see metaphysical concoctions not as underpinnings but as the canopies of baroque four-poster beds. . . . Metaphysical theories purport to interpret what we already understand to be the case. But to interpret is *to interpret into* something, something granted as already understood. Paradoxically, metaphysicians interpret what we initially understand into something hardly anyone understands, and then insist that we cannot do without that. To any incredulous listener they'll say: Construct a better alternative! But that just signals their invincible presumption that metaphysics is the sine qua non of understanding.

How could today's philosophy have reverted to the once moribund *vieux jeux* of metaphysics? The British and American idealism of a century ago, a metaphysics still hospitable to religion, died some time ago. At Yale it died a little later than elsewhere. . . . Yet with the rise of analytic philosophy something paradoxical happened. This movement began in a series of revolts, across Europe and America, against all forms of metaphysics. And lo, even before mid-century, some of its ablest adherents began to make the world safe for metaphysics again. Since then we have seen the growth of analytic ontology, analytic metaphysics, and it thrives today.

Or so it seems. I say that metaphysics is dead. What I see is false consciousness, a philosophy that has genuinely advanced beyond the past, but a philosophy that misunderstands itself.

2. ONTOLOGY REBORN

So what is our task today? The metaphysical enterprise, I argue, subverts our understanding both of our own humanity and of the divine—be it real or unreal—by its development of a detailed, intricate understanding of simulacra under the same names. One example is the purport of discussing the God of Abraham, Isaac, and Jacob while actually focused on the God of the philosophers. But the same sort of replacement by theoretical simulacra characterizes the enterprise throughout. In doing so it honors the letter while losing the spirit of every subject of significance in human existence. Our task: to show it up for what it is, demonstrate its impotence with respect to real questions of any importance, and bring into the light the precise way in which its mighty labors address simulacra of no importance at all.

How shall I go about this? I propose that we consider a very simple question or problem, admittedly in the domain of metaphysics, but the simpler and more elementary the better. If the discipline is shown up even there, the interested reader may then consider whether those flaws and failures do not also characterize more ambitious examples. If we had set about this three hundred years ago, we might very well have chosen the simple question, Does God exist?[2] Today that would not be a very good choice. Freedom or personal identity would be a good topic to choose, if it were not for their complexity, in which we would lose sight of the forest for the trees. We need a different example, one that should look sufficiently simple to us today.[3] I submit that the methodological critique will bear on the enterprise quite generally.

3. DOES THE WORLD EXIST?

To show you both the impotence and the collateral damage wrought by metaphysics, I must choose a question at once simple to answer, yet touching on something intuitively of genuine importance to us. The following question is surely among the very simplest we can ask:

Does the world exist?

The question is *not* whether the external world exists. I am not raising any Cartesian doubts. It is true: if we can ask this question, or any question at all, then we exist; and so, *something* exists. Let's agree in addition, right from the start, that we have no doubts about the reality of our bodies, our brains. But what about the world?

If the question seems trivial to you, that is because the answer seems so obvious. Surely even a child can answer it, once it has learned the words? But it is not trivial in another way: it does concern something of great importance to us. It is in the world that we live and breathe and have our being. We do not think the world is well lost for love or at least for anything short of love. . . . We can hardly think of any philosophical subject without speaking of the world.[4] So here it is: we have a question that intuitively matters greatly to us yet should be exceedingly simple to answer.

Doesn't the answer seem obvious to you? We are all part of this earthly ecosystem, which is part of the solar system, and that is part of the Milky Way galaxy, and so forth. Surely this progression has an end, a final term? And that is what we all agree in calling the world.

Oh, oh . . . The moment we have made this "obvious" answer explicit, we are reminded of famous proofs of the existence of God. Those demonstrations tend to prove the existence of something and end with the words "and that we all agree in calling God."[5] But those arguments we now all agree in calling unsound! So we had better look carefully at this supposedly obvious answer to whether the world exists. The earth, the sun, the planets, the Milky Way galaxy, and so forth, they all exist, all right. But is there in addition to all these real things also a thing, a totality, if you will, of which they are parts? Now we have a metaphysical question!

The "obvious" answer looked like a small argument or proof. If this ever-increasing series of physical systems exists, then so does its "sum." That argument can be contested. Indeed, we can, Mad Hatter–style, object by counterexample. You might as well say: All of us belong to the set of humans, which is part of the set of earthly things, and so forth; therefore there must be a set that contains everything. That conclusion does not follow and is false in modern mathematics.[6] Such analogies show at least that the putative small "proof" is not a proof. So, the metaphysical question does not have a completely obvious answer after all.

To this the metaphysician adds then: So the world does not *obviously* exist. Please let this raise your suspicions at once. We had a question that we understood to be at once significant and easy to answer. The metaphysician made the question precise in his or her own way and observes that it is not easy to answer.[7] But before we subject this transformation to closer scrutiny, let's give the metaphysician a bit more rope. Let's simply ask, then, about the world that does not obviously exist: Well, does it exist or doesn't it?

4. A SPECTRUM OF THEORIES

Whether the world exists is in fact a traditional question of metaphysics. Indeed, it encompasses three questions: What is a world? Does the world exist? Are there perhaps other worlds as well? These questions, including that of the plurality of worlds, were clearly posed by Aristotle (*De Caelo*, 276b–279a). In fact, Aristotle formulates the precise question that tends to constrain cosmology to a single universe. If the laws of nature are universal, how can their domain separate into distinct, mutually isolated worlds? In Aristotle's physics, each of the elements tends when unconstrained to go to its natural place. Thus if fire and earth exist in a hypothetical other world, they would tend to move naturally toward the same place as our earth and fire do. Therefore these worlds would not be distinct after all.

In modern philosophy those questions received a precise formulation in Kant's pre-Critical writings. During that early period Kant was still engaged in the type of metaphysics that he would shortly afterwards deconstruct, so we should not hold it much against him.[8] The first section of his *Inaugural Dissertation* defines a world as "a whole which is not a part." This definition answers the first question but leaves the second and third open. Is there a whole of which every actual thing is a part? If there is, is there only one? Must there be?

Actually, at first sight Kant has not given us a very good definition. Look at this chair: it has parts (for example, its legs) but is not itself part of anything else. But it is not a world, is it? There is one heavy-handed way to deal with such an objection. Kant could simply insist that our ordinary commonsensical way of taking this chair to be separate and not part of something is mistaken. He could say that it is part of something bigger, together with all the other furniture in this building, for example. But then he would be giving in to one of the temptations that make for really bad philosophy, surreptitiously and underhandedly turning the ordinary word "part" into technical jargon while ostensibly keeping it intact.

A better response is open to him. He can point out that in this example I trade on context, on the context-sensitivity of our language. A moving company would count this chair as part of the furniture, an estate manager count it as part of the house, and an astronomer as part of this planet earth. In one context it is a whole, which is not a part, but in another context it is correctly called part of something else. This is a correct observation about our ordinary uses of the word "part." But of course, Kant then needs to refine his notion of "world" accordingly. For it would not suit his purpose to say that in some contexts a chair is one of many worlds.

Therefore, to address the traditional metaphysical questions, Kant must first remove such context dependence. The way to do that is to settle on a single context, in which everything short of all there is counts as part of something else. We need a God's-eye context, to coin a phrase. For this absolute perspective Kant turns to physics; and that means, for him, to Newton's *Principles* and *System of the World*.

Ha! Given Newton's title, is it not possible to read an ontic commitment to the existence of the world from the accepted science of his day? No, as Kant understood, it is not so simple. Newton recognized several sorts of things: there is Absolute Space, and there are all the material bodies in that space. First question: should we think of the world as something (big, a material thing) in that space, or is Absolute Space part of the world? Not a question a scientist bothers his head with! Even if we say the former, is there really one big material thing that has all material bodies as parts? Or are, say, all the galaxies equals among equals, all of them wholes that are not parts? Or, reflecting on the analogy with sets, is each finite amount of material part of a larger amount, with every whole a finite thing that is also a part, wholes without end, and no whole at all of which everything is part?

We have an important lesson here for philosophy of science. Kant has to supply his own answer; he cannot read it off the science. In that respect, his situation was the same as ours today. Ontology cannot be read off scientific theories, although everyone has a go at reading ontology into them. Kant takes his inspiration from Newton's theory of force. What are the conditions requisite for the composition of an aggregate or multitude *(multitudo)* into a whole or totality *(omnitudo)?* The principle of composition, according to Kant, is mutual interaction. With that principle in place (added to science) Newton's Law of Universal Gravitation implies that all material bodies together form a totality , which is not part of anything else. Hence the world exists.

Notice also that, just as in Aristotle's case, we have a unique world here, or at least a unique material world, since all material bodies are part of one thing. Although on a more abstract level we can imagine other clusters of things, in mutual interaction but not in interaction with us, they can't very well be clusters of material things. At least, they cannot if we assume the literal truth of the law that all material bodies exert gravitational force on each other. So by putting together this package of a definition, a context of discussion, a principle, and a current scientific theory, Kant solved this problem of metaphysics.[9]

This would all have been more satisfactory if we had never noticed the context dependence or the addition by fiat of new principles to press a highly respected scientific theory into service for metaphysics. Kant himself tired of this game shortly afterward.

The very same questions that preoccupied Kant, before he freed himself from the vestiges of seventeenth-century metaphysics, re-emerge, however, in the twentieth century. They are explicitly posed in Peter van Inwagen's *Material Beings* (1990). Under what conditions is one thing [a] part of another? Or, equivalently, but in his words, "When is it true that there is something y such that the x's compose y?" Van Inwagen has his own answer and points to a variety of rival answers. I will not discuss the details. Most of these answers, as van Inwagen also notes, do not imply that the world exists. You may or may not consider that a drawback. One of those answers, however, has received more attention than most, and it does imply that the world exists: David Lewis's *On the Plurality of Worlds* (1986).

Lewis defines a world as the sum of all things spatio-temporally related to a given thing. (Another way to put this: the sum of a maximal collection of mutually spatio-temporally related things.) So what about the actual world? As you read this, you realize that you are one actual thing and that I am a contemporary located at some specific distance from where you are. So you realize that I belong to the same world as you do. There may also be other worlds, namely, if there are some real things that do not have a spatio-temporal location relative to yours or mine.[10] On Lewis's view, the world does exist. How is that? The phrase "the world" denotes the actual world: the sum of all things spatio-temporally related to a given actual thing. Does it exist? Well, that depends on whether the sum of this particular collection of things exists, on whether they compose something. Lewis provides an answer: within reason (and that includes this case), every collection has a sum. Therefore, the world exists.

This answer is a postulate. The postulate is that if a collection has a certain specified character, then its sum exists. This postulate is logically contingent, not provable, of some use to Lewis's metaphysics, introduced specifically to answer such questions. The postulate is spelled out in the context of a logical theory (mereology) developed with great technical virtuosity.[11] Such achievements in logic, which so often buoy up our contemporary philosophy, are indeed admirable. Logic by itself is vacuous. So all we have learned from this is that it is consistent to assert that the world exists.

But I did not ask whether the existence of the world can be consistently postulated! I asked: Does the world exist?

We have formulated the question and possible answers. Isn't that what it is to really understand a question, namely, to know what its possible answers are? It is; hence we have so far achieved a prolegomenon to any future definite answer to this question. But now, how are we to answer it? How do we go on?

5. SCIENTIFIC STEPS BEYOND SCIENCE?

How can we go on? This is precisely the problem addressed by analytic ontology. It is clearly time for us to take a close look at how this philosophical development understands itself. Analytic ontology was introduced by Willard Van Orman Quine, in his justly celebrated essay "On What There Is." It begins with a critique of traditional metaphysics. But then it restates the great question *What is there?* in hygienic form. To answer this question is the aim of ontology, which can now be pursued in a scientifically respectable way. Actually, this project takes two forms, one apparently modest and the other ambitious. The modest is to bring to light the ontic commitments of our best theories in science; the ambitious is to continue science so as to answer questions scientists do not ask, but in the same way as science answers its questions. The modest project may be no more than a deep-going study of the sciences, although perhaps charged with a contentious presupposition about what such a study will bring to light. Leave that aside for now. Let us consider the more relevant ambitious project of an ontology to go beyond answers to questions already dealt with by the sciences themselves. This is the project to engage in metaphysics as an extension of science, putatively pursued by the same means and realizing the same values.

This ambitious project can only proceed on the basis of some understanding of science, of how science answers its questions. Thus analytic ontology presupposes a philosophy of science. One part of my critique will concern the philosophy of science it has in practice presupposed. In my view that has certainly not kept up with actual developments.[12] The genuflection toward science among Quine's heirs has all too often been toward a naive caricature purveyed by the past generation of philosophers at whose knees Quine himself learned it.

TACTICS OF DEFENSE

Ontology, in the analytic vein, has one very good dialectical tactic. Suppose we bring an objection, for example, to materialism or physicalism in one of its forms. Then that objection can be dismissed if such an objection would, if cogent, equally apply to science. If the objector does not want to criticize science on the same grounds (if science is either sacrosanct or clearly successful in this context), that ends the matter.

This is very effective. For example, it allows us to immediately put aside the positivist critique that metaphysics is neither verifiable nor falsifiable. For after all, much of science isn't verifiable, either. Quine already emphasized this: ontology is in this respect "of a piece with" theoretical physics. The existence of quarks, or of the Big Bang, cannot be conclusively or directly verified or falsified. Our science faces the tribunal of experience as a whole and is forever underdetermined by the deliverances of experience. Since that is how it is with science, it must be allowed for ontology. As for the goose, so for the gander.

But how much of this defensive tactic is rhetoric? There is one striking difference between this goose and her gander. When a science, in its theoretical development, comes to a crossroads and can choose one direction or another, how does it choose? Consistency, both in itself and with the uncontested parts of the rest of science, is certainly a touchstone. The metaphysician can claim this touchstone as well. But it would be ludicrous to suggest that consistency alone is operative on the side of science. In science, every effort is made to put theory and nature jointly to the question, as harshly as by any Inquisition, and empirical evidence trumps all.

How can we reconcile this difference, which leaps to the eye, with the insight that in the end it is only the whole of science that stands to confront the whole of experience? The point is that along the way, in local choices between local alternatives, relative to assumed background, the empirical sciences do have something else to go by, besides the consistency guidelines set by logic. The sciences deliberately submit themselves to natural selection by empirical evidence, locally as well as globally. Any parallel that ontology can point to here pales by comparison.

The metaphysician has a reply to this objection, which ushers in a second defensive tactic. True, there are no ontological experimentalists. Logical consistency, it is true, leaves all logically consistent ontologies on a par. But when an ontology is offered as a reasonable, valuable, significant extension or continuation of science, consistency is clearly not the only criterion. Other values and desiderata are operative as well. By those criteria, a given ontology might even turn out to be head and shoulders above the rest—the only "good" extension of science into significantly uncharted territory. A second parallel to science is claimed at this point: the other values operative in metaphysical theory choice are among those operative in scientific theory choice as well!

The most cited extra value for theory choice, whether in science or metaphysics, is explanation. This was true when metaphysics dealt in proofs of the existence of God as sine qua non for explaining the universe. The demand for explanation is what drove those medieval wagons in the Cosmological Argument and the Argument from Design. It is still so in analytic metaphysics today. Metaphysicians who claim continuity with science typically claim that scientists infer to the best explanation, just as metaphysicians do.[13] So, if scientists proceed by inferring to the best explanation, and if this sort of inference is also the vehicle that propels metaphysics, metaphysics is truly the continuation of science by the same means. Again the gander claims the privileges he attributes to the goose.

But there are two points of contention. We may begin by allowing that scientific reasons for theory choice include explanation. But on one hand, what counts as scientific explanation may face harsher criteria than what counts as explanation in metaphysics. On the other, theory choice may not, as far as science requires, issue in belief. What I mean is: the choice among theories in science may be a choice to accept in some sense falling far short of endorsement as true.[14] In the present context, the obvious area of scientific theorizing to consider is cosmology. Does this branch of physics work with a well-defined notion of world, and does acceptance of its theories imply belief in the existence of a world in that sense? Can Quine's students and disciples unearth its ontological commitments? Or is there another way to understand the achievements of this and other branches of the physical sciences? I'll leave this here as the telling open question. (See further the appendix on scientific cosmology.) In my view, the presupposed philosophy of science is neither common sense nor common wisdom.

But I have a second point of contention that goes much deeper and indeed, I think, goes to the heart of the matter.

CHOICE IN A VACUUM

The very phrase "inference to the best explanation" should wave a red flag for us. What is good, better, best? What values are slipped in here, under a common name, and where do they come from? The appeal to explanation brings out into the open the glaring fact that we have a risk-taking pursuit of truth. Science is brave and dares to enter dangerous waters. Empirical science goes for bold conjectures and audacious hypotheses, it offers them as basis for prediction and action while the iron is still hot and conclusive evidence still infinitely far beyond reach. If metaphysics, presumptively the purest pursuit of truth, relies on inference to the best explanation, it finds itself in that imperiled boat as well. But now, once more, precisely where this parallel is claimed, a striking difference leaps to the eye.

Just what are the gains, what are the risks? Are they not very different? How is such risk taking to be rationally evaluated?

You will have understood me correctly if you now see science and analytic ontology caught in a Pascalian wager. But for science it is a real wager, and for ontology it could merely be pretend. To evaluate or even understand a wager, we need to know the risk and gain. We need to know what can be gained or lost in such a wager and also the chances of gain and loss. So what have we here?

If the wager is on a choice of theories or hypotheses, then from a God's-eye view, success consists in selecting the true and failure in choosing the false.[15] As in all success and failure, however, although there is value in winning as such, there are also collateral value and damage that win and loss bring along with them. If we pursue metaphysics in order to form beliefs about what there is, then the possible gain is true belief and the risk is falsity. So it is in science. But, first of all, what of collateral value and damage? And second, what are the chances of each in the metaphysicians' game?

In science, the stakes are great for all of us: safety, food, shelter, communication, all the preconditions for life in peace and justice that a successful science can enhance. The risk of acquiring some false beliefs matters little in comparison. The risks of enhanced forms of mass destruction and global poisonings do matter. So the case for pursuing science is not open and shut, but we can understand the case to be made. Most important for us, here, the acquisition of false beliefs, by itself, apart from their practical, empirical consequences, is no great matter in its contrast class of practical risk and gain.

That is very far from how it is in metaphysics. There the gains to be contemplated are those of having true beliefs (for example, about whether the world exists or many worlds exist) and of being in a position to explain (for example, what we mean by our modal statements). The risk is precisely that of acquiring false beliefs. The specter faced here is that we may end up having explained all that is dreamt of in our philosophies by intricately crafted postulates that are false. If there is collateral value or damage to all this, it certainly goes unmentioned in analytic metaphysics. So all there is to evaluate is the loss and gain of true beliefs *simpliciter*.

In the end, individual philosophers may bring their own subjective probabilities and personal values to this evaluation. But philosophy is a communal and historical dialogue. Analytic ontology cannot claim scientific respectability if all it has to show for itself is a *formal* parallel. Now it is time to appeal to concrete, specific values and probabilities to be offered for common acceptance to the philosophical community. Where is the metaphysician who shows us how likely it is that inference to the best explanation in ontology will lead to true conclusions? Why is he or she missing?

Where is the metaphysician who makes the case that the gain of explanatory power outweighs the risk of ending up with a tissue of falsehoods? What is this gain, what is the good, how is it weighed against truth? If simplicity, strength, coherence, and all those other explanatory virtues are to be placed in the balance against truth, may we please be shown the balance, the gauge, the units, the scale? As long as we have nothing like that, the defense of ontology as scientific points only to the form its theory and theory choice take.[16] But nonsense can come in the same form as wisdom. Form is nowhere near enough.

In any case, a little common sense suffices to show the disparity between science and metaphysics so well hidden by this common form. Consider the real history of Newton's physics, compared to what might have been the history of Cartesian dualism. Newton's physics reigned dominant for two hundred years. It gave us false beliefs but many benefits. I don't think anyone will say "It would have been better if Newton had never lived!" Imagine that Cartesian dualism had not been so conclusively rejected by the late seventeenth century but had also reigned for two hundred years. Would we say that the false beliefs that metaphysics gave us had been but a small price to pay for the ease and the intuitive appeal felt in its explanation of the human condition?

FALSE CONSCIOUSNESS IN PHILOSOPHY

Pascal's wager rings hollow precisely when the probabilities are just anybody's guess and the values dubious or the stakes negligible. How likely is it that a truly successful, coherent, explanatory ontological hypothesis is true? Who can say? Let the probability be subjective if you wish, but tell me, then, how does it connect with our other shared opinions—if at all? Let the values too be subjective, if you wish, but tell us, how do they connect with our other, shared values— our common values?

But most of all, please admit that this putative pursuit of truth runs on a fuel of probabilities and values extraneous to its enterprise. For what is there inside this project besides the delight in puzzle-solving? Then let us focus on those extraneous opinions and values: What are they? Until they are supplied, ontology has only the form of a rational inquiry in which the form of theory choice is rational. Even if we were to agree that theory choice takes precisely the same form in ontology as in science, nothing would follow by way of rationale for ontology. The agreement would supply ontology with only the barest of credentials, hardly going beyond mere consistency.

This is my main point and the point that I will explore further in the other lectures. Philosophy itself is a value- and attitude-driven enterprise; philosophy is in false consciousness when it sees itself otherwise. To me, philosophy is of overriding importance, to our culture, to our civilization, to us individually. For it is the enterprise in which we, in every century, interpret ourselves anew. But unless it so understands itself, it degenerates into an arid play of mere forms.

6. THE FORM OF SUCCESS, AND ITS FAILURE

I'm tired of coherent nonsense!

TOM STOPPARD, *The Real Thing*

To conclude, I wish to return once more to our guiding example: Does the world exist? However we deal with this question, we should not lose sight of our sense, inarticulate as it may be, that the world we live in is something of crucial significance to us. That significance should not be lost on any construal of what we mean when the word "world" appears in our discourse.

There are philosophers outside analytic philosophy who have struggled with this sort of question. Analytic philosophy can rightly pride itself on having produced the greatest critical arsenal the world has ever known. But analytic philosophy does not always hold itself to its own standards.

It is easy enough to criticize the logic and grammar of such statements as "nothing noths" and "the world worlds." But the author of such a text invites grammatical criticism, giving its language a deliberately unfamiliar and suggestively defective form to draw attention to philosophical perplexity. Criticism is not as easy if philosophical texts strive mightily to preserve grammatical and logical form, to express themselves in familiar-looking language. Then "form criticism" (if I may adapt that term) is pre-empted; defects and perplexities are hidden deep below the linguistic surface. Such tactics are infinitely more deplorable. We should not relinquish the stringent demands on intelligibility at the heart of analytic philosophy in exchange for mere compliance with logic and grammar!

"WORLD" IS NOT A COUNT NOUN

The world we live in is a precious thing; the world of the philosophers is well lost for love of it.

But even to say this is not accurate. If we think that way, we have already fallen into the trap that we willingly entered when we began the exposition of the analytic "cosmology." As I pointed out then, Kant's pre-Critical discussion could not start unless the word "world" was first decontextualized. The many loving as well as derisory ways in which we use the word "world" are not constant in reference, and often they are not referring uses at all. In order to understand our actual thinking, as opposed to its philosophical caricature, we need to pay attention to this.

My heading may be misleading. The ordinary word "world" has in fact many ordinary uses as a count noun; I discuss some of them below.[17] But none of these are at all the distinctive philosophical use found in recent ontology that we have been discussing here. As to that philosophical use, we can now conclude that there is no reason to think that it refers to anything, if indeed it is intelligible at all. But what about our ordinary way of speaking and thinking?

Below I cite dictionary examples, but for now consider the following: "All the tears in the world won't help you now" and "Not a single judge in the whole world would believe you." In both of these we could take "world" to stand for the entire universe, assuming that there is such a thing. But equally, we can take "world" to stand for something smaller or more delimited, though not explicitly specified: the whole of human history for the tears, the whole of current humanity for the judges. In each case we could also have utilized a purely quantificational phrase: "All the tears there are or ever have been . . ." or "Not a single judge alive today . . ." If we now add the "world" phrase again, we do not get nonsense but only rhetorical redundancy. ("All the tears there are or ever have been in this world . . . "). The additional "world" phrase is empty: it has no relevant effect on the content (which is not to deny that the domain of discourse is a relevant parameter and that we could take "the world" to denote that set or alternatively some putative object composed by its members). The schematic use, in other words, allows us or the context to select a count noun or noun phrase, with some real or putative denotation or other, as capturing the currently intended range of the quantifier.

Let us see how this accords with the standard record of English usage, the *Oxford English Dictionary*. This source explains that the etymology of "world" is "wer" (man) plus "ald" (age, life)—thus "age of man," "life of man." It is not easy to see how this temporal concept allowed for the second, roughly spatial, cluster of senses that are now clearly more common.[18] The major headings under which the *OED* lists examples of use are the following:

I. Human existence; a period of this.
II. The earth or a region of it; the universe or a region of it.
III. The inhabitants of the earth, or a section of them.
IV. Idiomatic uses and phrases.

Classification of the examples under these headings suggests that both context and explicit content are used to hypothesize denotations for the term when found. For the first heading a striking example commenting on Henry VIII's divorce mentions "[o]thers which foretold this dolorous doleful wretched world that followed." A related locution, old but still used, is "of the world," by which religious denote the secular sphere of life. "The Roman world" denotes a part or period of human existence.

Perhaps the most common uses of "world," however, fall under the first part of the second heading: to denote the earth or a part thereof. *Around the World in Eighty Days* is a story of an earthly circumnavigation. *Paradise Lost* says of Adam and Eve that "The World was all before them, where to choose Their place of rest" and means the earth, not the galaxy. When W. S. Gilbert wrote "It's Love that makes the world go round," he meant no more. The New World, of course, is part of the earth, as is the Old and the Third. The request to "imagine a world free of hunger and poverty" may sound like I am asking you to think of a possible world, a truly philosophical request. But it really asks you to imagine the human race here on earth free of hunger and poverty and what things would be like then.

"World" is also used to denote larger systems (the second part of heading II), and then it occurs readily in the plural. Before the twentieth century, disquisitions on the plurality of worlds often concerned other planets, stars, solar systems, galaxies. This yielded idioms concerning great quantities and vast distances: "they are worlds apart," "I would not stand in her way for worlds." Sometimes the demarcation is less natural, more abstruse, or more fanciful than those astronomy gives us. Locke claims that "the intellectual World is greater and more beautiful than the material World."[19] Somewhere in between are the world of physics or chemistry, the inorganic world, the outdoor world, the underworld, a Boy's World.

With some of these we may have strayed into classification III: The inhabitants of the earth, or a section of them. The *OED* lists the world of fashion and the learned world and quotes "Two noblemen, whose names are as eminent in the poultry world as in rank" from the *Poultry Chronicle* of 1854.

Finally, worlds can be something like mythical regions: the nether world, the world to come, a better world, the dream world, the world of gods and heroes. To this sub-cluster belong Dante's "With Virgil . . . visited the nether world of woe," Shelley's "gleams of a remoter world / Visit the soul in sleep," Tennyson's "second world" and "world-to-be," and Fitzgerald's dismissive lines in the *Rubayyat* (xxv) about "All the Saints and Sages who discuss'd Of the Two Worlds so learnedly." It is among such purported regions of reality magically accessible to us that I think we should locate the worlds discussed in the following conversation, famous among children, from C. S. Lewis's *The Lion, the Witch and the Wardrobe:*

"But do you really mean, Sir," said Peter, "that there could be other worlds—all over the place, just round the corner—like that?"
"Nothing is more probable," said the Professor, taking off his spectacles.

The dictionary proceeds on the assumption that "world" always denotes something, some supposedly existing entity or system, but not that it always denotes the same thing. In each example it seems that we could take that something to not exhaust all there is but rather to encompass some relevant class or region. When we interpret quantifiers such as "all" and "some," we specify a domain of discourse. But (a) we do not require that domain to be designated by any expression in the statement, (b) the domain we specify need not be a physical entity, it can easily be a set, (c) we take its identification to be contextual, and (d) the identification is typically, even in context, largely underdetermined. The "world" phrase that seems to point to this domain of discourse may help to determine it or may only signal the need to do so. If this is correct then we can often enough regard "world" as either not standing for anything or else denoting a set. Moreover, when we do regard it as standing for something (even a set), its referent is contextual; there is no single thing that it denotes in all such occurrences.

As an instructive similar example, less in common use but equally hovering at the edge between technical precision and philosophical reification, I want to mention "isomorphism." There are many important general insights expressed in statements in which this noun occurs "all by itself," so to speak. Mathematics describes its objects only up to isomorphism; that is an important point about mathematics. But this air of linguistic self-sufficiency is deceptive; the term is context-dependent. To say that structure A is isomorphic to structure B means that there is a one-to-one correspondence between them that preserves certain operations and relations. That is an explication of the vaguer phrase "A and B have the same structure." But explication, as usual, forks in many directions, and in this case remains itself vague unless those "certain" operations and relations are specified.

In mathematics, the way to precision is straightforward. If I ask whether two groups are isomorphic (in those words, using the word "group"), then I am asking about correspondences that preserve the group operations. It may still be added that the two structures are very different in other respects. For example, the elements of one are permutations and the elements of the other are operations on a Hilbert space. There is a very precise sense in which the two entities have the same structure and an equally precise sense in which they do not. But what if I ask the question about two physical entities, or one physical and one mathematical? Is this pendulum, a physical table-top model, isomorphic to the one in your study, is it isomorphic to the mathematical model described in your physics text?

It seems that we can ask of such things only whether they have the same structure under a certain description. In that case we must specify the description before the question can be completely identified. There are, however, philosophical views according to which that is not so in principle. Such views impart a definite and complete sense to the question whether two physical entities have the same structure, whether they are, so to speak, totally isomorphic. For example, when van Inwagen lays out his assumptions at the beginning of *Material Beings,* he says that the world is particulate, that is, every material being is composed of parts that themselves have no proper parts ("mereological atoms"). Add to this any of the varieties of antinominalism that entails that there is only a restricted set of real relations (as opposed to arbitrary sets of pairs, triples, or other sequences). Then it makes sense to ask of two structures whether they are isomorphic, *tout court,* without qualification. For that means : Is there a correspondence between their mereological atoms that preserves all the real relations?

Relative to some philosophical views, therefore, "isomorphic" is not, in the end, a merely schematic or context-dependent term. There is, according to such views, a straightforward, noncontextual assertion of isomorphism. (A particular assertion may of course be restricted, by constraints due to contextual factors in discourse, but that is a general point about all terms.) The rest of us, lacking such a philosophical view, can use the term "isomorphic" without qualification only in a schematic way. That is, lacking such a view, we must take a bare assertion of isomorphism to be not a full-fledged statement but a statement schema. Statements are produced therefrom by "filling in the blanks."

The very same point may be made about uses of "world." The form "All . . . in the world are . . ." is schematic in several ways. The "in the world" phrase is itself a blank, to be filled in. That blank is filled in when the domain of discourse is specified for the quantifier. There are again philosophical views relative to which this is not so, in the end. These are views according to which there is a single thing, THE WORLD, which is the ultimate and complete candidate that can fill every such blank. The rest of us, lacking such a view, must do what the editors of the *OED* do: for each occurrence of "world" we identify some plausible region, system, or set of entities that delimits the statement's domain of discourse. In other words, we treat the general and unqualified use of "world" as schematic only, relying on contextual factors to turn the schema into a statement.

To sum up, then, here is my suggested alternative to the idea that "world" is a count noun. It is instead a context-dependent term that indicates the domain of discourse of the sentence in which it occurs, on the occasion of utterance. It plays this role sometimes by denoting the domain (a set) and sometimes by purporting to denote an entity of which the members of the domain are parts. In the latter case we need not take that very seriously (it may be metaphor, colorful language, rhetorical extravagance); only the indicated domain of discourse is important.

This also explains why the world is something of importance to us, why we would not want to lose touch with the world we live in. For in any concrete context, the word "world" refers to a domain of crucial significance for the shape and texture of our lives. (There just is not one single domain that has that significance in all contexts.) Here is a much-ignored criterion of adequacy for any philosophical talk about worlds: that it should pay more than lip service to such significance in its putative subject.

7. A DILEMMA FOR THE CONSCIENTIOUS

The entire metaphysical discussion of the world's reality failed to go beyond the form of substantive hypotheses. To show that, let us imagine how a truly conscientious analytic philosopher would eschew the seduction of familiar wordage put to technical use. She looks to mereology and notices that in ordinary discourse the part-whole relation does not even seem to be transitive. After all, we philosophers are an important part of the university faculty, but are our knees part of the faculty? So she begins by introducing the technical term "Spart" and lays down the following principles:

1. If A is a part of B, then A is a Spart of B;
2. Spart-of obeys the axioms of basic mereology;
3. a Sworld is, by definition, something which is not a Spart of anything else.

At this point, two decisions await. One is whether to add existence postulates, such as that certain definable Ssums of given entities also exist. Such postulates settle the question whether the Sworld exists or many Sworlds, exist. The other decision is whether to drop all those initial sibilants and thus stake out a position in ontology.

Before the second decision (or some other such way of connecting with nontechnical discourse) is taken, this philosopher has no philosophy. That is still the case if the theory is extended into a truly virtuoso performance of abstract system building. But the second decision, I say, cannot be hidden or made surreptitiously, nor do we end up with a real philosophy if it is made blatantly sans rationale! Therefore, at this point, the real work would only just have begun; the "hard problem" (to adapt another catch phrase) would not yet have been broached at all. But that work would take us outside the enterprise of analytic metaphysics, which is in the final analysis only a formal exercise with its motivation and rationale suppressed from view.

What happens if she relaxes the demand for rigor? Having created a language system only distantly related to known human or even philosophical interests, it might seem fortunate, might it not, that there are already words in common use, (to wit, "world" and "part") which play almost all of the role of "Sworld" and "Spart"? If we suppress the initial sibilant, we will sound as if we are making perfect sense, at least logically and grammatically. We may then encounter some stares that we take to be incredulous, since our statements do not accord with the pre-understanding of "world" and "part." With regard to his more substantive metaphysics, David Lewis has quite rightly remarked that an incredulous stare does not amount to an argument. But in the case I am imaging here, perhaps the stares are not incredulous. Perhaps, instead, they express a sense of being utterly nonplussed.

It seems to me that however we continue this rational reconstruction of the philosopher's art, we reach a negative verdict on its works. One possible continuation is to say that in the philosopher's mouth, "the world exists" is only a funny way of saying "the Sworld exists." Since "the Sworld exists" has such a thin veneer of meaning, this transformation is needed to give us a sense of familiarity. But then that sense of familiarity is a delusion and the question of credence, of credulity or incredulity, does not even arise.

The other possible continuation is to say that on the contrary, through this careful construction, the philosopher has found a stronger guarantee of meaningfulness and literal significance. No discourse at all is meaningful in any more full-blooded sense than this. The criteria explicitly met are all the criteria there are; hence they are the sufficient marks of meaning—ipso facto, this discourse makes sense. "Sworld" is intelligibly related to "world," taking over a carefully selected family of uses, regimenting them, and is then used to make new, logically contingent, fully intelligible assertions. If we are careful not to let other usages of "world" creep back into our professional discourse, then "the world exists" is a perfectly good way of saying "the Sworld exists."

The unfortunate negative verdict forced on us by this second line of reasoning, which grants sufficiency to such lenient standards, is that it is very easy, all too easy, to make sense. We can sit in our closets and in a perfectly meaningful way, kneading and manipulating language, create new theories of everything and thereby important contributions to ontology. In other words, to put it a little more bluntly, this "world play" we engaged in here is but idle word play; although shown to be meaningful, it is merely idle word play nevertheless. On both verdicts, ontology is not what it purports to be. But to me the second verdict is the more devastating one.

8. A WORLD WELL LOST

Let's return for a moment to Pascal, to complete the parallel with the seventeenth century. The objection I have to seventeenth-century metaphysics is that it replaced its own real subjects of inquiry by simulacra, sometimes consciously and deliberately so. In Descartes' posthumous work *The World, or Treatise on Light* we see this very explicitly.[20] This is a treatise in theoretical physics. But at a certain point Descartes suggests that we momentarily set aside any effort to account for what has been observed or what the real world seems to be like. Instead, he suggests, let us construct the world that God would have created if he wished to make a world perfectly transparent and intelligible to the human mind. Let us construct and study this abstract simulacrum, instead of the observed and observable phenomena themselves. That is the methodology Descartes announces here:

> For a short time, then, allow your thought to wander beyond this world to view another, wholly new one. . . .
>
> Now, since we are taking the liberty of imagining this matter to our fancy, let us attribute to it, if you will, a nature in which there is absolutely nothing that anyone cannot know as perfectly as possible.
>
> And my plan is not to set out . . . the things that are in fact in the true world, but only to make up as I please from [this matter] a [world] in which there is nothing that the densest minds are not capable of conceiving, and which nevertheless could be created exactly the way I have made it up.
>
> Were I to posit in this new world the least thing that is obscure, it could happen that, within that obscurity, there might be some hidden contradiction . . . . Instead, being able to imagine distinctly everything I am positing there, it is certain that, even if there be no such thing in the old world, God can nevertheless create it in a new one.[21]

Of course, two things follow pretty quickly. First of all, transparency to the human intellect turns out to be compliance with the strictures of the mechanical philosophy. This view of nature, to which Descartes and his contemporaries adhered, requires mechanical "pushme-pullyou" explanations for all phenomena. Second, lo and behold, the constructed world fits all the data of observation and can be offered as faithfully representing the real world after all!

This way of proceeding is not such bad methodology here, for in physics nature soon gets its turn. The Cartesian bubble was burst in the next generation. In metaphysics this methodology is also prevalent, but on one hand not so explicitly acknowledged and on the other hand not subject to the same sort of natural selection. It has, however, the same drawback: the criteria of intelligibility are automatically those of the currently popular philosophical trends.

The most salient example of this in seventeenth-century metaphysics was actually the construction of a God who is perfectly intelligible to the human mind, while constantly proclaimed as beyond human comprehension. This God is omniscient, omnipotent, omnibenevolent . . . let's call him the O-O-O God for short. Does the construction succeed in fitting any data? Well, the biblical and medieval practice of "proof-texting," in which the data are selected texts by authorities (in other respects so much decried by this time), emerges here as determining what any concept of God must match. Perhaps this part is not so interesting. In fact, the seventeenth century seems as cavalier in its treatment of religion as the twentieth-century metaphysics is of science. More to the point for the philosopher: Does the construction succeed on its own terms? Now there is an interesting problem that can generate endless philosophical labor.

In that example the immediate challenge is the problem of theodicy: How can pain and evil exist if that philosophical God exists? Don't misunderstand me—there is a religious problem of pain and of evil.[22] But the philosophical labor expended on theodicy accords that problem hardly a glance. The focus is instead precisely on that lovely logical problem of the consistency of the O-O-O God's existence with the presence of evil. It is a fascinating problem for logic, but it is not much different from the children's puzzle of what happens if the irresistible force meets the immovable object. Nor of much more importance.

Even analytic metaphysicians uninterested in religion succumb to this fascination with the logical problems of theodicy. But I point to it only as an instructive parallel. The constructed God is not so different from the constructed world. Both are abstract simulacra of something real and important whose appeal lies mainly in the logical problems they engender and the virtuoso displays of ingenuity we can then enjoy.

Let me end with a short credo. I am an analytic philosopher. I fully appreciate the tremendous contributions of analytic philosophy, in its great diversity ranging from Russell and Moore's revolt against idealism through the varieties of conceptual, linguistic, and logical analysis that followed. But I believe that philosophy can be very different from the above logical exercises pursuing the illusions of Reason. Indeed, a great deal of analytic philosophy is not like that at all and has made real and lasting contributions to the Western philosophical tradition and its self-understanding. After this critical beginning, the first positive task I want to undertake is to show how philosophy can be something other than metaphysics, so that we need not remain stuck in these trivial pursuits.

What Is Empiricism and What Could It Be?

[W]hen empiricism itself, as frequently happens, becomes dogmatic in its attitudes towards ideas, and confidently denies whatever lies beyond the sphere of its intuitive knowledge, it betrays the same lack of modesty; and this is all the more reprehensible owing to the irreparable injury which is thereby caused to the practical interests of reason.

— KANT, *Critique of Pure Reason*

If we reject metaphysics, the speculative art, is there something left to do in philosophy? There is indeed a strong antimetaphysical tradition in philosophy, namely, empiricism. Is that simply a thing of the past, something we have long left behind in our philosophical journey of the past two thousand years? I do not believe so, and I propose to enter on a quest: What is empiricism, and what could it be, if it is to be a viable philosophy today?

One. In Search of a Tradition

1. SKETCH OF THE TRADITION AS USUALLY UNDERSTOOD

Empiricism is not a single, specific philosophical position, but there is a tradition of philosophical positions that we call empiricist. When we teach history of philosophy, we single out several long-standing rival traditions and identify their major adherents. In the case of empiricism, we point to modern British empiricism as an important part: Francis Bacon, Hobbes, Locke, Berkeley, Hume, John Stuart Mill.

To this we add both pre- and post-history. Before Bacon there were the late fourteenth-century nominalists at Oxford and Paris, strongly involved in the beginnings of the scientific revolution (as dramatically portrayed in Eco's *The Name of the Rose*). After Mill we point to Comte and the French Positivists, the English and American revolts against German idealism, and the Vienna and Berlin Circles, which developed Logical Positivism and Logical Empiricism. We are even willing to add more ancient examples: the Skeptics who took over Plato's Academy, and even Aristotle to some extent—thus admitting that it is a matter of degree (Aristotle was not an empiricist, really, but he was more empiricist than Plato . . .).

Apart from a list of names, can we identify this tradition in some more principled way? What makes it *one* tradition?

2. HISTORY OF THE WORD "EMPIRICISM"

The British empiricists did not call themselves the British empiricists. Worse: they said explicitly that they were not empiricists! This becomes less puzzling when we realize that the word had originally a quite different though not unrelated meaning.[1]

The earliest use appears to refer to a school of physicians (Empirici, as opposed to Dogmatici or Methodoci) who professed to eschew theory and to draw their rules of practice entirely from observation and experience—the accumulated experience of the medical profession. When we find the word in Francis Bacon, it has already been generalized beyond medicine. Bacon uses it to characterize an approach to what we now call *science* as opposed to philosophy: "Those who have practiced the sciences have been either empiricists or dogmatists. The empiricists, like the ants, merely collect and use: the rationalists, like spiders, spin webs out of themselves. But the way of the bee lies in between: she gathers materials from the flowers of the garden and the field and then by her own powers transforms and digests them; and the real work of [science] is similar."[2] Bacon's usage is simply followed, I think, by Leibniz in the preface to his *New Essays:*

> [B]easts are sheer empirics and are guided entirely by instances. While men are capable of demonstrative knowledge *(science),* beasts, so far as one can judge, never manage to form necessary propositions, since the faculty by which they make [inferences] is something lower than the reason which is to be found in men. The [inferences] of beasts are just like those of simple empirics who maintain that what happened once will happen again in a case which is similar in the respects that they are impressed by.... That is what makes it so easy for men to ensnare beasts, and so easy for simple empirics to make mistakes.

Leibniz is thus identifying the empiricists' method with naïve numerical induction. John Stuart Mill has something similar in mind, but his usage does extend beyond Bacon's and Leibniz's. Mill includes among the empiricists the philosophers who take it that the ants are right, so to speak. Included, then, are what we would now call philosophers (as opposed to scientists), if they endorse the methodology that Bacon called empiricist. Mill distances himself strongly from empiricism even in this broader sense; he thinks it is a very bad methodology. And so we see the last great representative of British Empiricism saying: "When this time shall come [the time in which the right method is followed in all areas of inquiry], no important branch of human affairs will be any longer abandoned to empiricism and unscientific surmise."[3]

3. CODIFICATION BY THE HISTORIANS:
THE DEFINING CRITERION

So where does our current use come from? Crucial was the nineteenth-century emergence of professional historians of philosophy and their desire to write a triumphalist history of the modern era. They saw Kant as the great victor, having produced the synthesis that overcame thesis and antithesis in early modern thought. So they wanted there to be two great philosophical schools in the seventeenth century, radically opposed to each other and equally wrong, overcome and *aufgehoben* by Kant's transcendental idealism.[4]

Well, call those warring schools—verbally following Bacon—the rationalists and the empiricists. Distinguish them first geographically, between Continent and Sceptered Isle, then look for a more principled criterion. For that criterion they took a salient issue from Leibniz's essays against Locke: innate ideas. Locke held that the mind is originally a tabula rasa on which experience writes, Leibniz that it is like a block of marble, already structured to some extent through its inner striations, which experience sculpts. That is then taken to be the defining difference between the two schools.[5]

Once codified, the criterion became the staple of textbook writing. I found a nice example in Princeton's Firestone Library, a little book called *The Problems of Philosophy*—not far from another book by that title. The Stuart Professor of Logic at Princeton University in 1898, John Grier Hibben, published this introduction for his undoubtedly rapt students. Its sixth chapter is devoted to the "problem of knowledge," which he said was introduced by Locke and comprised two parts, the source of knowledge and its nature. With respect to the former part, he distinguished two schools. The first is rationalism: the source is primarily in the mind itself, which is immediately aware of certain fundamental principles that give form to the material supplied by sensation. The second, which includes preeminently Locke, Condillac, Hume, and Mill, is "the theory which refers all knowledge to experience as its source, namely, empiricism" (97). These two schools are then followed by the critical school of Kant, sloganized by the dictum that the Understanding makes nature but does not create it, thus giving proper due both to the mind's work and to something foreign for it to work on. This story, which the Princeton students heard in Professor Hibben's classroom, is precisely that "standardized" version.

4. IMMEDIATE INADEQUACY OF THE CRITERION

With our hindsight it is easy to see that this criterion was about to run into difficulties. It is a criterion based on views of how the mind works, deriving from a dispute that arose well before psychology separated itself as an autonomous discipline. But that separation was in progress precisely at this time—the time also of Frege's devastating critique of psychologism in philosophy.

Quite apart from that, the criterion's inadequacy has by 1898 already become manifest in textbook writing. For Hibben continues his story by telling his students that there also exist some empiricists now; they are called Positivists, after August Comte's "Positive Philosophy," and they live in France. On the face of it, his classification may have seemed correct by his criterion, given that Comte "insisted on the positive facts of experience, the facts which form the subject matter of science, as the sole basis of our knowledge" (100). But it is at the same time a far cry from the innate idea controversy, as is obvious even from Hibben's nutshell presentation of Comte's view:

> Comte regards all knowledge as circumscribed by the general laws of science which have been experimentally determined, and which account for the sequence of phenomena, the measurement of their intensity, and all their quantitative relations, but which, however, are silent concerning the underlying ground of

these phenomena, and their significance. . . . The end of knowledge, according to Comte, is the more perfect systematization of
the sciences, in which task all metaphysical presuppositions
must be strenuously avoided. (101)

This sounds much more like what empiricists say in the twentieth
century than anything we have come across yet. It is not psychology;
it does not relate to sensations, associations, or other operations of
the mind. It concerns methodology, thus returning in that respect to
what Bacon and Leibniz had in mind and to questions of epistemology that can be separated from psychology. That is precisely what
the empiricists of the next few decades would regard as central to the
tradition they intended to continue.

5. SKETCH OF THE TRADITION CONTINUED:
THE RECURRENT REBELLION

After this abortive effort by the historians, should we conclude that
the entire tradition was but a figment of our imagination? I don't
think it is; but the tradition must be identified in some different way.
I can't do it at once, nor by a simple open-and-shut criterion or
definition. But I want to draw your attention to one salient feature to
begin. The story of empiricism is a story of recurrent rebellion
against a certain systematizing and theorizing tendency in philosophy: a recurrent rebellion against the metaphysicians.

That is why we are ready to call Aristotle more of an empiricist
than Plato and speak of an empiricist turn at that point. Aristotle
called Plato's followers back from high theory to empirical inquiry.
That is also why we think of the late fourteenth-century nominalists
as the parents of British empiricism: they staged a rebellion against
an Aristotelian tradition that had wandered far away from Aristotle's
empirical focus. The British empiricists are best seen as critics of
Continental systematizing. They are very weak as systematic phi-

losophers but do not see that as a failure. Similarly, the positivists and later empiricists staged yet another new beginning for empiricism, in their critical opposition to the metaphysics of their day.

What exactly are the targets of the empiricist critique? As I see it, the targets are forms of metaphysics that (a) give absolute primacy to demands for explanation and (b) are satisfied with explanations-by-postulate, that is, explanations that postulate the reality of certain entities or aspects of the world not already evident in experience.[6] The empiricist critiques I see as correspondingly involving

(a) a rejection of demands for explanation at certain crucial points and

(b) a strong dissatisfaction with explanations (even if called for) that proceed by postulation.

I will refer to these as the first and second characteristics of empiricism. Others may be added as we go along.

Let us make this concrete with specific examples. Suppose that, in a philosophical way, I do not understand ethics or science or religion. It might be one thing to take me by the hand and lead me into relevant experience. That might allow me to acquire a deeper sense of insight into those aspects of human existence. It would be quite another thing—and to the empiricists of little or no value—to postulate that there are certain entities or realms of being about which ethics (or science, or religion) tells us a true story.

Yet that is what philosophers have often tended to do: to "explain" ethics by the contention that ethical principles are just the (putative) truths about values, scientific theories the putative true summary of the laws of nature, and religious doctrines the putative true description of a divine, extra-mundane reality. Such tendencies presuppose that unless we can think of the relevant text as purporting to be a true story, there is no explaining or understanding the subject at all.[7] Empiricists have a threefold response: to deny, first, the value of any such "explanation," second, the reasons anyone might have for thinking it to be true, and third, the legitimacy and appropriateness of that demand for explanation itself.

So the empiricist tradition consists of a loosely associated series of recurrent rebellions in a recurrent form of philosophical dispute. But we still have not answered the question: What, in general, counts as an empiricist philosophical position? Criticism of others is all very well, but isn't there also something more positive, something constructive, something by way of empiricist creed?

Two. Critique: What Empiricism Cannot Be

We are trying to determine what empiricism is and what it could be. Perhaps we have an inkling now. I propose to look for clues next in twentieth-century critiques of empiricism.

6. THE PERIOD OF EMPIRICIST CRITIQUE OF EMPIRICISM

Somewhat paradoxically, the most incisive criticisms are associated with philosophers who may themselves very well be regarded as within the tradition. I have in mind four: Husserl, Reichenbach, Feyerabend, and Quine. I will not go into detail about what they say here, but I'll try to extract and condense the crucial points. (I'll elaborate further in the appendix.) There are two main lines of critique, not unconnected. The first shows that modern empiricism was associated with the idea of "foundations of knowledge." There can be no doubt (the critics recalled) that all of our knowledge *begins with* experience. But the idea that experience *provides the foundation* and source of knowledge they attacked as untenable. The second critique goes deeper: it shows that this foundationalism was conceived of as, in effect, a metaphysical thesis of just the sort against which empiricism stages its recurrent rebellion.

7. FOUNDATIONALIST EPISTEMOLOGY:
DOOMED TO VICIOUS CIRCLE OR INFINITE REGRESS?

As representative here I'll take Reichenbach, who called his own philosophy "logical empiricism." Reichenbach asserted that modern empiricism had ended in disaster.[8] But he spoke as a representative of a new empiricism, diagnosed the crucial error that had precipitated the disaster, and could point to his own practice as free from this error. The error, he said, had been to accept the aims for philosophy laid down by the rationalists. The rationalists reached for *demonstrable* knowledge of ourselves, our world, and our place in that world. Empiricists meekly and mistakenly accepted that goal as the criterion of adequacy for philosophy. Only thus, Reichenbach thought, could he explain the empiricist engagement in a foundationalist epistemology whose self-destruction dragged empiricism down with it.

The rationalists' aim, as Reichenbach saw it, was this: philosophy should give us a theory—significant, substantial, informative—about what there is and demonstrate its correctness. The empiricists could not accept that any such thing could be demonstrated on the basis of reason alone. Accepting nevertheless that the adequacy of our beliefs should be demonstrable in some way, they postulated a foundation for knowledge. All legitimate concepts were to be reducible to those applicable in sense experience, and all knowledge was to be derivable from the facts known by experience. The deliverances of experience furnish the data, and what is known is precisely what can be derived from those data.

But this philosophical strategy proves self-defeating. Whether the foundation be postulated to lie in reason or in experience, this epistemological bootstrapping is bound to fail.[9] Would such a demonstration not have to rest on a basis at least as content-full as the theory to be demonstrated? At first sight the demand for such foundations is circular. If we could find a foundation for knowledge, however, and a guaranteeably reliable construction of all knowledge on that foundation, the task would be completed without circularity. Only now a regress threatens: What about this foundation and method of construction? Circle or regress, choose your poison. Modern empiricism had fallen into the trap, after its incisive critique of rationalist metaphysics, of trying to reach for the same unattainable end.

8. REACHING DEEPER: WHY STONEWALLING CAN'T WORK

There might seem to be a third option besides vicious circle and infinite regress. An empiricist might just assert:

> The described foundation in experience is a source of truth with certainty.
> Our particular way of extrapolating beyond experience, to form expectations of future experience, preserves truth and certainty.

That is my position, he or she might say; I assert it and reject any request for justification. But this stonewalling fantasy shows only that the trouble goes much deeper than the misfortunes of foundationalism by itself. For what is this sort of assertion if not a thesis about what the world is like? It says that we are in a fortunate situation, in having this reliable source of opinion, and adds perhaps that there is no other source. That is a factual thesis.

I do not want to stop to consider the usual sort of challenges, such as how the empiricist could possibly claim to know, or have reason to believe, that this thesis is true. The much worse problem I see is this: we are talking here about the very basis of empiricism, supposedly, and it looks like precisely the typical target for empiricist critique. If that is what becomes of the empiricist rebellion, then it turns into its own enemy.

This is contentious; let us now back it up with an argument. Since this is a crucial issue for the argument of these lectures as a whole, I shall in fact present the argument twice over. In the first round I shall display the very general characteristics of empiricism that lead to its defeat if thus naïvely formulated. Then I shall state the argument more discursively as it would apply to debates between, on one hand, several such empiricists, and on the other, such empiricists and the metaphysicians they oppose.

To begin, then, to be an empiricist is to take a certain kind of philosophical position. But what is that? What is a philosophical position?

Typical examples that come to mind at once (nominalism versus realism with respect to universals, dualism versus monism on the mind-body question) are clearly views of what we and the world are like. They say that certain kinds of beings are real (universals, mind) and how they are related to each other. To have such a view, then, is to believe something. For example:

> To be a mind-body dualist = to believe that mind and body are real, distinct substances.

If we take this as the definitive cue we arrive at the following (meta-)philosophical principle:

> Principle Zero:
>   For each philosophical position X there exists a statement X+ such that to have (or take) position X is to believe (or decide to believe) that X+.

This X+ we may then call the dogma or doctrine of position X. Not just any statement X+ will fit here, of course. To believe that there are flying saucers does not qualify as taking a philosophical position.

But perhaps the belief that there are monads or universals or alternative possible worlds does so qualify. (Why?)

If Principle Zero is correct (and this is a big question, the moment the principle has been formulated), then it must yield a corollary for empiricism. There must then be some statement E+ such that

(NE) To be an empiricist = to believe that E+ (the empiricist dogma).

The mnemonic name "(NE)" stands for "Naïve Empiricism." Naïveté is not exactly a disqualification for philosophy. Still, I do not advance Principle Zero as obviously correct. We need to see where all this leads us. The question we face is: What statement could possibly play the role of E+ in (NE)?

If there is such a statement as E+ it is the dogma that sums up empiricism. But what role would it have to play?

Here I must draw a bit more on the history of empiricism, namely, on its admiration for the empirical sciences. If we were to advance some candidate for the role of E+, it would have to furnish the basis for the critique that the empiricist rebels aimed at their targets in metaphysics. But what would it take for E+ to furnish such a basis? It would itself need to be invulnerable to that critique (that is, be the sort of thing which that critique leaves standing). At the same time it would have to imply the falsity, untenability, or meaninglessness of all metaphysics. Can there be such a proposition?

More important, how can this question look to the empiricist? Clearly E+ cannot be a tautology, so it must be a factual thesis. To be invulnerable to empiricist critique, a factual thesis must be of the sort exemplified by scientifically respectable hypotheses. Here we have a clue. One crucial fact about science is very important to the empiricist. In science, disagreement never puts anyone automatically beyond the pale. This has to do of course with the empiricist conviction that no factual claim is a priori. But we need not appeal to any deep epistemological principle here. In science disagreement is not impiety, and doubt is not treason, no matter what the content. That feature is very salient in the empiricist case for taking empirical science as our paradigm of rational inquiry.[10]

A candidate for E+ could be something like "Experience is the one and only source of information." Its exact content does not matter to our current argument, as long as it purports to be a factual thesis. The following will apply, mutatis mutandis, whatever that thesis is.

> Corollary to (NE):
> Empiricist critique of X = demonstration that X is incompatible with (contrary to) the empiricist dogma E+.

The third characteristic of empiricism:

> (c) As in science, so in philosophy: disagreement with any admissible factual hypothesis is admissible.

Now we have the resources for a reductio ad absurdum argument: Contraries of E+ are not compatible with E+, yet must be admitted!

On one hand, (c) tells us that contraries of E+ must be admissible to the empiricist. This is simply so because E+ is a factual thesis, a statement that is contingently true or false, so disagreement with it is admissible. On the other, the status of E+ as empiricist dogma guarantees that its contraries are not admissible—that is the corollary to NE. Empiricism, in trying to frame a doctrine of its own, has talked itself into a corner.

That is really the end of the argument, but now I will go through it again in a slightly different way. The situation is this. Suppose empiricists rest their critique on any factual thesis about what we are like or what the world is like. What should they do, then, if a metaphysician disagrees with that thesis?[11] Empiricists say, "Disagreement among us is always possible and always allowed; let us both explore the factual hypotheses we favor." But if this is their response to the metaphysician, they are then and thereby giving up on the idea of a radical critique of metaphysics.

The above argument, taken as a whole, is a reductio of "naïve" empiricism. Though naïve, that view is not unattractive; it goes as follows. There can be many different empiricists, but they are empiricists because they all share a certain dogma, E+. Though they share other characteristics, the belief that E+ sums up the entire position; it is what makes them empiricists. Some of those other shared characteristics (which must therefore derive from that shared belief in their common doctrine) are a common style of critique directed at metaphysics and a common admiration for the empirical sciences. They also include a conviction that when it comes to holding and disputing beliefs, the dialogue must take an undogmatic form: "as in science, so in philosophy." Beyond what they share, each may add further principles and views, provided those additions are compatible with E+.

Let's first look at that supposed lesson from science. It concerns a favorite theme in empiricism: that the empirical sciences are undogmatic, that the very spirit of empirical science is the antithesis of dogmatism. But that does not imply that at any stage at all, every factual hypothesis is admitted as worthy of consideration. Who would now so admit the idea that the earth is flat? Yet that counts as an admissible scientific hypothesis in a wider sense. We have rejected it, but it could be or could have been admitted as possibly true at an earlier stage. Some as yet unrefuted hypotheses fare actually no better in practice. Wesley Salmon gave the example of a scientist reacting to some idea of Scientology: "As a scientist I cannot reject this before we have collected evidence, but when we have I will!" Nevertheless, there is a basic degree of respect evident even in this response. Admissibility in its most general form allows any disagreement with accepted scientific opinion in principle to be respected, even if in practice we have gone clearly beyond the point where it is worth our time or effort. Empiricists similarly mean to rule on no purported fact about what there really is. They reject the idea that we could have a priori access to any such information. Thus they allow any factual disagreement within the bounds of the admissible. Metaphysics is another matter. (But how? Naïve empiricists are here in the process of talking themselves into a corner, remember; let's follow them a bit further.)

Thus one empiricist, Peter, will say quite different things about another empiricist, Paul, than he will say about the metaphysician Paulina. Peter will say, "I disagree with Paul, but the mistaken principles and beliefs he adds to E+ are admissible [within empiricism] because they are compatible with E+." To Paulina he will direct a critique, possibly based to some extent on views he does not share with Paul; but he will add a critique on which he and all other empiricists agree. Since E+ sums up the basic empiricist position, that shared critique must derive entirely from E+. Thus if Paulina holds principle Q, that shared critique must amount to: "the truth of Q is incompatible with E+." (There are subcases here: E+ might simply imply that Q is false, or Q might be the sort of thing that E+ classifies as nonsense or as neither true nor false, for example.)

Now the other shared characteristics begin to make trouble. They are meant to derive entirely from the shared belief in E+. But if philosophy is to have the same ethic of belief as science, what does that entail? It entails that no factual hypothesis at all is to be ruled out from the outset. Any factual hypothesis must in principle be given over for empirical investigation. What there is, and what the world is like, is not to be a matter of intellectual punditry; all putative matters of fact are admissible in that sense. Perhaps E+ says as much. Perhaps it says something like "Experience is the only source of information," from which the empiricist may then derive "So there can be no a priori demonstration or refutation of any factual claim." But E+ is itself precisely such a factual hypothesis. This means that its contraries are also putative matters of fact. So they must be admissible in the same way as empirical hypotheses are generally in the sciences. Unfortunately, since E+ is the dogma that sums up the entire basis of this empiricism, it is also the sole basis for any empiricist critique of metaphysics. It follows now that by the empiricist's own lights, any empiricist critique can therefore be legitimately countered as follows: "The target of your critique is a claim contrary to E+, hence equally admissible as a hypothesis and not to be ruled out from the outset." There is now either no longer any bite to the critique, or else it bites its own tail. This impasse is unavoidable if E+ is itself a factual statement about what there is or what the world is like. So now naïve empiricism has painted itself into a corner and is in effect reduced to absurdity.

I don't think I'm being fanciful. If the empiricists' position consists, in accordance with Principle Zero, in the assertion or belief of a factual thesis, then they have no way to demur from the very sort of metaphysics they typically attack. This is modern empiricism's second, and I think much more serious, disaster. There cannot be such a proposition as E+. There is no factual thesis itself invulnerable to empiricist critique and simultaneously the basis for the empiricist critique of metaphysics. So either empiricism reduces to absurdity or—we have finally come around to it--Principle Zero is violated, and can be violated, and a philosophical position need not consist in holding a dogma or doctrine.[12]

Three. What Empiricism Could Be: Philosophical Stances

The problem with naïve empiricism appears to lie in the very idea of (NE) itself. Being an empiricist cannot consist in believing some statement about what the world is like. But is there any other alternative? Yes; and in fact we have displayed the alternative already in the way we discussed the empiricist's recurring rebellion. We have in fact throughout, though implicitly, been dealing with philosophical positions that cannot be captured in dogmas.

9. THE RECURRENT REBELLION RE-EXAMINED: WHAT SEPARATES EMPIRICISTS FROM METAPHYSICIANS?

In characterizing the forms of metaphysics that empiricists attack, I emphasized the demand for explanation and for satisfaction with certain kinds of explanation. For empiricists I listed rejection of explanation demands and dissatisfaction with and disvaluing of explanation by postulate. Moreover, I listed the empiricists' calling us back to experience, their rebellion against theory, their ideals of epistemic rationality, what they regard as having significance, their admiration for science, and the virtue they see in an idea of rationality that does not bar disagreement. Notice that not a single one of these factors is a belief.[13] The attitudes that appear in these lists are to some extent epistemic and to some extent evaluative, and they may well involve or require certain beliefs for their own coherence. But none are equatable with beliefs. Implicitly, then, we have already been relying on a view of philosophy that belies Principle Zero.

10. HOW TO VIOLATE PRINCIPLE ZERO: THE STANCE

So here is the proposal: a philosophical position can consist in something other than a belief in what the world is like. We can, for example, take the empiricist's attitude toward science rather than his or her beliefs about it as the more crucial characteristic. Then we are led to the following suggestion of an alternative to Principle Zero. A philosophical position can consist in a stance (attitude, commitment, approach, a cluster of such—possibly including some propositional attitudes such as beliefs as well). Such a stance can of course be expressed, and may involve or presuppose some beliefs as well, but cannot be simply equated with having beliefs or making assertions about what there is.[14]

11. THE STANCE AS WILL AND IDEA

Suppose that empiricism is a stance rather than a thesis; how does that get empiricism out of trouble? For we could raise the issue of allowable disagreement all over again. Can we not say: the metaphysician disagrees, has a different and incompatible stance, but disagreement does not make one unscientific, irrational, or impious. . . .

Not so fast! Disagreement within science over a factual hypothesis keeps everything within the scientific family. But if empiricism is a stance, its critique of metaphysics will be based at least in part on something other than factual theses: attitudes, commitments, values, goals. Now it is quite clear in the example of empirical science that disagreement in that sphere does not stay within the scientific family. A disregard for evidence, a refusal to submit one's ideas to natural selection by relevant experiment or to engage in vigorous testing when nature itself does not put one to the test (these are some examples, none of them factual beliefs!) can certainly take one beyond the scientific pale. So the paradigm of science does not suggest that disagreement in the sphere of attitudes, commitments, values, and goals is invulnerable to empiricist critique. On the contrary, it suggests that it is. Feyerabend gave us a memorable description of such a disagreement in action: "the distinction between the crank and the respectable thinker lies in the research that is done once a certain point of view is adopted. The crank usually is content with defending the point of view in its original, undeveloped, metaphysical form, and he is not at all prepared to test its usefulness in all those cases which seem to favor the opponent. . . . It is this investigation . . . which distinguishes the 'respectable thinker' from the crank. The original content of his theory does not."[15] The crank, in other words, exhibits a very different attitude toward empirical investigation and exploration, which in addition points to a difference in attitude toward the proposed or advocated theory.

Four. Example of a Stance Misunderstood: Materialism

To the Vienna and Berlin circles my proposal would not have sounded alien; quite the contrary. In much of their work they expressed precisely the contention that empiricism is a stance rather than a factual thesis or theory.[16] Yet later philosophers in the analytic tradition have not generally tended to adopt such views of what philosophy is or can be. As a further defense I will now attempt to show that empiricist positions are in that boat together with some major putative exemplars of metaphysical theories about what the world is like.

One popular plea for metaphysics rests on the idea that for the good of science, scientists must start with provisional realism—there are unobservable causes for all observable phenomena or some such thesis—and presumptive materialism—matter is all there is, so those causes are all material mechanisms of some sort. I will concentrate here on materialism. Physicalism and naturalism are not precisely the same as old-fashioned materialism (all these isms come in various flavors and colors), but in the present context, the differences will not matter much. The argument will go through, mutatis mutandis, if we substitute, for example, "physical" or "supervenient on the physical" for "material."[17]

To begin, then, let us take the putative metaphysical theory summed up in the thesis: matter is all there is. This may sound a little dated, but is actually not far from current formulations.[18]

sounds debatable: surely it must be either so or
pearances are deceiving. Genuine debatability
ıding of what the suggestion actually means. A
resupposition is at stake: Does presumptive ma-
terialism ... ... ase make any difference to science at all? By "in
this sense" I mean, in the sense of assumptions, theses, factual claims
about what there is and what there is not.

13. WHAT IS MATTER?

Does the thesis that matter is all there is rule out at least some kinds
of theories, so that they are not even candidates for scientific exploration? I will argue that this is quite illusory. There may, however, be
a certain orientation, attitude, or stance associated with this thesis—
which does affect science as well as practical and intellectual life
generally—for which this thesis functions as code. If that is so, then
materialism may be a prime example of false consciousness in philosophy. For in that case materialists may take themselves to be
maintaining a theory while they are in reality merely expressing
attitudes, in ways that lend themselves to such expression only under
conditions of confusion and unclarity.

The thesis "matter is all there is" certainly sounds like a substantive factual claim. Does it not rule out Descartes's mind-body dualism, Aquinas's souls, spirits, entelechies, cosmic purpose? If those
are substantive factual claims, then a thesis that contradicts them
must be, too.

But we cannot simply assume that all those putative metaphysical theories really are what they sound like, if we are about to
question the status of any one of them. The contradiction may also
be just appearance. A contradiction may be merely verbal. For ex-

ample, if a Cartesian says to a materialist "Matter is not all there is," then of course there is a contradiction on the syntactic level. One uses a sentence that is the negation of the other one. This syntactic contradiction is there, then, regardless of whether either materialist or Cartesian is making any sense at all. The materialist thesis will genuinely rule out the Cartesian view only if each can be made clear enough so that the denial has some genuine content (and even then it may not).[19] The precise truth conditions for these various claims require at least that there is a genuine, and not just a verbal, distinction between what is material and what is not material.

Suppose that the thesis is indeed the important part of materialism. Then something follows from this about what materialists will find it important to do. In that case they will certainly not rest until the distinction between matter and what is not matter has been made so clear that the thesis is a factual claim, which can clearly be either true or false. But if they do not, then by *modus tollens* we should conclude . . . what?

What would count as something that is not material? Descartes said that matter is extended and mind is not; mind thinks. But if that is not a stipulative definition, it is certainly wrong. Otherwise we would have to say that Hertz's massive point particles, if they exist, are not material. Equally we would have to say that Hartry Field denies materialism when he claims that space-time points are real, concrete individuals. And Field is well known for his insistence that any philosophical account he would accept must be compatible with materialism.

It may be unfair to take Descartes as our whipping boy. Do more recent putative statements of materialism fare much better? Typically they start from some version of received scientific opinion, perhaps with some anxiety about being up to date. They will not say that atoms or elementary particles are all there is, since they know that there are trees, persons, and rocks as well. But they will say that everything is composed solely of atoms or elementary particles. If we take this seriously we shall, I wager, once more land in an untenable historical parochialism. When Newton introduced forces in addition to bodies, did he deny the thesis? Forces are not composed of particles. When Huyghens's waves-in-the-ether theory defeated Newton's particle theory of light, was that a setback for materialism? Surely not, although the ether was a continuous medium, not particulate. When a recent article in a physics journal bore the title "Particles Do Not Exist," was that a denial of materialism? The author's argument was that particle number is not relativistically invariant, so how many particles there are is as relative as left/right, up/down, rest/motion.[20]

There are, of course, still other attempts to identify precisely what it is to be physical or material. One to be found quite often is to equate the material or physical—almost nonchalantly—with what is located in space and time. Is that a good criterion for distinguishing what is material or physical from what is not? There does not seem to be a satisfactory conceptual connection. First of all, angels, demons, and God himself have been said to appear fully at certain places and times, although they are usually cited as paradigm examples of the nonphysical. These are, of course, examples of entities that are able to manifest themselves in space-time but are not at all times localized there. Should we then refine the criterion to something like "what is physical is precisely what is at all times fully localized in space"? It does not seem so, for elementary particles as conceived by the Copenhagen school of quantum mechanics are presumably physical but do not meet that criterion. As the electron is captured when it hits the television monitor screen, it has a particular location, but it did not have a well-defined spatio-temporal trajectory beforehand. Indeed, it is easy to show in the quantum mechanics developed at that time that if a particle's location is at a given moment in a well-defined finite spatial region, that condition will not last very long at all. So the electron is, as it were, going in and out of space. Is this, then, an example of the nonphysical? Did these physicists introduce immaterial substances into physics? It seems better to conclude that the spatio-temporal location criterion does not match materialists' understanding of their own thesis, either.

Whenever philosophers take some general feature of physics and use it to identify what is material, what happens? Physics soon goes on to describe things that lack that feature and are altogether different. When that happens, does materialism bite the dust? Surely not! But if materialism were really, purely and simply, some such thesis as "everything is composed of elementary particles," I could not so readily say "Surely not"!

14. TWO MOVES FOR MATERIALISTS

Soi-disant materialists have certainly taken cognizance of this difficulty. When their most important terms are tied to current scientific theories, they must die with those theories; but if not, they seem to lack content altogether. That is a dilemma. In response, they have opted for one of two moves. Some have attempted to formulate very specific theses relating to the putative subject matter of psychology, argued that these are empirical, and offered the results as a specific version of materialism. Others have pinned the thesis down by nailing it to a specific science such as physics, by means of a completeness claim for that science. It seems to me, and I will try to show, that neither move leaves us with materialism as an identifiable substantive thesis.

THE FIRST MOVE: MATERIALISM AS SCIENTIFIC HYPOTHESIS

Place argued that it is tenable to say that certain events and processes traditionally classified as mental (for example, sensation) are identical with events and processes in the brain.[21] That this is indeed so he labeled as materialism and argued that it is in fact a scientific, empirical hypothesis.[22] The described "mental" events and processes have a certain complexity, which brain events and processes may or may not have. Empirical evidence for such higher complexity would disconfirm the hypothesis. The name "materialism" is also given to this or closely similar claims about the psychological by, for example, David Armstrong.[23]

I have three preliminary questions. First , not every replacement for what I have called the thesis can be accepted as the "real" materialism; can this one? The principal question before us is what exactly the materialist's main thesis could be. We should perhaps accept any seriously offered contender. But if we could identify certain familiar psychological events and processes with physiological ones, we would hardly be finished with the traditional concerns of materialism. That a person has a purpose, for example, does not consist in any specific type of occurrent event or process; nor that her sins are forgiven, that she is in a state of grace, or that she is precious beyond rubies. And these are only examples about persons; what else may there not be between heaven and earth never dreamt of in materialist philosophy? I don't want to be fanciful, but merely establishing that sensations are brain states seems hardly more than a drop in the bucket for the materialist. The virtue of such a ringing thesis as "matter is all" was to settle the hash of all such stuff once and for all.

The second preliminary question: Does the description of the "mental" or the psychological in terms of which the replacement thesis is formulated do justice to its intended concern? Armstrong was rather more conscious than was Place of the second preliminary question when he was debating Malcolm, a Wittgensteinian. Today he would also have to contend with putative failures of functionalism, arguments that no computational theory of consciousness could even in principle be successful, and demonstrations that truth conditions for belief attributions must have historical and social parameters outside the believer.

But leave these debates aside. Here is the main question: Supposing the empirical claim is false or is scientifically investigated and found wanting, will there or will there not be a fall-back position to call "the real materialism after all"?

It would be a poor game if after much scientific strife the loser could say, "that's not it at all, that is not what I meant at all." Well, what if we accept Place's or Armstrong's formulation, and their empirical claims are found wanting? Suppose, for example, that no neurological process can be identified that can even in principle predict human decisions. The next empirical question would be: What probabilities can be assigned to the (neutrally described) actions being decided on, conditional on the states of the central nervous system? If these probabilities cannot even in principle be made as near zero and one as we would like, is that the end of materialism?

Think of the exact parallel: no quantum state will predict the exact time of radioactive decay. The probability of decay within a given time period cannot be brought arbitrarily close to zero or one no matter how much information we get about the physical situation. Is that the end of materialism? It is not; and neither would materialism come to an end if what humans do could be related only probabilistically to their brain states. People would simply be more like bits of radium than we had suspected. A favorite belief of the materialists would have to be relinquished, but they would all know how to retrench. Human behavior would simply be more like radioactive decay than we had thought, that is all. The spirit of materialism is never exhausted in piece-meal empirical claims.[24]

THE SECOND MOVE: WHATEVER IT TAKES

If you press a materialist, you quickly find the most important constraint on the meaning of the thesis. That constraint is simply that it should be compatible with science, whatever science comes up with. That is contrary to what some of them say. If, they say, certain phenomena could not be explained purely in terms of material factors, then the scientific thing to do would be to give up materialism. But, holding the thesis, they make the bold conjecture that this will never happen. That what would never happen?

If that question cannot be answered with a precise and independent account of what material factors are, there is still one option. That is to nail a completeness claim to science or to a specific science such as physics. The instructive example here is Smart, who begins his essay "Materialism" with an offer to explain what he means: "By 'materialism' I mean the theory that there is nothing in the world over and above those entities which are postulated by physics (or, or course, those entities which will be postulated by future and more adequate physical theories)."[25] He quickly discusses some older and more recent postulations in actual physics, which make that "theory" look substantive. But of course the parenthetical qualification makes that discussion completely irrelevant!

Smart may believe, or think that he believes, the "theory" here formulated, but if he does, he certainly does not know what he believes. For of course he has no more idea than you or I of what physics will postulate in the future. It is a truly courageous faith that believes in an "I know not what"—is it not?

Indeed, in believing this, Smart cannot be certain that he believes anything at all. Suppose science goes on forever, and every theory is eventually succeeded by a better one. That has certainly been the case so far, and always some accepted successor has implied that the previously postulated fundamental entities (known, after all, only by description) do not exist. If that is also how it will continue, world without end, then Smart's so-called theory—as formulated above—entails that there is nothing at all. Let's not be too quick to celebrate this demonstration of clear empirical content.

In a clear indication that he is at least subliminally aware of the problem, Smart quickly adds some extra content. Not content with his initial formulation once he realizes that it is compatible with emergent properties, holism, and the irreducibility of biology to physics, he says, "I wish to lay down that it is incompatible with materialism that there should be any irreducibly emergent laws or properties, say in biology or psychology. . . . I also want to deny any theory of 'emergent properties' " (ibid., pp. 203–4). We should read this as an *amendment* of the above definition of materialism. The "theory" formulated above, taken by itself, did not imply any of that. Just how does Smart know that his initial formulation was inadequate? Is he telling us that he knows that either physics will forever eschew emergent properties or else materialism is false? Since quantum physics may provide, at this point, a clear example of holism (as argued, for example, by Paul Teller), should we conclude that materialism may already have come to an end?

Of course not. Faced with the consequences of his own idea— that materialism should be whatever it takes to be a completeness claim for physics—Smart started backpedaling. Everything that is "repugnant" to him (to use his phrase) may eventually come to be incorporated in future physics. So Smart adds, in effect, that physics will be false if that happens. But faced with that consequence, no materialists will stick by him if he sticks by that. They'll point out, quite rightly, that he was of a "classical" mind, and as so often happens with the older generation in physics itself, quite unable to assimilate new visions of the structure of the *material* world.[26]

15. MATERIALISM AS FALSE CONSCIOUSNESS

So is it all just a matter of scientific reactionaries with their self-trivializing theses dressed up as uncompromising metaphysical constraints on science? No, it is not. All this effort to codify materialism bespeaks something much more important: the spirit of material-ism. Materialism is a hardy philosophical tradition that appears differently substantiated in each philosophical era. Each instantia-tion has its empirical as well as its nonempirical claims, which inter-pret for that era, in its own terms, the invariant attitudes and convic-tions that I call here the "spirit of materialism."

How shall we identify what is really involved in materialism? Our great clue is the apparent ability of materialists to revise the content of their main thesis as science changes. If we took literally the claim of a materialist that his position is a simple belief, we would be faced with an insoluble mystery, for that belief would then consist in the claim that all is matter, as currently construed. If that were all there was to it, how would such a materialist know how to retrench when his favorite scientific hypotheses fail? How did the eighteenth-century materialists know that gravity, or forces in general, were material? By the end of that century, Baron d'Holbach's *Système de la Nature* defined materialism on the European continent, but it had become scientifically obsolete only a generation or two later. Nothing in d'Holbach's description of nature allowed for the new theories of light, electricity, and magnetism.[27] How did the material-ists know in the nineteenth century that the electromagnetic field was material, and how did later materialists persist in this conviction after the ether had been sent packing?

Perhaps a materialist could reply that it is possible to measure certain quantities and that this is his cue to what is material. But that cannot provide the criterion needed. Just think again of the transi-tion from Cartesian to Newtonian physics. Newton identified forces as the causes of changes in states of motion. Accordingly, if you measure the direction and rate of change of momentum, you obtain a description of that cause in terms of its effects. The recipe for measuring force direction and magnitude is exactly to measure those effects. But even if the effects are motions of material bodies, it does not follow logically that the cause is material. As far as logic is concerned, one could add consistently that these causes are immaterial, spiritual—even mental, if Mind does not need to be someone's mind. But instead the forces are said to be material just like the extended bodies so classified before. If this is a claim to knowledge, the materialist must seemingly have some rather mysterious power: a knowledge that the newly introduced entities have the *je ne sais quoi* that makes for materiality.

It is quite clear now: the new conclusion that the newly introduced entities are material too is not a matter of knowledge at all. But what is it, then, in this metaphysical position, that guides the change in content, which it would be pedantic to signal with a change in name? If the "physicalist" or "naturalist" part of this philosophical position is mainly the desire or commitment to have metaphysics guided by physics, then it is something that cannot be captured in any thesis or factual belief. If the position does not mainly consist in such a desire or commitment, then what is it? This knowing how to retrench cannot derive from the substantive belief which is (at that time) identified with the view that all is physical. So what does it derive from? Whatever the answer is, that, and not the explicit thesis, is the real answer to what materialism is.

Hence I propose the following diagnosis of materialism: it is not identifiable with a theory about what there is but only with an attitude or cluster of attitudes. These attitudes include strong deference to the current content of science in matters of opinion about what there is. They include also an inclination (and perhaps a commitment, at least an intention) to accept (approximative) completeness claims for science as actually constituted at any given time.[28] Let us call these the first and second characteristics of materialism. Given this diagnosis, the apparent knowledge of what is and what is not material among newly hypothesized entities is mere appearance. The ability to adjust the content of the thesis that all is matter again and again is explained instead by a knowing-how to retrench that derives from invariant attitudes.

This does not reflect badly on materialism; on the contrary, it gives materialism its due.[29] But it does imply that only the confusion of theses held with attitudes expressed, which yields false consciousness, can account for the conviction that science requires or implies materialism.

16. MATERIALISM WITHOUT FALSE CONSCIOUSNESS?

I mean the above as a diagnosis of materialism, not an indictment or refutation. Its incarnation at any moment will be some position distinguished by certain empirical consequences, and these will either stand or fall as science evolves. But whether they stand or fall, materialism as general philosophical position, as historical tradition in philosophy, will survive. Given this, however, there can, for that very reason, be no question of regarding materialism as an assumption at the foundations of science. There is no "presumptive materialism" that constrains scientific theories to consistency with certain determinate factual theses. Materialism itself is not so constrained, and it survives by changing so as to accommodate the new sciences.

We may take this in part as explanation of something that materialism has in common with other hardy perennials of philosophy. Besides the theses on which the day's materialists take their stand, and which vary with time, there is also such a thing as the "spirit of materialism," which never dies. False consciousness can be avoided in two ways:

(1) the philosopher may lack that spirit and be genuinely concerned solely with certain definite factual questions about what there is, or

(2) the philosopher may have that spirit and not confuse its expression with any particular view of what the world is like.

The latter, however, may never yet have been instantiated among philosophers.[30]

Nevertheless, the second option is the really interesting one and similar to the one I would favor for any attempt to continue the empiricist tradition. The problem for materialists will then be to identify the true materialist stance and for the empiricist to identify the true empiricist stance (or the spectrum of true empiricist stances). Being or becoming an empiricist will then be similar or analogous to conversion to a cause, a religion, an ideology, to capitalism or to socialism, to a worldview such as Dawkins's selfish gene view or the view Russell expressed in "Why I Am Not a Christian." That is so, and not perhaps a prospect to everyone's liking. But let us not color the project with guilt by association. If I am right, all the great philosophical movements have really been of this sort, at heart, even if different in purport; what I favor is that we should do what we do without false purport.

Five. What Could Philosophy Be, Then?

I have now argued that empiricism must be a stance rather than a thesis and that materialism is in fact a stance, but misunderstood as a thesis about what the world is like. There are two points I would like to make in conclusion. The first concerns just what philosophy in general is and can be, once we escape from the confines of Principle Zero.[31] The second concerns precisely how these two stances of empiricism and materialism differ from each other.

The most immediate reaction I have received to this idea of philosophy as stance is: But then how can philosophical differences ever be settled? What is philosophy going to be, if it is a matter of differing stances, and how can we ever come to agreement in philosophy?

That is a little ironic—was it so easy then to settle disputes over those factual theses? Just how long did it take to settle those disputes over the reality of universals, the nature of knowledge, skeptical doubts, objective necessity in nature, and so on? How easy was it to reach agreement on those issues?

What is behind the question is probably something like the following. Since the differing stances also involve value judgments and attitudes toward life, love, and laughter, their basis may be thought to be purely subjective, merely subjective, and not susceptible to rational debate. But if that is indeed what is behind it then I cannot really take it seriously. After all, we have learned something since those heady but simplistic days of *Language, Truth, and Logic*. On one hand, we know very well how to defeat the simplistic philosophies that make values just a matter of subjective preference, dismissably relative. On the other, we too are members of a highly politicized open society in which ethical and ideological differences are precisely what are most up for debate. We need not look far to see that rational discourse is possible on matters that touch our values, attitudes, and commitments. So I'd just like to say: look around you, take part, welcome to the real world! But in fact there are examples in philosophical debates that begin in putative factual disagreement and turn out to hinge on value judgements.[32]

Stances do involve beliefs and are indeed inconceivable in separation from beliefs and opinion. The important point is simply that a stance will involve a good deal more, will not be identifiable through the beliefs involved, and can persist through changes of belief. I think I can illustrate this very well by reflecting on some ways in which the materialist and the empiricist stances differ from one another—and simultaneously show how rational disputation is possible and relevant, even if it cannot settle an issue definitively.

For both these philosophical positions I found it crucial to point to certain attitudes toward science. Both involve a very positive attitude toward the empirical sciences, but not the same attitude. Characteristic of materialism is a certain deference to the content of science. This deference takes two forms: the belief that the scientific description of the world is true, in its entirety or near enough, and at least a strong inclination toward completeness claims for the content of certain sciences. "This is true, and nothing else is true" would express such a claim. Because of the difficulties surrounding such claims, and the dim appreciation that the claim is less important than the deference it betokens, we usually hear something else, something like "What else *is* there?" But that too is only a challenge masquerading as a factual question.

Empiricism may also be approached through reflection on its positive attitude toward science. But this admiring attitude is not directed so much to the content of the sciences as to their forms and practices of inquiry. Science is a paradigm of rational inquiry. To take it as such is precisely to take up one of the most central attitudes in the empiricist stance. But one may take it so while showing little deference to the content of any science per se. Berkeley, Leibniz, Mach, Duhem, to name a few, worked mightily on philosophical accounts of science, in a very positive, even loving vein, while thoroughly critical of the foundations of physics of their time. How do we live in a world in which, to the best of our knowledge and belief, all our best most fundamental scientific theories are false?[33] We live in it by the lights of science as practice, as search, as rational form of inquiry par excellence.

For the materialist, science is what teaches us what to believe. For the empiricist, science is more nearly what teaches us how to give up our beliefs. All our factual beliefs are to be given over as hostages to fortune, to the fortunes of future empirical evidence, and given up when they fail, without succumbing to despair, cynicism, or debilitating relativism.[34]

Scientific Revolution/Conversion as a Philosophical Problem

For last year's words belong to last year's language
And next year's words await another voice.
— T. S. ELIOT, "Little Gidding"

How shall we develop the empirical stance, to continue the empiricist tradition? The problems I'll address in the remaining lectures all belong to epistemology: the realm of knowledge, belief, and opinion. That realm has throughout been the empiricists' central philosophical concern. If we cannot today accept the epistemologies of any of our empiricist predecessors it is because we—all of us in Western culture—have come to see ourselves and our relation to nature quite differently than we did before. In this lecture and the next I will take as focal point a question that belongs very specifically to the twentieth century. The last lecture will also deal with questions broadly epistemological, though with a different focus.

Focusing on a single question, however central, would be a small game if we occupied ourselves merely with the question itself. What makes it worth the candle is that we can let it function as a probe, a touchstone, the occasion to explore prospects for renewal in empiricist epistemology. That is what I mainly mean to do. The focal question is this: How are we to understand scientific and conceptual revolutions?[1] Are there really such radical, deep-going changes as philosophers such as Norwood Russell Hanson, Paul Feyerabend, and Thomas Kuhn described? I can state my response quite simply. Yes, there are such changes, so radical that they are characterized by a remarkable historical asymmetry. From the posterior point of view, the prior can be made intelligible and the change ratified. From the prior position, however, the posterior view was absurd and the transition to it possible but incapable of justification.[2] Taken together, these two points may seem less an answer than a paradox. Somehow the two will have to be brought into a delicate balance if the answer is to stand. I will try to do so in this lecture and the next. I hope to provide a prolegomenon to any future empiricist epistemology. Some major traditions of modern philosophy surviving in mainstream analytic theory of knowledge will have to be discarded.

One. The Problem: Our Rejected/Celebrated Past

Around the middle of the twentieth century our view of the empirical sciences began to shift. Through the writings of historically oriented philosophers such as Hanson, Feyerabend, and Kuhn we began to see their evolution as a sort of punctuated equilibrium. Received scientific opinion tells us a great deal about what the world is like. But this opinion, the scientific representation of the world, goes through radical, revolutionary changes. Thomas Kuhn introduced his picture of long periods of normal, paradigm-dominated science separated by revolutions. Even that may sound rather sanguine now. In the sciences we see a large human predicament mirrored: epistemic trauma and crisis in science mirror our evolution through many histories of crisis and trauma.

That there had been revolution in the history of science was not by itself a novel idea. Galileo, Boyle, Descartes, Newton were scathingly explicit about their radical break with Aristotelian physics and

Ptolemaic astronomy. The evangelists of relativity, the quantum, and biological evolution were no less explicit about the enormity of their breach. But these were triumphalist views that relegated the past to error. Contrary to that triumphalist rhetoric was actual scientific practice. That practice lives by the criterion that it must retrospectively account for past success and remain undogmatic about future vindication.[3]

This phenomenon of our cognitive life poses a major problem for philosophy. In retrospect, we can see the changes we went through—from suffering through reversal to recognition, to use the Aristotelian phrase—as fortunate. But was trauma overcome by reason or by lucky epistemic mutation? Can we have a conception of knowledge, belief, and opinion in which such radical, revolutionary changes are intelligible as rationally endorsed responses to crisis? The old philosophical chestnuts of induction, abduction, confirmation, and "proportioning one's opinion to the evidence" by some sort of recipe or rulebook had lent themselves well to triumphalism. But we are forced now to a more nuanced view of ourselves as quite possibly, at any moment, in the same situation as those who had to go through the traumatic conversion experience from a "classical" to a "contemporary" world picture. To this more nuanced view those philosophical chestnuts had little to contribute.

Here we have a touchstone for the adequacy of our epistemology. For empiricism this is a truly major problem. An extremely liberal empiricism might lead to the pessimistic, skeptical conclusion that those revolutions constitute a rupture in rational scientific progress. A similarly extreme conservative "fundamentalism" would imply a purely rational, rule-governed hidden process underlying precisely the endorsable changes in science. That conservative view would relegate trauma and discontinuity to the realm of appearance alone. Neither view can do equal justice to both sides of the phenomenon. One plays down the real experience of epistemic dislocation, the other ignores the retrospective rational endorsement of certain such transitions in our own past.

Why is our problem a philosophical problem and not simply the difficulty of understanding an opaque psychological transition? The reason is that these changes come with explicitly posed calls for decision—to accept the new theory, conceptual frame, world picture, or to reject it—and yet rational decision theory is at a loss to either steer or account for them. This I will argue in detail.

1. EPISTEMIC TRAUMA, REVOLUTION, CONVERSION

In 1913 Niels Bohr proposed a new model of the atom that made no sense within the context of classical physics. But his model accommodated a large body of recent experimental findings recalcitrant to theoretical representation. The questions this model raised for classical convictions ran deep. When an electron passes from one stationary state to another, how does it choose which (lower energy) state to jump to? How does it decide at what frequency it is going to vibrate? How does a photon, emitted during such a transition, choose the direction in which to move? Without answers, nature appears to be indeterministic. By classical criteria, however, a theory is not finished before it has displayed the phenomena as part of a deterministic process. Rutherford, Einstein, and Raleigh were skeptical, dismayed, or dismissive. In Goettingen the assumptions were found too bold and fantastic: "If it's not nonsense, at least it doesn't make sense." Born called it "queer and incredible"; and still all of these men admitted that the impressive empirical success showed that there must be something to this queer, incredible theory.[4] There was considerably worse to come; indeterminism in nature was the least of it. Yet within a few decades, the quantum revolution could claim the allegiance of the physics community, and questions as to its coherence and intelligibility were largely moot.

When Einstein's special theory of relativity reached these American shores, it found a physics community that had every right to speak for itself.[5] William F. Magie's presidential address to the American Physical Society in 1911 expressed one clear reaction: "In my opinion the abandonment of the hypothesis of an ether at the present time is a great and serious retrograde step in . . . physics. . . . How are [the supporters of the theory of relativity] going to explain the plain facts of optics?" Was he expressing the considered opinion of the society's members? If anyone had a claim to knowledge of what is and is not genuine physics, it was they. Yet within a very few years they relinquished that opposition to relativity.

Although surprisingly fast, these transitions were neither peaceful nor easy. The trauma tends to be quickly forgotten, perhaps repressed, simply not understood by the postrevolutionary generations. We need to look back to contemporary accounts. With respect to the theory of relativity's reception in Europe, Reichenbach (actively involved in the theory's conceptual assimilation) wrote tellingly:

> It is obvious that each philosophical school selects from the theory of relativity exactly those philosophical issues that appear interesting from its particular vantage point, and either accepts, rejects, or "interprets" the physical theory depending on whether or not the theory agrees with the doctrines of the school. This accounts for the amazing variety of opinions, the violent controversies about the importance, consistency, and scientific applicability of Einstein's discoveries. The kaleidoscopic chaos of opinions is heightened, in turn, by the participation of the general public in this controversy.[6]

Although even-handed, this is still a passage written by an advocate, more deeply immersed into the theory's conceptual foundations than almost any other philosopher of the time. Thus Reichenbach is already engaged in the retrospective task of accounting for the prior lack of understanding and error, as seen from the postrevolutionary perspective. His critique of various philosophical responses reveals quite graphically just how incomprehensible the new world picture was from the prior "classical" point of view.

As we now look back, there are a number of such major transitions in our view of nature. The first great scientific revolution in our Western tradition occurred in the fifth century B.C., when visions of a flat earth layered between water and air gave way to the view that the earth is round. The evidence was empirical, carefully compiled from the visibility of stars as sailors passed the island of Rhodes on their way to or from Egypt, the length of shadows at equinox in southern Egypt and Alexandria, and so forth. But the elimination of the cosmic up-down asymmetry of the previous worldview was the first great relativity revolution, relativizing the zenith to places on earth. In Aristotle's cosmology that great asymmetry had given way to rotational symmetry (with a fixed center). Up-down was downgraded to relative status. The Copernican revolution and its Galilean chapter are of course the best documented and most intensely studied. There space acquired translational symmetry and lost its privileged center while Galileo's kinematic relativity abolished the distinction between rest and constant motion. The later revolutions of relativity and quantum theory are of course the freshest on our minds.

Given that transitions from old to new, from the familiar to what was initially alien, are actual, they must be possible. There must be ways in which someone caught up in one way of thinking can transit, in principle anyway, to another way. On the other hand, this does not imply that the felt unintelligibility was an illusion. At least in sufficiently mathematized disciplines, it is quite possible to demonstrate rigorously the limits of translation or assimilation. As one example we can think of how the mathematician Beltrami showed how certain non-Euclidean two-dimensional spaces can be embedded in our familiar Euclidean three-space. That allowed one to think, briefly, that new views of space that were entering physics could always be regarded as just placing our material world in a specific, possibly rather strange, region of Euclidean space. But once it was shown that many of the space-times in models of general relativity do not admit of any such relation to the space+time of Newtonian physics, the game was up. The transition to the new view of nature was to a view that was literally and logically incapable of being accommodated in any way within the previous view.[7]

These conceptual overturnings are not peculiar to the empirical sciences alone. There have been great changes in our conception of what it is to be a person, or conscious, or moral. Some of these changes are at least loosely associated with those in science. That is not nearly all there is to them. No changes in science could by themselves force us to see other tribes, races, or cultures as truly human, worthy of respect, and having the same basic rights as ourselves, for example. Other illuminating examples of other-than-scientific conceptual revolutions occur in religion. Saint Paul came back to the Jerusalem community that he had persecuted, but now as the Apostle to the Gentiles. Whether it was through Paul or through Peter that this community came to accept that someone could become a Christian without becoming a Jew, I do not know. But think of what had happened by the time they accepted that. The rejected doctrine had been an unquestioned, hardly even articulated, central part of their new worldview. In the Jerusalem community some had known Jesus himself, had been closely involved in the Gospel story, and had never understood this Gospel differently. If anyone had claims to knowledge, it was they. But they relinquished that claim.

Such crises are similar to those in the history of science: the claim, new to the Greeks of the fifth century B.C., that the world is round; Galileo's claim that the earth is not at rest, nor at the center of the universe . . . Now we say that we know these things, but at the time each of these was a call to radical conversion.

In each of these examples the old conceptual scheme certainly seemed to have no room for the new belief, or even to allow it as sensible—yet was radically changed over a historically short period. By the time of Socrates' death in 400 B.C., the earth was a sphere at the center of a spherical universe; within one generation after Jesus' death, Christianity had become a universalist religion; by the end of the century of Galileo's censure, the universe had no center and the earth moved.

What characterizes a radical change in view, as opposed to a mere change in opinion? As with almost any distinction, there will be a gray area; one kind will shade off into the other. But the literature points to four striking features to explain the sense of epistemic trauma so richly attested to in the writings of those who lived through such changes. First of all, there is an old or "classical" framework, left behind in favor of the new. Certain old notions are discarded, now seen as having fallen apart under the probing of nature and thought.[8] But second, in some areas comparison is possible, and there a recognized success succeeded a failure. In the *locus classicus* for the historical appreciation of such epochs, Kuhn writes: "there must be a conflict between the paradigm that discloses anomaly and the one that later renders the anomaly lawlike. . . . [T]he successful new theory must somewhere permit predictions that are different from those derived from its predecessor. That difference could not occur if the two were logically compatible."[9] This second characteristic is part of the requirement for "royal succession" of scientific theories, to which I will return in the next lecture.[10] So is the third: that the new framework allows for an explanation (in its own terms, of course) of the old framework's successes and of how it was possible for the old, faulty, or false theory to have succeeded in those ways. (With this sort of success the unintelligibility of certain older notions is then marginalized and relegated to the unimportant.) But I will focus here on the fourth characteristic. This one has to do with the view from before, specifically the view of those who see the successor appearing on the horizon, so to speak: the new view is literally absurd, incoherent, inconsistent, obviously false, or worse—meaningless, unintelligible—within the older view. We might call the third characteristic the retrospective intelligibility of older views and the fourth the prospective unintelligibility of the new.

Both engender problems for understanding. If the new views were prospectively unintelligible, how was a transition possible? And if in the transition some aspects of the past are decisively disowned, how can that past be retrospectively understood? This lecture addresses the first question; the second will be our focus in the next lecture.

2. THE PROBLEM OF RADICAL CONVERSION
AS A CRITERION OF ADEQUACY

The problem is simple to state. Imagine yourself looking back to your past self, or to our communal past. Say: I can now understand quite well how I thought at the time, but I see that by those earlier lights what I now think makes no sense at all. How was it possible for me to go through that fortunate change? That I now see it as fortunate and vindicated does not at all mean that it was rational, reasonable, or rationally acceptable at the time. So should I applaud bursts or binges of irrationality as acceptable crisis response? Should I glory in having done precisely what I would now forbid myself in the name of Reason? Should I give up my commitment to rational management of opinion, since I now applaud that previous unratifiable change of mind? Or am I just mistaken to think that my present views were absurd or unintelligible then? Is the whole idea of radical conversion, of true revolutions in scientific thought or elsewhere, an illusion?

This is a major problem for epistemology but one that traditional epistemology has hardly broached at all. There is no doubt that people can frame almost any sort of belief, no matter how egregious to "common sense." We know many examples of people who do—and actual implies possible. The question for the philosopher does not concern psychological possibility but rationality. Is there any *rational* way I could come to entertain, seriously, the belief that things are some way I now classify as absurd? Since I include myself in this world, and conceive of myself as a being capable of living in this world, any far-reaching change in how I take the world to be affects how I conceive of myself. Can I really, rationally come to see myself as anything beyond one of the familiar sorts of pigeon that fit one of the familiar pigeon holes handed to me by the tradition I'm taught in school? This is not simply an individual problem. Is there any rational way in which our civilization could come to see itself as something that did not fit its own accepted taxonomies? There was a pat answer not long ago. We emerged from superstition and myth into science and practical wisdom through a method (the scientific method, Reason) guaranteed to lead all its true practitioners into the light of truth. This triumphalist autohagiography of Reason has had to give way—not to irrationalism but to a more accurate and realistic autobiography that respects the very criteria we call scientific.

So here is the problem for epistemology: we take ourselves to have knowledge and to know what it is to be rational. Yet we also look back and see that in our past our presumed knowledge went into crisis, and the crisis was resolved in ways that burst the very categories of our then-putative knowledge and reason. We could perhaps think of ourselves as so superior to our past that these reflections are now irrelevant—and maybe that is the natural episte-mological attitude. But what if we acknowledge that we could be in that position again?[11]

The epistemologist confronted with radical conversion, whether in religion or science, faces the same question at a higher level. There were times when epistemology itself needed to undergo radical changes and did so. Can we coherently acknowledge that we could be in that position again? This problem is a touchstone for episte-mology and a fortiori for empiricism, if an empiricist position is to include an epistemology in its stance.

Two. Frameworks for Solution

Our focal problem is the intelligibility of conceptual revolutions. But the overall aim is to explore prospects for an empiricist episte-mology adequate to this and other challenges. So first we step back to acknowledge a deep philosophical divide in approaches to knowl-edge, belief, and opinion.

3. TWO FORMS OF EPISTEMOLOGY

The twofold division of epistemologies I propose will cut across some familiar categories and produce some unlikely bedfellows.

Willard Van Orman Quine's "Epistemology Naturalized" fa-mously contends that rightly understood and cleansed of confusion, traditional epistemology leaves a residue only of questions for em-pirical science (cognitive science) and for logic.[12] "The Death of Epistemology" is a phrase more likely to be associated with Rorty or Foucault, but in analytic philosophy the epithet should clearly go to Quine: Epistemology is dead. First God, now epistemology. Where will it all end?

Naturalized epistemology, engendered by this article, should not be philosophy at all but part of cognitive science, if Quine's conclusions are accepted. Fine, let's not quarrel about disciplinary titles.[13] The point is that its products should be theories with clear empirical content and should be constructed in the framework of the accepted science of the day. What strikes one as most likely to be missing is the traditional concern with values and evaluation. What is rational, what counts as transgressing the bounds of sense or of reason, how is it rational to manage and update our opinions? Such questions can appear in the writing of a scientific theory of cognition only in two ways: as questions about what values a certain population actually has and as questions about under what conditions those values can or are likely to be realized. Is a given procedure an effective means— by descriptively identified criteria of effectiveness—to a certain— also descriptively identified—goal? That is in part an empirical and in part a logico-mathematical question, and thus it falls within the scope of such a theory. Asserting such a theory (about what values a population actually has and what the effective means to their realization are in their environment) definitely does not involve the expression of any value judgment. Weber's injunction to the social sciences to produce only value-neutral descriptions is fully obeyed.[14]

But later efforts to naturalize parts of philosophy have not obviously honored this constraint. In Larry Laudan's "normative naturalism" and Ronald Giere's "philosophy of science naturalized," the views developed sometimes do and sometimes do not appear to involve value judgments as well as empirical and logico-mathematical assertions. Admittedly, a large part of their work does consist in the development of such a factual theory, a contribution to cognitive science. When it seems that the epistemological position nevertheless involves a value judgment, it is because the writer is identifying with a certain community, for example, the scientific community, as he or she conceives of that community and its goals.[15] I shall use the term "objectifying" to refer to an epistemology that clearly consists in a factual theory writing project about cognitive functioning.[16] If the appearance of value judgments being involved in, for example, Laudan's or Giere's position is correct, then they are not simply developing an objectifying epistemology.

The category of objectifying epistemologies is not restricted to Quinean types of naturalized epistemology. It also includes, as far as I can see, various metaphysical and theological epistemologies both past and present. There too we can easily see a slide into nonobjectifying positions. Consider Alvin Plantinga's epistemology, with its emphasis on "proper functioning": we have knowledge when we have acquired true justified beliefs through our properly functioning natural means. We may see this as a factual theory (metaphysical or theological rather than empirical) about the cognizing subject and cognitive functioning. But the word "proper" raises an eyebrow. The concept of proper functioning clearly applies in the first instance to artifacts. Artifacts function properly when they do precisely what they are designed to do. It seems therefore that we can speak of humans functioning properly in the area of cognition only if we think of them as either created, or trained and educated, in accordance with a certain design--whether the design of a Creator or of a society that trains and educates its members. So far so good; this can still be a factual assertion, either about creation or about society. But if the philosophical view includes subscription to or endorsement of that design then that "proper" becomes one of the philosopher's own terms of positive evaluation. In that case the view is no longer an objectifying epistemology, even if it has a large subpart that is or has the general syntactic form of one that is.

Now I have indicated what an objectifying epistemology is; I will spell this out some more below. I have also displayed one way in which there can be nonobjectifying epistemologies. Are there other ways? Presumably so: any development of a view in epistemology that does not consist entirely in the construction of a factual descriptive theory of cognition will be thus. I will offer as examples certain approaches to epistemology that do not engage in the construction of a scientific, quasi-scientific, or metaphysical theory of the processes of cognition. These examples happen to have another more salient characteristic as well: they give central importance to the will and the role of decision. Thus they are voluntarist epistemologies (a term that I will here use with minimal connotations).[17] Do we really have good examples of such approaches, which on one hand reject the "theory" format in their view of what knowledge and opinion are like and on the other give a central role to volition? We may detect something like that in Saint Augustine, in Descartes, and still more so in Pascal, but most of all in the American pragmatists and some of the analytic philosophers they influenced. The latter include Reichenbach and to a lesser extent, in some moods, Carnap (but I think that such an ostensibly neopragmatist thinker as Quine lost the crucial thread).[18]

Individual philosophers never fall neatly on one side or the other of such a divide, of course, as we shall see even more clearly when I describe these two strains in epistemology. But meanwhile you will have noticed some strange company—for today's naturalists often present themselves as in every way opposed to natural theology and to most metaphysics as well! Once you contrast them to the voluntarists, however, you can see naturalism falling quite clearly on the same side as natural theology.

4. "OBJECTIFYING" EPISTEMOLOGY

In response to the example of Saint Paul, not to mention Galileo and Copernicus, one may feel a very natural temptation to write a theory. To at least one of those three all of us will attribute some new knowledge that he brought into the world, effecting a radical change in our cognitive situation. But how? We are quite unlike the immaterial intelligences of heaven and hell. Compared to them we are much more like plants, beasts, and manmade machines. But we must also have possibilities of insight and cognition closed to those "lesser" beings. Thus the task we may see for ourselves is to describe (to write a theory in the narrow sense of a systematic factual description of) what we are like and how we function, when we function properly in certain specified respects. On that basis we can then answer the question of what is possible for us by way of knowledge or "adequate" beliefs or opinions. The result will be a theory: possibly a scientific theory, belonging to cognitive science or one of its empirical subdisciplines, or possibly a metaphysical theory about the grasping of essences or the like. Or it may be something in between, a quasi-scientific, more or less metaphysical, hybrid. The point is that this will be a theory in the narrow sense of a systematic factual description.

If you ask yourself for examples of epistemologies, you are most likely to think of such theories, of what I am calling "objectifying" epistemologies.[19] In recent jargon, there are externalism, internalism, and reliabilism; in somewhat less recent terms, inductivism, foundationalism, and so forth.[20] From the Middle Ages we remember the doctrine that knowledge is possible because of the *adequatio mentis ad rem*. Starting with Descartes, modern philosophers constructed variants on such "guarantees" of the accuracy of our mental representations with respect to their extra-mental objects. Once some separation set in between philosophy and scientific psychology, it became possible for Frege to rightly decry the continuing psychologism in epistemology and for Husserl to be rightly converted by Frege's critique.[21] But as Philip Kitcher ably brought to light, twentieth-century analytic philosophy largely turned against this Fregean insight in epistemology after having honored it so thoroughly in philosophy of logic, mathematics, and language.[22] This psychologism tends now also to take a rather mechanistic form in its alliances with cognitive science. Rudolf Carnap put his finger on the Zeitgeist when he declared the central problem of epistemology to be the design of a robot that can simulate our every intellectual capacity. For that, in his—and many of his contemporaries'—view, was how alone we can achieve self-understanding.

This theory-writing project has an elementary problem to face. If we are to write a theory about our cognitive activities and their adequacy, we'll have to draw on the very theories that encapsulate our present view of the world. But if we do so the result will simply rule out as impossible any way of coming to know that we ourselves don't fit our present view of the world.

Imagine such a theory of knowledge. Suppose for example that it is based on a science that describes us as animals born with instincts and drives that shape response to experience, with all experiential access circumscribed by these animals' physiology. Then that theory of cognition cannot have as a theorem that under certain realizable conditions we will come to know that we are not thus. Quite the contrary! It will imply that any conceptual revolution taking us out of that current scientific view would be an example of cognitive dysfunction, of failure, of error, and fall under the heading of how error is to be explained.

Perhaps many would say: "Well, that is right, for this basic view of the world is true." Fine, but of course that is what every generation says of its most fundamental beliefs. The problem, that no such epistemology can classify conceptual revolutions at that level as anything but error and failure, is a general feature. A different epistemology based on a medieval science might similarly classify as error any intellectual development leading to a view of cognition as completely conditioned by our physiology. To put it quite generally: any objectifying epistemology must imply that I will be in error if I come to believe that I am something not captured by its description of what I am.

Could I rationally become someone who takes our current theories of how we function in the world to be radically mistaken? Answer this on the basis of what we are according to that current view, and the answer may indeed very well be yes. But that answer will come with a corollary: that this change would be just one of the many ways in which I can fall into error, to be explained on the basis of our limits, shortcomings, and imperfections. The sorts of change described as conceptual revolution will take their place in the category of serious error to be avoided, with prescriptions for how to avoid it. These sorts of changes will be proclaimed as the errors of those who don't use induction, won't accept falsification by the evidence, refuse to infer to the best explanation science affords, let their bodies deteriorate so as to obstruct intellectual proper functioning, and so on and so forth. A few good lessons in the scientific method or the rules of right thinking will be in order. . . .

Not everyone will see this as a shortcoming.

Writers on naturalism are well aware of what I have pointed out here and often enough willing to accept this feature as something to stand by. They take resting one's epistemology on the currently accepted scientific world picture to be what it is to be rational, let alone scientific or intellectually respectable.[23] Well, that is really the only thing to do, if you think for example that epistemology must be cognitive science—if you take it that the project of epistemology is to write a theory of cognition.

But at every historical moment the current such epistemology will classify certain future conceptual revolutions under the heading of pathology—and no such epistemology will survive those revolutions if they occur. In other words, this sort of epistemology fails to give us a view of knowledge that is invariant under such transformations. Under these conditions we will be able to see the relevant conceptual and scientific revolutions only as divided into the "correct" ones that led us toward our current science and the "errors" that may lead us or might have led us away from that accepted truth.[24] I submit that the epistemological problem of radical conversion, or if you like, conceptual revolution, is an unsolvable problem for objectifying epistemologies.[25]

The point may be obscured in subtle ways. One such way is to think: an objectifying epistemology consists of a theory (for example, a theory of cognitive psychology), but the epistemologist is holding that theory merely as a working hypothesis. That epistemologist is then quite possibly capable of the judgment that we may in the future arrive at opinions contrary to that theory and do so correctly. This reflection is correct but does not ameliorate the problem. For the point is then that he or she is imagining the falsity of that theory and is concurrently classified by that theory as someone whose opinion is either incorrect or incomplete.[26]

None of this is a reason for not engaging in cognitive science. Empirical science can in principle provide descriptions and representations of any process we engage in, including our theory choices and other epistemic activity. But the philosopher engaged in objectifying epistemology must face a choice: either to become an empirical scientist (the pursuit of armchair science should not be an option here!) and to forsake the greater traditional ambitions of epistemology—or else to be content with an epistemology that fails on the touchstone of leaving room for radical scientific and conceptual revolutions in certain areas.

5. VOLUNTARISM IN EPISTEMOLOGY

What alternative is there? There is no way to write a theory of cognition while escaping from our general beliefs about what we and our world are like. We cannot construct a presuppositionless theory, a priori, independent of our current science, theology, metaphysics, or whatever else we have accepted as knowledge. But neither can we construct a theory based in our current knowledge base and still make sense of the very idea that we might be in the position of the pre-Copernican, pre-Galilean, pre-Newtonian, the pre-Einsteinian, that is, capable of correctly attaining, through a conceptual revolution, a true insight radically at odds with that current knowledge base.

How do we escape from this straightjacket? By rejecting the project of objectifying epistemology. We imperfect, finite beings, thrown into this imperfect, fallen world, are engaged in an "enterprise of knowledge."[27] We are engaged in epistemic pursuit, so to speak, pursuit of epistemic goals, of cognitive gain (to coin another phrase), individually and as a community, a culture, a civilization. About this volitional, intentional activity we hope to discourse illuminatingly without writing a theory about it, at least in the narrow sense of "theory." Some approximate parallels in other areas may help. There is a considerable difference between Clausewitz's *On War* or the ancient Chinese *The Art of War*, which are books of military strategy, and books such as John Keegan's *The Face of Battle* that describe how war is actually conducted. Similarly, most books on chess do not provide theories of chess-playing in the sense of systematic descriptions of the activities of participants in the game. Instead they investigate the tactics and strategies appropriate to certain criteria of evaluation, explicated or made precise in certain ways.

The above (characteristically voluntarist) description of our human epistemic condition faces its own special question. The extent to which epistemic pursuit can be successful will certainly depend on what is true about us and about the world in which we live— hence on empirical fact. But what that dependence means depends on what counts as "successful." This in turn depends on what exactly that pursuit is, that is, what is its defining aim, its telos. Only if we can answer what we are after in this enterprise can we even begin to determine how much of it hinges on our doing something well or badly and how much on contingent fortune.

What I have just said embodies the distinctive approach to knowledge of the pragmatists, though foreshadowed in history in the way I indicated above.[28] This sort of approach actually takes two forms, quite appropriately paralleling two strains in ethics.[29] In ethics we can discern one strain in which all moral judgments are taken to harmonize with each other: although there may be varieties of goodness, moral judgment concerns what will be better or best all told, and such a judgment is presumed (perhaps I should say presupposed) to be always possible. I'll call this the "axiological" strain, for it sees all moral judgment as deriving from a value scale. The other strain consists of philosophers who just can't accommodate so much on any single scale, and accordingly tend to think in terms of imperatives rather than value. For them the heart's command incarnates a moral realm, but it is not univocal; it may harbor all the tensions and conflicts for which human hearts are known These hearts' disharmony derives not just from their own frailty and sin but comes about in part because that moral realm itself is not monolithic or harmonious in the right way. That second strain I shall call "deontological." We can now discern a similar division in epistemology.

WILFRID SELLARS'S IRENIC AXIOLOGY

Remember that voluntarism in epistemology has its own special question. We recognize in our selves and our civilization an enterprise of knowledge, a cognitive pursuit, and many traditional questions of epistemology can be directed to this subject. But before we can answer any of the relevant questions about it, we face another question: What is the telos, the defining aim of this enterprise?

Wilfrid Sellars, himself once a Yale philosopher, had an answer fairly far removed from the practical sphere. The enterprise of knowledge is defined by its aim, which is to become intellectually and practically at home in the world. This, he added, is achieved by attaining for oneself the status of explainer, the one who can answer why-questions, so to speak, *ex cathedra*—to answer these questions in the first place for oneself, of course. But the criterion for our own status in our own eyes has much to do with how we see others as perceiving us. Therefore the communal standards for explanation will figure in the intended end and in the measure of its attaining.[30]

Sellars's view brings out first of all just why it is so important to answer the voluntarist's main question. Remember, that question is about an activity we are all engaged in all the time, and it asks, What is the point? We need an answer if we are to have any idea about what standards or criteria of adequacy to apply. To give one example: arithmetic mistakes in your bankbook may result in bouncing checks. Objections to such specific consequences have their own rationale, which may not transfer to distinct but similar cases. Faulty arithmetic can also result in poorly calibrated weather predictions whose consequences, however dire, may not include bouncing checks. Nor can we pretend that there is no connection between the two faults. The point is that only if we have a good general idea of what end is meant to be served by the activity will we have a good general idea about how to evaluate performance, tactics, and strategy.

Fine, we agree to the importance of some answer of the sort Sellars gave. But any rival answer about the aim of the epistemic enterprise could conceivably do as much for us. Once the aim is specified, we enter the sphere of practical or instrumental rationality, the practical syllogism and its ilk. That is true no matter what the axiology placed at bottom.[31] So, how shall we evaluate Sellars's specific answer, then? We need to see if the evaluation it engenders agrees with our pre-understanding of the matter. If it does not, we must either reject Sellars's view or else change our understanding.

As one virtue, Sellars could today claim to provide the rationale for a rule for which many philosophers show an inordinate liking: inference to the best explanation. The practice, it is said, in both science and daily life, is to infer the truth of the best explanation of our evidence. The best explanation of his father's death, given all of Hamlet's evidence, confronts him with his mother's guilt; irrational, then, to see her in any other way. Similarly in science: our current theories provide the best explanation we have of all known observable phenomena; irrational, then, not to take them as true. Irrational why? Because the very aim of forming and managing our opinion is to achieve that state of being at home in the world. But that happy state requires us to be able to explain what we see on the basis of our beliefs about what there is. The very point of tending our opinion is to put us in a better explanatory position with respect to the world we live in. So of course that rule of inference to the best explanation has a ready rationale!

But with this recognizable putative virtue comes an equally important objection. Sellars's view is not apodictically correct.[32] We do want explanations—who would deny that? But should we place that desire at the very heart of our epistemic enterprise and identify its fulfillment as the sine qua non of being at home in the world? To do so gives way to the overwhelming demands that Kant identified as leading to the illusions of Reason. Indeed, this rule of inference to the best explanation, at first attributed to scientific practice and everyday life, is the very vehicle for traditional metaphysical longings. So here we may be seeing a rather familiar spectacle: the philosopher reading his own desire to eliminate wonder into the entire world outside his study.

Sellars put one special value on a pedestal and elevated it to the status of the Good as sought in our epistemic strivings. We need not deny the value: it is certainly a good to have explanation when we can have it. But is it a supreme or overriding Good? And may there not be many values people embrace in this region? Indeed, may we not be living here, just as in the moral sphere, with the possibility of irreconcilable conflicts and tension?

This is not an egregious suggestion. In fact it brings us to the deontological strain of voluntarist epistemology.

WILLIAM JAMES'S EPISTEMIC IMPERATIVES

Almost exactly one hundred years ago William James addressed the philosophy clubs of Yale and Brown Universities on precisely this issue in his lecture "The Will to Believe."[33] James was not unaware of the *Drang nach Erklaerung* such as Sellars expresses to us, but he gave it a subordinate place as the "sentiment of rationality."[34] In its stead he proposed that our epistemic enterprise is conducted with two ends in view. The two desires he identified in this role are the desires to believe truth and to avoid error.

If we tend to the garden of our beliefs and opinions, we will see it flourish and grow, with many more beautiful plants, fewer and fewer weeds. This gardening metaphor is apt but a little disquieting. To increase our flowers, we fertilize and spray, but these treatments are good for the weeds as well. To decrease the weeds, we cut and burn and may even resort to some weed-killer—all of which degrade the environment and affect the flowers too.

So it goes with our opinion. If all we wanted was to avoid error at all costs, we would cut our opinion down to the bare bone, perhaps end up believing tautologies only. That would drastically lower the information content, and we would not be believing much of the true story about anything. The other extreme is as bad. If believing truths was our only aim, we could just believe everything and be sure to catch the truths in our net. That, as A. N. Prior once said, would certainly end *logische Spitzfindigkeit* once and for all.

We can't emphasize too much that these two desires introduce tension and conflict. We are not in the godlike position of simply and infallibly choosing for our beliefs all and only what is true. All we can do is pursue these two goods, and in this pursuit we cannot jointly maximize informativeness and expected accuracy. The two values so introduced are not simply two desirables; they pull us in opposite directions. They cannot be jointly maximized; to some extent, each is gotten at the expense of the other.[35] So the two desires by themselves are an incomplete package; they do not yield a well defined telos for opinion. That telos should be the search for a properly or well balanced body of opinion, with some equilibrium of information and security. Notice the third ingredient that has slipped in: the balance, the good proportion, the golden ratio, the measure . . . of truth believed as against error avoided. Now, although truth and error are objective categories, handed to us by nature itself, so to speak, this measure of balance is not! How are we to supply it ourselves?

In this regard Isaac Levi speaks of our individual risk quotient. Well, yes, that is an important personal factor, differing from the stout of heart to doubting Thomas and vacillating Hamlet. It is our own, we have a right to it. It is not something objective, in which we can simply follow nature's suit. Suddenly, if that is the clue, the responsibility for a crucial value judgment has landed on us ourselves.

Once we have admitted this, it is easy to spot other value judgments at work. We certainly do not have a simple desire for information, period. Levi speaks here of desiring relief from agnosticism. Perhaps we do sometimes desire such relief, and it may well be the very same desire James identified as the "desire to believe truth." But we do not desire such relief across the board! We are happy enough not to have any opinion on a multitude of topics. Instead we want information about what concerns us, what we count as relevant. That is the fourth ingredient, so to speak. As we are weighing the value of increasing our information content against the higher risk of falsehood in our beliefs, we'll certainly take into account what that information is about and what sort of information it is. Otherwise we'd be obsessively reading encyclopedias and dictionaries, *People* magazine and the *National Geographic*.

So James was not exactly right in his identification of aims. We need to relativize, or to recognize sensitivity to context, in these two desires. Part of our judgment here, a very important part, derives from our opinion of what others will want from us. We are part of an information economy,[36] in which certain sorts of information are much more valuable than others. This is, as in Sellars's view, a matter of community. *Enfin,* the values involved here are quite different from mere desires for truthful information and freedom from error. Some are independent of the relative weight of information versus security. To put it briefly: neither the logic of belief and knowledge nor the theory of subjective probability can address more than a severely abstracted aspect of our epistemic life.

How does this neo-Jamesian view compare to Sellars's? First of all there is the way conflict and tension are built into the very enterprise. If one of our major aims is to avoid error, we do have a general rationale for correcting our arithmetic wherever it is in play. But given that we have at the same time another aim, we realize that correcting our arithmetic does not get overriding importance. If we are pretty sure we stayed within certain error limits, we can often safely go on with our business despite a few such flaws. We cannot take this too far. Near the end of the continuum we see the importance of truth increasing sharply, but still, a continuum it is. However, any measure on this continuum by which we may balance the two desires and find a point of equilibrium, we will have to supply ourselves. Neither logic nor empirical study will take away this element of choice or the value judgment involved in that choice.[37]

The point is general. Once we think about our epistemic life as part of this more general information economy, in which our value judgments play a crucial role, the very conception of a methodological cookbook with precise recipes or other sorts of "inductive logic" loses all plausibility.[38] This general point can be made even on Sellars's view (as antidote to Carnap's robot) but is much stronger on James's since the tensions between our crucial epistemic goods make for an end in view that is beset with conflicts and tensions. The value judgment that supplies a measure of balance between our separate desires is up to us; the choice is momentous, and it is unavoidable.

So far, so good; but there is one very large problem that James does not seem to see and on which I can touch only briefly here.[39] It is a problem of coherence. Whatever our reasons are for believing or for changing our minds, they are in many cases not reasons for belief in a strict sense. In the strict sense, a reason to believe a given theory, say, must be something that makes that theory more likely to be true. I cannot coherently say, for example, "I believe in angels, for that belief has great therapeutic value for me, but I agree that such a therapeutic value does not make the existence of angels any more likely." Nor can I say that I made up my mind to believe that the theory of evolution is true despite insufficient evidence, because this theory unifies biology and increases the informativeness of my total set of beliefs. At least, I cannot while adding that neither of these virtues makes a theory more likely to be true. Well, perhaps I can say it, but then I must be understood as either confessing an incoherence in my opinion or else owning up to ulterior motives for the belief. For the very point of belief is to have something, some picture of what things are like, of which we can say: that is how I think it is, period.

A belief is still a belief if it is held for ulterior motives. But in such a case we have to say something like: "I realize that this was not a reason for belief; it did not make the matter any more likely to be true, but still, that is how or why I came to believe it." In the case of a scientific community, it is easier to draw contrasts that tend to escape us in private, individual epistemology. There are many reasons to accept a good theory if only because a good theory has many uses and is valuable in many ways. Thus a scientific community can reasonably come to accept a theory as a basis for prediction or explanation and as a framework for the design of further research for the very good reasons provided by the scientific credentialing process.[40] Many of these legitimate reasons for acceptance fall outside the reasons for belief, in that they do not make it more likely that the theory as a whole is "tracking the truth." Hence we should distinguish acceptance from belief. In the case of private opinion on little matters of fact the boundaries are not as clear as for the uses of theories in science. A good deal of what James describes beyond the desire to avoid error seems to me to lie on the side of acceptance as distinguished from belief. But the communal epistemic enterprise of science, which is the proximate topic of this essay, is the enterprise of managing its body of accepted hypotheses, where out and out belief is not of equal relevance.[41] Therefore I propose to leave this distinction aside in our present context and follow the traditional terminology, in line with James's discussion.[42]

6. THE PROBLEM OF REVOLUTIONARY CHANGES IN VIEW: NOT YET SOLVED

Although I introduced these forms of epistemology mainly by example, it will have been clear enough where I stand. William James came nearest, among the various views I highlighted, to the true character of our epistemic life. Our aim in the epistemic enterprise is indeed more complex than he indicated, since the desires for truth and avoidance of error are contextually qualified by our interests and values. This adds, however, only more tension and more calls for judgment, in which neither Reason nor factual knowledge can eliminate the burden of responsibility. In opinion as in action, we place our stakes and take our chance.

How does our major problem—the question concerning conversion and conceptual revolution—look now, in the light of voluntarist epistemology? Certainly we have obtained some leeway. The element of personal decision, values, and volition has entered and received a legitimate place in our epistemic life. By itself, however, this element is no cure-all, and in fact it provides an immediate remedy only for the smaller ills. If I have a conflict, for example, between seeing a student and reading a colleague's paper, and can find no higher value to decide the matter, I may justly take the responsibility for deciding. The consequent inescapable problem of dirty hands is not so great. Similarly, the voluntarist may wish to say, for the decision about when to accept a hypothesis, when to make up one's mind that the evidence has become sufficient. But is that right?

That we can just make up our minds, when evidence and reason reach their limit, makes easy sense when the stakes are low and the choice not momentous. Even then, it can perhaps make good sense only for a hypothesis that is already a live option for us, one we understand and already count among the significant alternatives to be taken seriously. Is revolution/conversion a case in point? Genuine revolutions in the arts, the sciences, ideology, or the conception of the state or of nationhood are surely not ones in which the stakes are low. Worse: they do not issue in views that were accepted as already live (or even intelligible) options anterior to the revolutionary episode. And with this reflection we seem to face our starting problem all over again.

Let us count our gains. We have surely fulfilled a necessary condition for making sense of such revolutionary developments with the entry of volition and values. Both the Sellarsian and the Jamesian epistemic agent can be driven into a corner by new experiences and new ideas. The agent pursuing the overriding value of explanatory harmony may find his or her epicycles multiplying inexorably, the weight of needed hidden variables increasing, the baroque adjustments in the light of new experience finally unbearable. Similarly, the person who has been proceeding with a definite risk quotient, and definite values for various sorts of information, may find that expectations are more and more frequently disappointed. Continually lowering the risk quotient is but a temporary palliative, until thinking has become so hidebound as to suffocate itself with security. At some point only a leap of some sort (a leap of faith, a "throwing away of the prior," as Bayesians say) will provide escape. Important for the philosopher, if we pass through such changes, the view of ourselves as engaged in such an epistemic pursuit with its governing desires and constraints can remain invariant throughout.

The concomitant conception of rationality is crucial here: rationality is but bridled irrationality. Throughout such changes we can continue to view ourselves as acting reasonably—I should say, as acting in a way we can endorse to ourselves as reasonable. Changes in view are not rational because they are rationally compelled; they are rational exactly if they are rationally permitted, if they do not transgress the bounds of reason.[43]

And yet there is a lacuna here, for a mere assurance of permission or coherence, however reassuring, does not amount to understanding. We still face that problem of the prospective unintelligibility of the new. So we must look into the permitted decision processes to gauge whether such radical changes in view as are found in scientific revolutions are truly intelligible to the voluntarist eye. Do they really stay within the bounds of reason, even so liberally conceived? What we find will not be immediately very satisfying.

Three. The Impasse: Enter Emotion

What happens in such a situation of severe epistemic hardship and increasing despair? These are precisely the sorts of crises in which the envisaged alternatives can change, with radical changes no longer necessarily precluded.

7. IN TRANSIT PERILOUS: CONDITIONS FOR REVOLUTION

As Kuhn, Feyerabend, and others have graphically demonstrated, the old deteriorating framework will not be given up until and unless there is a genuine rival on the scene. Hence we have two conditions for revolution: despair at the deteriorating status quo and a viable rival. But can these be seen as such at the time?

In one sense, the first can be understood well enough by the lights of prior opinion and understanding. That is, we can tell that our expectations are disappointed, that the earlier rate of success has diminished, that we have been working fruitlessly on our current projects. But from the point of view still dominant at that time, this is classified as due to the complexity and recalcitrance of nature, including our own human nature. When the going gets tough, the tough get going, isn't that right?

No, somehow this despair about the human condition has to turn into a sense of rebellion against the received view of what that condition really is. But how can it? By the lights of that received view, such "consciousness raising" is really consciousness lowering.

And what about the second condition, the perception of a serious rival to the received view? Succinctly: How can we possibly understand and count as a viable rival something that is absurd by our present lights? And how can something be a genuine rival to our present way of seeing and conceiving ourselves-in-the-world unless it is absurd by our present lights?

So here we have the further problem, which is not evaded by voluntarism in epistemology. We can't very well exercise the will on options unless we can see them as genuine options. How can we make intelligible to ourselves the process of choice, which takes us into options that we could not see as genuine options beforehand? We cannot satisfactorily relegate this to the subconscious or to physiological mechanisms behind the subjective scenes. Augustine does not cease from reflection, Einstein does not become tongue-tied when speaking with the other physicists. Nor do we just hope to wake up in a new mind or brain some day, with our conceptual perplexities dissolved into thin air. Quite to the contrary: there is a continuing inner and outer dialogue throughout the conversion experience—even though some of it is certainly devoted to expressing puzzlement and lack of understanding at what we are going through just then.

There must be a transition in which this status changes, a transformation of our situation that affects precisely the field of choice. First of all, our situation must deteriorate by our own lights, and second, the new option must have appeared, although neither the deterioration nor the new option is as yet seen as such.

8. PASCAL'S WAGER AND ITS LIMITS

> There are three things I need to think of when I climb: the probability of a fall, the consequences of a fall, and my own ability to judge the first two.[44]
> —LYNNE HILL

In William James's "The Will to Believe," our seminal essay in empiricist-voluntarist epistemology, Pascal's paradigm for decision making occupies a central role. Ostensibly, the decisions made in the course of the epistemic enterprise follow that paradigm. This is balm to our contemporary ears, for during the century since then this decision paradigm became the basic format for decision theory in economics and for "Bayesian" epistemology. But James takes this up, as Pascal does, in the very context where rationality seems most perilously in danger, exactly where that paradigm itself seems to be betrayed by its creator: Pascal's Wager.[45]

Blaise Pascal turned away from science and mathematics after learning from his Jansenist friends that scientific curiosity is just another form of sexual indulgence. But his writings thereafter did not fail to display a certain debt to this earlier indulgence, as becomes clear if we read the wager after looking at his correspondence with Fermat.[46] The letters, however, do not spell out general conclusions. This is probably in part because of the assumed common agreement on the basic approach, succinctly summarized in *The Port-Royal Logic* as follows: "To judge what one must do to obtain a good or avoid an evil, it is necessary to consider not only the good and the evil in itself, but also the probability that it happens or does not happen; and to view geometrically the proportion that all these things have together."[47] That passage, presumed to be Pascal's contribution to this influential logic text, presents the paradigm of rational judgment found in the correspondence and extrapolated in the wager. The person who judges and decides must determine the "value of the hope"—as Huygens so engagingly calls it—involved in each possible alternative before him.[48]

How does one determine this value? Geometrically. We must consider the value of each possible outcome and also its probability and then "view geometrically the proportion that all these things have together." As simple example, consider the decision to buy or not buy major medical insurance. Each action then has an expectation value that is the sum of the costs and benefits weighted in proportion to those probabilities. You will lose money either way: the cost of the insurance if you don't fall ill, and that cost plus the deductible if you do. But you are no dupe: you have placed a monetary value on the fear and possibility of ruin. Moreover, you have taken into account the probabilities of sickness and health.

With this basic insight into how one calculates the value of the hope in mundane projects, we now approach the project in which the stake is one's life and the hope eternal bliss. On the face of it, Pascal's Wager is simply this: you must choose whether to believe in God or not. If you do, and He exists, you will have eternal bliss. If you do not, you will have only this life (whether He exists or not). However small the probability that He exists, the value of eternal bliss so far outweighs the pleasures of a life of unbelief, given its scanty three score years and ten, that the expected gain of believing is the greater by far. So, believe!

That is a caricature, and even its defects are not very instructive; we need a closer look at Pascal's text itself. My reading of this famous passage will have three parts. First, we need to see how Pascal distinguishes the argument in the wager from demonstration. Second, we have to gauge what he thinks to accomplish by framing a certain choice in these gambling (that is, decision-theoretic) terms. Finally, we should take a careful look at the argument and ask how the limits of decision-theoretic reasoning appear in it. Our focus throughout is to be on the conceptions of reason and rationality in this text.

It is not true that Pascal offers his reasoning as a demonstration that, once we properly appreciate our situation, we are rationally compelled to believe. He does not set out to demonstrate (as he has so often been portrayed as doing) that it would be irrational for us not to believe. Starting with "Let us now speak according to our natural lights," Pascal argues that there can be no "rational grounds for their [the Christians'] belief." This is the introduction to the wager. Therefore, the wager passage does not purport to provide such rational grounds. Instead the wager is presented in answer to the charge ("it does not absolve those who accept it") that if a belief is without rational grounds then one ought not to have it.

"Ought" is not exactly unequivocal. The assertion "one ought to—" could be elaborated as "it would be immoral not to," "irrational not to," "imprudent not to," "un-American not to," and so forth. Here the sense must surely be the first? But however we construe the "ought," the charge is clearly based on the contention that one ought not to believe anything except what one is rationally compelled to believe. This view of rationality has a dual, as we saw above, that rationality is but bridled irrationality: rational belief is belief within the bounds of reason—that is, permitted (as opposed to compelled) within the dictates or criteria of reason.

On the former view Pascal could have no answer to the charge. Thus the first conclusion we must draw is that the "bridled irrationality" view of rationality is implicit in Pascal's text. I take it that this "permission" view of rationality is signaled when he writes, "Reason cannot make you choose either, reason cannot prove either wrong," and adds a little later, "Since you must necessarily choose, your reason is no more affronted by choosing one rather than the other." The decision-theoretic paradigm serves, then, to go beyond this point. Using it, Pascal means to indicate how there are still distinctions to be drawn among beliefs when neither they nor their contraries are compelled by reason and evidence.

Pascal does present his probabilistic reasoning, transposed from the gaming table to a more fundamental gamble: "Every gambler takes a certain risk for an uncertain gain, and yet he is taking a finite risk for an uncertain finite gain without sinning against reason." Further, he writes, "You have two things to lose: the true and the good; and two things to stake: your reason and your happiness; and your nature has two things to avoid: error and wretchedness." But as reasoning these remarks play a quite different role from the traditional arguments of natural theology. The only claim is that such a procedure does not sin against reason.

At every point where a question arises, Pascal emphasizes that reason cannot provide an answer. Yet the line of argument leads you to a conclusion. So you may want to object: Is this conclusion—that you should believe—not rationally compelled if the line of reasoning is cogent? Pascal does say, after calculating the value of the gamble, "And thus, since you are obligated to play, you must be renouncing reason if you hoard your life rather than risk it for an infinite gain, just as likely to occur as a loss amounting to nothing." But the choice of words to the contrary, the fact is that he has not produced rational grounds for belief. For he has given no evidence, nor purported to; the gamble has exactly the same expectation value for any given individual if God does not exist as if He does, and its value to you cannot provide evidence that He exists.

Does this probabilistic reason at least remove the need for choice, in the sense that the advice it yields always prescribes a unique course of action? Such a uniquely directed sense of rationality does not go with the conception of bridled irrationality. It belongs instead to the idea that it is irrational to believe or act except when rationally compelled. The latter view appears in the voice that says, "But I will condemn them [the Christians] not for having made this particular choice, but any choice . . . : the right thing is not to wager at all." That is not Pascal's voice; it is the same voice that leveled the charge to which the wager responds.

If probabilistic reasoning does not remove the role of choice and will, what does it accomplish? This challenge is still usually presented in some such form as this: Suppose Blaise Pascal and a Moslem Achmed Pascal both offer you their wagers in this form: They ask you to state your value for a life unhindered by faith, and also your probability that their faiths are true. You do, and then each shows that if you believe, your personal expectation value of the outcome is so great that the gain of believing far outweighs the loss. This result is then taken to show the utter worthlessness of Pascal's reasoning. William James's correct response was that the wager is applicable only to those options that are live for the person involved.[49] If belief in a given hypothesis is not a live option for you, then the wager's argument does not get off the ground. If the Christian faith confronts you as a live option, then Pascal's text has its relevant application for you, and otherwise not. Note the very curious, to traditional eyes, personal form; reasoning in its traditional conception cannot have this context and person sensitivity. Such a status has always been considered incompatible with the objectivity of reason. Fine, then; this is not objective reason. But if the option is a live option for you, then the "reasoning" is applicable by you to your own situation—that is all.

If only the Christian and not the Moslem faith is a live option for you—as it was in Pascal's circle—then the objection gets no purchase at all. Suppose, however, that both the Christian and the Moslem faith are live options for you. Then the story brings out a clearly inescapable element of choice that Pascal's persuasion cannot (and need not, and must not) eliminate. For in this situation Pascal must say, with even greater justice: "But to which view shall we be inclined? Reason cannot decide this question. Infinite chaos separates us. At the far end of this infinite distance a coin is being spun which will come down heads or tails. How will you wager? Reason cannot make you choose either, reason cannot prove either wrong." He wrote this passage before the decision analysis; but we have to say it again, in this variant, after the analysis. And you cannot take two of these courses, nor half of one and half of the other. Nor, finally, do the suggestions of prudence (tossing a real coin, say) seem better than an insult to the person who must choose.[50] Not to decide at all may be to go for zero expectation. That is the one course of action that has absolutely nothing to recommend it, except that you have made no choice between alternatives that reason did not dictate. (A little consolation there.)

What should we conclude, then, about the method of reasoning? After following it through we may find we have reason for something, ipso facto, without having gained a demonstration that we are rationally compelled this way or that. Can we generalize this?

Of course, if someone refuses an almost sure thing, we can accuse him of irrationality; but accusations trip so easily to the tongue. If we generalize the particular conclusion of the preceding paragraph, we will say: It is never irrational to take, or to refuse, a gamble (always excepting so-called Dutch Books!),[51] although one may have reason to do so. For how could one be rationally compelled to have a higher or lower risk quotient?

By this I mean the following: Expectation or expected gain is not known gain. Thus the consideration that one action has greater expected gain than another does not show that it is the better one to choose. If you choose the unbelieving life, you are certain that you will not sacrifice those "noxious pleasures, glory and good living." Stepping back, you may decide to proclaim that you are risk-averse and will not stake what you have.

It may be objected that this does not make you an exception to the rule of maximizing expectation, if taken most generally. Whatever choice you make, you can be represented (in a more elaborate model) as having factored in further values, namely, your attitudes toward the gamble as such. That is definitely so; but notice what this implies if used as a general defense. If so used, it entails that we can never really convict someone of violating the "maximize your expected value" maxim. It is a gambit that would work not only for the actual choice made but equally for any different choice. Thus the very defense of that Bayesian picture implies that we can never establish that a given gamble is what reason compels us to take. Choice and its responsibility never slip from our shoulders; no recipe for rational behavior can remove them.[52]

So the typical objection to the wager (what if we are addressed simultaneously by a Moslem Pascal?) actually ends in strengthening the wager's real point. But the conclusion I take to be there from the beginning in Pascal's text. The probabilistic reasoning presented as exactly the pattern of reasoning proper to the human situation is not, indeed is never, of the same sort as demonstrations that purport to provide rationally compelling grounds. Their relation to rationality is more subtle. First of all, they are relevant only in a context in which such personal factors are present as which options we accept as live options for us, and how we value things—not to mention how we personally assess the various probabilities and what we set as our personal risk quotient. Second they make sense only on a conception of what is rational or rationally endorsable that is entirely at odds with the traditional "compelled by reason" conception. With this more nuanced probabilism now placed within our voluntarist epistemology, let us return to our focal problem.

9. SCIENTIFIC REVOLUTION/CONVERSION AS A DECISION PROBLEM

retical problem does scientific revolution pose for deci-
y? When we come to the sorts of decision involved there,
nplated outcomes make no sense from the anterior point
imagine that we need to evaluate an outcome that is, by our
ights, ourselves speaking and thinking nonsense, while far-
much better. Does that make sense? It seems that this
we true abdication of reason, and not just because we classify it as a bad outcome, an outcome with a low value. We are not coherently framing a decision for ourselves here. For how can we tell that what we now see as material welfare in that kind of future will be cognized as such then? And if it is not, what about a future in which we are by our present lights well off, and by our lights then miserable or suffering a great loss? Perhaps we can suppose that in

contemplating this decision I see myself laughing and outwardly cheerful in that future. But given the opacity to me now of what my words and body language then mean, I really have no access to how things really seem to me then. Will this cheerfulness be the false face adopted in despair of ever regaining what I have lost? None of these difficulties appear in the ordinary everyday case where we can assume that our future way of thinking about ourselves will be the same as it is now, factual details aside. That, however, is precisely what we cannot assume here. There is therefore no rational way of deciding upon such a transition, if rational means "rational by the lights we have beforehand." But any other way is to lower oneself into true intellectual perversion, is it not?

Imagine yourself totally inside a scientific world picture that is becoming burdened with more and more blatant anomalies, severe calculational difficulties, failing predictions, and epicycle-laden explanations. An alternative appears; some people are beginning to talk about a strange new theory that makes absolutely no sense and violates the most basic commonsensical expectations of what nature can be like. What is still classified as a satisfactory outcome? To solve the problems, of course. Taking some absurdity seriously does not count as a solution. Even if it did one would have to be an imbecile to expect that it will be vindicated by future experiments. If you stop for a moment to envisage yourself converted to those strange new ideas, you see yourself stooping to blatant nonsense, you hear yourself babbling with (c'est le bouquet!) an air of having explained the inexplicable.

What could possibly change this evaluation? What we need to find is this: something that can play the role of changing the basic parameters of our problem situation, the very parameters on which decision-theoretic reasoning depends. As an empiricist, one cannot simply add this something by postulational fiat. Is there anything in our experience to play this role?

10. SARTRE AND PASCAL:
BREAKING THE DECISION PARADIGM

We've come to the very limit of Pascal's initial decision paradigm now. This is the place where we are called to decision. The "maximize your expectation" formula is not applicable. That formula presumes to have as given exactly what is now at issue. We are caught in a catch-22, a double-bind, the sort of problem from which there is no exit unless the terms of the problem itself are changed. I propose that we look at one approach to this very sort of predicament: Sartre's essay on the emotions.[53]

Sartre begins his essay with some putatively mechanistic accounts of emotion. They take the plausible form of characterizing emotion as effecting a substitution of the bearable for the unbearable. Thus a woman confessing to her therapist finds herself unable to go on; she begins to cry. A man ordered to do a task that puts him in danger weakens, shakes, becomes short of breath, and his place is taken by another. Someone is treated with condescension by a bureaucrat and suddenly stops filling out the forms, tears them up, shakes a fist, and shouts. In each case the behavior that the situation demands but is too exigent is discontinued and replaced by "setback" behavior that the actor can carry out.

Sartre points out that these mechanistic (hydrostatic?) accounts trade on an ambiguity. They purport to utilize only nonteleological terms: certain pressures build up, a breakdown occurs, and one form of behavior is replaced by another. But their appeal is due to a quite different feature. We have a sense of explanation because we automatically hear the theory as asserting that the new behavior (as well as the giving way to certain feelings) is adopted in order to solve the person's problem, in order to provide a way of responding to the situation that does not make the same impossible or unbearable demands. This "in order to" makes it not a mechanistic but a tele-ological account that points to purpose and function.

That is precisely the right way to go, according to Sartre. We will understand emotion when we characterize it in terms of function, in terms of the role it plays in such a situation. When we give in to those feelings, we are transforming our situation radically. For example, when I want something from someone I will not normally count stealing, extortion, or assault among my options. But if I become angry enough at that person, I will see him or her as evil, execrable, guilty, despicable, undeserving of what he has, deserving of ill treat-ment. . . . Then the options have changed. What I classified earlier as an immoral option now turns up among the just. This is not a causal account. That I see him as thus or so, and that I am angry at him, are not two distinct facts, they are inextricable. What is it, precisely, to be angry? Anger does not consist in a state of the cortex, blood pressure, adrenaline level—except in the sense that dancing or ca-ressing someone consists in motions of the limbs. To become angry means to come to see things in a different way, as unjust, as deserv-ing of violence and rejection. "Anger" is a term in person-discourse, not in physics or physiology. The changes in value judgment are among anger's most distinctive identifying features.

Thus, on Sartre's account, the central factor in emotion is a certain kind of change in view that transforms our subjective situa-tion. This gives emotion a definite cognitive and volitional func-tion.[54] At the same time, this change fulfills the wish to live in a bearable, acceptable situation. But it generally does so in a way that is from the prior point of view more analogous to superstition or voodoo than to effective action:

> It is a transformation of the world. When the paths traced out
> become too difficult, or when we see no path, we can no longer
> live in so urgent and difficult a world. All the ways are barred.
> However, we must act. So we try to change the world, that is, to

live as if the connection between things and their potentialities were not ruled by deterministic processes, but by magic. . . . The impossibility of finding a solution to the problem objectively apprehended as a quality of the world serves as motivation for the new unreflective consciousness which now perceives the world otherwise and with a new aspect, and which requires a new behavior. (pp. 58–60)

This is not tenable as a general theory of emotion.[55] In contentment, joy, happiness, affection, and many other emotionally charged situations we are not moved by a wish to change the world from unbearable to bearable. Sartre's attempt to put all emotion into this frame is Procrustean, as appears quite clearly in his awkward description of joy: "the joyous subject behaves rather exactly like a man in a state of impatience. He does not stay in one place, makes a thousand plans which he immediately abandons, etc. . . . Joy is a magical behavior which tends by incantation to realize the possession of the desired object as instantaneous totality." (pp. 68, 69) This may be true of some cases of joy but is a far cry from most or from the most typical.[56]

Sartre's account is right in one way, however: emotion can have precisely the function he describes, and this is an important aspect of what emotion can be and can do. The person who shakes a fist and shouts in anger is not so far from the one who sticks pins in a voodoo doll.[57] In that state of anger, those activities are felt as satisfying, whereas from the unemotional point of view they are pathetic or gratuitous. In emotionally difficult situations we become, I cannot put it otherwise, superstitious: fearful, we dare not speak a name or name a possible outcome whether fortunate or disastrous; in grief and regret the old photos we save are guarded like greatly treasured relics; in happiness we see every tree and stranger as a smiling spirit. Most of all, Sartre is right to describe the transforming role that emotion can play.

Such a transformation is evident, for example, in Kafka's *Meta-*

morphosis, in which events place the young man Gregor's family in an unbearable situation. They cannot treat the son as they would an insect, they cannot relate to the son as to an insect, no matter what form he now has. But they also cannot change the situation by effective action. There is no cure, nor is there any effective way to lessen the burden on the family while that insect is a person. The situation changes through emotion—among other things, through the sister's uncontrollable sobbing anger while calling on the parents' allegiance to her well-being—which can change their world to one that is bearable, intelligible, acceptable, a world in which it is simply not true that this insect is her brother.

We can certainly see such transformations through emotion in the terms of the decision paradigm whose anomalies they are. The values of the possible outcomes of various actions are changed, in a way that changes the action itself into something different. Thus the immoral rejection of a son upon his worse-than-cancerous affliction changes into the rightful removal of a gruesome insect. The assessment of various outcomes as satisfactory or disastrous changes, although from a purely neutral point of view the action and outcome have not changed. Physically, chemically, physiologically there is no change at all. Another, still more clearly cognitive, aspect of the situation also changes in emotion. What seems possible or probable, impossible or improbable is no longer the same. Incredible feats occur in the heat of passion, but we need not look at extreme examples. A happy person is optimistic, expects good things; an unhappy person has little by way of expectation. The worst seems the likeliest when we are feeling generally miserable; then we also take other people's negative judgment as the likeliest truth, on the scantiest of evidence.

But when those two sorts of aspects change, the situation as conceived in decision theory is what changes. What appears to us as satisfactory by way of action is entirely determined by these factors.

Change those factors and what is satisfactory or acceptable to us changes. Whereas before getting a job was the only satisfactory outcome, upon such a change the very act of eliminating that possibility may be the best—by hitting the interviewer or spitting in his soup, for example. The change will be emotional, through emotion, through a giving way to feelings that are from the prior point of view totally unworthy of us, with behavior that is thoroughly beneath us. But through this emotional experience, the prior valuation is now seen as puerile, dogmatic, myopic, reactionary.

The sober and dispassionate view of all this will not be exactly favorable. A subjective transformation is an escape; emotion is escapism. Sartre rightly considers it of a piece with magic or voodoo. Recourse to magic consists in the idea that situations can change by our wishes, dreams, incantations, rituals. In emotion we have recourse to a primitive sort of magic. Isn't emotional thinking precisely wishful thinking? It is certainly thinking transformed by something other than evidence. But in fact no other form of change is possible when what could be evidence for a rival is not classified that way simply because the rival is classified as an absurdity. So the pattern applies to conceptual revolution as well.

Of course, I do not mean to simply assimilate such revolutionary changes in our thinking to this primitive emotional magic. The connection between the two lies in a general pattern that applies to both. A change that makes intelligible something that was previously unintelligible must be in important part a change in attitude. If this change is not rationally compelled by the evidence but involves also an element of choice, we must note that it is a typical role of emotion to precipitate (or even mainly consist in) such a subjective transformation. None of the familiar emotions that anyone would list as feelings or passions may be involved, but what is involved is something that plays precisely that role. Therefore it is precisely what Sartre's theory would classify as an emotion as well.

Although emotion is clearly also a subject for psychology, we are here focusing on a role it can play in cognition. There is a logical gap between the prior and the posterior epistemic states when they differ on what counts as intelligible. Something is needed to play a certain role in the transition: the something we asked for at the end of the previous section. When emotion has the problem-transforming function that Sartre described, it plays precisely that role. Thus Sartre's description gives phenomenological reality to that something. That something is not a postulated hidden variable but something encountered in experience.

There is just one thing to add yet. When I emphasized how emotion looks to the sober and dispassionate, I had to emphasize what the passions have in common with escapism and magic. But there is something else to recall. The fact is that some of the greatest and most valued things in our past were possible only through emotion. Sometimes nothing short of passion will do.

11. NO EXIT?

The question of how we can view those revolutionary changes in our epistemic life, while endorsing them and yet maintaining our commitment to manage our opinion rationally, has itself been transformed in the course of our inquiry. It has now become a question about how to view the role of emotion in our epistemic and valuational stance and in the epistemic enterprise as a whole.

Somehow, the emotional transformations we have envisaged change how one sees the outcome of conversion to the new world picture. The conversion itself changes from something unintelligible to something that is certainly intelligible and allows for a rational posterior evaluation on its merits. If all of this makes sense, then we can accept the above transformation of our main question. But of course we have by no means yet established that it makes sense.

Certainly, the conversion was emotional, not dispassionate. The change was not arrived at, nor could it have been, through purely dispassionate deliberation. And finally, the posterior position is one that we now value as a more insightful way of seeing the world we live in. But even granted all that, it does not follow at all that the change, or the role of emotion therein, is understood. How can such a thing work? Fine, we can understand for example how Claudio's anger and despair are in part constituted by his changed view of Hero, from virtuous and true to deceiving and foul. But how could any emotion make meaningful to us what was patently absurd by our lights previously?

CODA

These are questions about how the revolution can afterward be seen as intelligible although the outcome was absurd by prior lights. To these I will devote the next lecture. Something crucial must be missing yet in our understanding of radical change in view, even if we have been on track and have uncovered much that needed to be understood. Some of our presuppositions must be keeping us blind or bound to traditional categories that left no room for a middle way between strict reason (deduction, induction, abduction, what have you) and the irrational *credo quia absurdum*. We'll need to delve further down. There are certainly enough directions as yet unexplored: further cognitive aspects of emotion as problem-solving, the overtly oversimplified picture of received scientific opinion in this discussion, the ramifications of how a communal or social epistemic enterprise can differ from that of an individual located in a community, to name only a few. All of these will appear to some extent in the next lecture. But one thing we have already gained. A new and viable empiricist epistemology must break radically with tradition if it is to be adequate to the way we have come to see ourselves during the past century. As I see it, some of the insights of pragmatism and existentialism pointed us decisively in the right direction. We will not get out of our philosophical double-binds without something like a metaconversion, in which all the false hopes of traditional epistemology give way to a new view of reason.

Experience
(Epistemic) Life Without Foundations

> Whorf, wanting to demonstrate that Hopi incorporates a metaphysics so alien to ours that Hopi and English cannot, as he puts it, "be calibrated," uses English to convey the contents of sample Hopi sentences. Kuhn is brilliant in saying what things were like before the revolution using—what else?—our post-revolutionary idiom.
>
> —DONALD DAVIDSON, "The Very Idea of a Conceptual Scheme"

> Meanings can change, but generally do so in the direction of an increased richness and precision of definition, so that we do not lose the ability to understand the theories of past periods of normal science.
>
> —STEVEN WEINBERG, "The Revolution That Didn't Happen"

A change in view is properly called radical or revolutionary only if the posterior view is absurd relative to the prior one. We do in fact see our past punctuated by radical change, by conversions that could not have been ratifiable or justifiable by prior lights. So why do we not see those changes as simply irrational, as a matter for the psychopathology of everyday life rather than philosophy? In some cases we do; more so perhaps when we see such changes in others' history and especially when we shared the prior view but resisted that change. In certain other cases we do see the change as irrational yet fortunate. Then we find ourselves ruefully admitting that we came to our present fortunes by luckily vindicated lapses of reason or leaps of faith, perhaps taken only in sheer desperation.

But we do not regard the great scientific revolutions in that way. First of all, development of a rival conception was by no means always an act of utter desperation. Neither Galileo's Aristotelian contemporaries nor Newton's Cartesian neighbors felt themselves at the end of their tethers. Second, we steadfastly endorse some of these changes as being in accordance with reason. Galileo, Newton, Darwin, Einstein, and the quantum revolutionaries can be depicted in retrospect as the true heirs of past insight.[1] So we still have our dilemma. On one hand, then, we are forced to acknowledge a chasm between the old and the new, and on the other, we must be able to see our present as a rationally endorsable continuation of the past.

This provides us with two major questions to address. First, how precisely do we display our endorsed results (our posterior views) as rightful successors of the old? We may call this the "problem of royal succession in science." When a new theory is advocated as replacing a previously accepted one, it must satisfy certain criteria that pertain not only to its current successes but also to its relation to its predecessors. Second (now taking for granted an irenic posterior view of the posterior view's relation to the prior), how precisely can we understand the transition as having been in accord with reason? To these two questions I will devote the first and second parts of this lecture; the third will ask for the moral of it all.[2]

One. After the Epistemological Impasse: Interpreting the Past

Pre- and postrevolutionary worldviews are incommensurable. Is that so? When we look back to the views we left behind we tend to think that we understand them and can separate what was good and retained from what was bad and discarded. Not all of that is anachronistic blindsight.

1. AMBIGUITY: OUR DECONSTRUCTIBLE LANGUAGE

Imagine an eighteenth-century Newtonian scientist to whom it is suddenly suggested that perhaps mass varies with velocity. That is absurd in his terms. In his models, mass varies only when material is added or lost. Moreover, whereas velocity varies from one frame of reference to another, mass does not. All of this is so basic to his way of thinking that he is just completely puzzled by the suggestion. It makes no sense.

So far this story seems to bear out our impression of incommensurability. There is no where to go, at this point, if we think of the Newtonian's language on the model of some logician's ideal. But although that Newtonian does not realize it yet (though his heirs in the next century came to do so), there are such ambiguities in this speaking and thinking that any three different logicians would likely construe it (extrapolate it to an unambiguous formalism) in three different ways. For in the Newtonian tradition, mass can be equally well characterized in three different ways: the proper mass ("quantity of matter," a certain constant value assigned to, for example, each atom), the inertial mass (a measure of its resistance to motion), and the gravitational mass (evident in the mutually induced acceleration of bodies at a given distance from each other).

Logically speaking, it is quite remarkable that these three values would coincide. So a logician would construe the word "mass" as standing for only one of them but say that the physicist's talk was ambiguous between the three. Now, in Einstein's framework, light has a constant velocity that no moving body can exceed. Therefore, if a force is applied so as to accelerate the body, the resistance to motion must increase as the velocity increases, so that it never achieves the velocity of light. In the second sense then (resistance to motion) mass does vary with velocity although in the first sense it does not.[3]

This example shows at least that the most precise language about nature we have, devised by the most precise of physical scientists, can harbor hidden ambiguities. Here we have the makings of one quick resolution of our dilemma. Conceptual revolutions bring such hidden ambiguities to light; or perhaps we should say, conceptual revolutions can occur when they come to light. So, is the posterior view unintelligible or demonstrably absurd to the prior? Yes, provided of course that demonstration is given in the ambiguous language of the past! But no, in the (retrospectively) disambiguated terms. A delicate balance between anachronism and hindsight. . . . Ambiguity does not stop at single words. Words can be ambiguously combined; rule following, no problem at all in daily life, is a mystery to philosophers for that very reason. For natural language, the language we live in, is inexhaustibly rich in the possible ways of being made more precise. The task of making our language, our rules, our laws, our theories more precise is an *unendliche Aufgabe*. It can never, even in principle, produce the undeconstructible text.

Paul Feyerabend, generally credited with introducing the idea of incommensurability, expressed this view incisively in his posthumously published *Conquest of Abundance:*

> I agree that if discourse is defined as a sequence of clear and distinct propositions (actions, plans) which are constructed according to precise and merciless rules, then discourse has a very short breath indeed. Such a discourse would often be interrupted by "irrational" events and soon be replaced by a new discourse for which its predecessor is nonsense. If the history of thought depended on a discourse of this kind, then it would consist of an ocean of irrationality interrupted, briefly, by mutually incommeasurable islands of sense.[4]

The solution to our dilemma rests, then, in the recognition of this character of the real language in use in which real science—and on the individual level, our real opinions and intentions—develop.

2. CRITERIA FOR ROYAL SUCCESSION IN SCIENCE

What this means especially is that the posterior view brings with it a very clear understanding of the prior, now superseded, theories. In this way it can grant them their proper place in the sun. Indeed, when it comes to "royal succession" in science—the replacement of older successful theories by new rivals—the pretender to the throne must show, by its own lights, why the older theory was as successful as it was. One of the main credentials for a new theory, offered as rival to an old one, is that it be able to explain and preserve the successes of the old theory. For example, the special theory of relativity entails that Newton's laws of motion are approximately correct for phenomena whose velocities are small in comparison with the speed of light, and the quantum theory entails that for contexts in which Planck's quantum of action can be regarded as negligibly small.

This does not, of course, qualify the point that the new theory, taken as a whole, contradicts the old theory, taken as a whole. After all, the old theory simply stated its own principles as universal laws of nature. Even that contradiction, however, must be understood to be of the new with the old theory as now understood. This new understanding of the old theory, which is of course one of its possible interpretations, or at least disambiguations, quickly takes root. Indeed, it does this so firmly that from the posterior point of view it is hard to see that there was a revolution at all. We see this nicely borne out in Steven Weinberg's 1998 review of Kuhn's work:

> It is true that there was a good deal of uncertainty about the concept of mass during the Einsteinian revolution. . . . But this has all been resolved . . . and in fact the term "mass" today is most frequently understood as "rest mass," an intrinsic property of a body that is not changed by motion, which is much the

way that mass was understood before Einstein. Meanings can change, but generally do so in the direction of an increased richness and precision of definition, so that we do not lose the ability to understand the theories of past periods of normal science. (50)

Our conclusion must quite firmly retain both perspectives. From the prior point of view, before its disambiguation and reinterpretation, the new concepts and theories are literally unintelligible. The disambiguation is also not, from the prior perspective, a harmless exercise, for it severs aspects whose identity has been a matter of tautology. From the posterior perspective, on the other hand, there is a "right" way to understand the old world-picture and it is quite possible, on that understanding, to explain how it could have been as successful as it was while literally false.

But this stereoscopic retention of both perspectives still leaves us with some of the puzzlement that haunted the last lecture. How does a rational community—or individual—move out of the prior view into the new? (I am not speaking here of the retrospective rationale; that we can now understand perfectly well.) Merely uncovering some ambiguities in word or phrase would certainly not account for that. Indeed, a little logical acuity would suffice to uncover any number of such possible splittings of concepts, and a good deal of such disambiguation actually happened in Mach's, Kirchhoff's, and Hertz's examinations of classical mechanics. The diagnosis we have so far fits small conceptual changes as well as radical ones and leaves no wonder only in the former. The distance between, for example, classical physics and the relativistic or quantum world is too vast to be satisfactorily accounted for by this alone.

So what has happened when a community, after considerable intellectual trauma, finds itself in a new conceptual frame? How did discussion within that community lead from one point to the unimaginable next one? Feyerabend's early critique of "classical" empiricism brought to light an ambiguity that goes much deeper than mere ambiguity in individual words or phrases. Modern empiricism's notion of experience harbored a major historical tactic for denial of genuine conceptual change. If experience speaks with the voice of an angel, then we have a constant bedrock on which to found both discourse and rational belief. After all, neither misunderstanding nor disbelief seems even possible in stories of angelic visitation! Any conflict in succeeding world pictures must, then, be due to error pure and simple. Revolution/conversion is, then, the easily intelligible phenomenon of how we shift from one bad extrapolation of that lucidly true message to another, whether worse or better. The search for a rock-solid foundation for knowledge was precisely the rock on which empiricism foundered.[5] As Feyerabend dismantles this empiricist fundamentalism, however, we gain an insight into how things actually work in a scientific (or religious) community so as to make revision at once possible and possibly radical.

Two. Experience: Empiricist Fundamentalism and the Open Future

> Experience is the name that everyone gives to their mistakes.
>
> —OSCAR WILDE

> Experientia docet? Experientia doesn't.
>
> —ALDOUS HUXLEY, *Antic Hay*

Empiricism has often enough been a tradition in disrepute. The school in medicine to which its very name refers was generally thought of as quackery by the more learned. Shakespeare's *All's Well That Ends Well*, act ii, has a typical bit of abuse:

> We must not
> So stain our judgment, or corrupt our hope,
> To prostitute our past-cure malady
> To empirics.

That the tradition eventually called empiricism fell into disrepute in modern philosophy as well was for the same reason, namely, for its naive way of basing everything on experience, naively conceived. Thomas Hill Green's introduction to Hume in the late nineteenth century provides the definitive verdict of history, or at least of the historians of philosophy at the time. In a closely argued exposé of Locke, Berkeley, and Hume, he showed how they conflated almost every rational function into a fiction (called experience) meant to serve as foundation for knowledge. We cannot be "classical empiricists," in the sense attacked by these later philosophers. Regrettably, much of that nineteenth-century critique remained equally applicable to some twentieth-century views in the empiricist tradition.

But the beautiful thing about philosophy is that philosophies die. New philosophy can then grow from the soil enriched by the dead. I will here explore Feyerabend's critique of classical empiricism, consciously paralleling a seventeenth-century Jesuit critique of fundamentalist Protestantism. Feyerabend's exquisite irony won't leave the Jesuit's position intact. There is a sense in which the Jesuit cannot survive his own critique. Nevertheless there is also a sense in which all the positions examined can survive—even poor, maligned empiricism. They do need to relinquish a certain amount of false consciousness. The very demise of the fundamentalist gambit brings into the open presuppositions that obstruct our understanding of how reasoned change in view can be radical and discontinuous, without surrender to the irrational. What Feyerabend laid bare is precisely how, in a fertile social context, the radical departures of the future are continuous with strands of an ambiguous past. The roles of emotion and imagination that we encountered above are not abandoned, but neither is reason.

3. FEYERABEND'S CRITIQUE OF CLASSICAL EMPIRICISM

The great scientific revolution of the sixteenth and seventeenth centuries was simultaneous with the great schism in Western Christianity, itself involving a radical conceptual shift on both sides of its divide. In religion one was faced with on one hand a venerable church tradition and on the other a revolutionary insistence on Scripture alone as basis for belief. The Jesuit, François Veron, set out to demolish the Protestants' "Scripture alone" rule of faith.[6]

As Feyerabend correctly observes, the Jesuit's argument is very general and applies to any simple foundationalist epistemology. So Feyerabend adapts it for use against what he calls classical empiricism—roughly, the view that what is to be believed is exactly what experience establishes, and no more ("experience is our sole source of information," as one might say).

I will first examine the argument, which is clearly very powerful. Second, I'll consider whether it is perhaps too powerful, whether it is in effect a skeptical argument. If so, and cogent, it would undermine any pretense to rational belief. Feyerabend himself points out why the argument could have had little force in the targeted Protestant community itself. But can we think of that community's epistemic stance as rational, rather than as mere double-think? Feyerabend leaves this in doubt, and yet, in a sly way, holds out the hope of a genuinely promising development. It is precisely on this hope that I hope to build.

THE JESUIT ARGUMENT, AND ITS PARALLEL FOR EXPERIENCE

Fundamentalism is characterized by the rule of faith: *Sola Scriptura.* That is: on religious matters, and indeed on anything on which the

Scriptures pronounce at all, Scripture is the one and only source of information. Believe Scripture and Scripture alone: that is the rule.

What if Scripture speaks on a certain subject but leaves some questions about it open? In many such cases one cannot afford to believe Scripture alone. Then the rule is presumably at least negative: to believe only, or at most, propositions in accord with Scripture. There may, however, also be strictures against adding to Scripture. If we interpreted "in accord with Scripture" in the minimal sense of "logically consistent with Scripture," that would most certainly not suffice! But now the question has already led us into the argument.

In philosophical terms fundamentalism is clearly a foundationalist epistemic position. For to hold this position is to identify a basis or foundation for all rationally permissible opinion or belief and for all knowledge claims in a certain domain.[7]

Classical empiricism, as Feyerabend characterizes it, has a parallel foundationalist position in epistemology. *Sola Experientia:* any claim to knowledge, any support for opinion, must come from experience; experience trumps all. Of course, we see the usual paradigm of empirical science hovering in the background. Note the role that controlled experiment and observation play in the empirical sciences; that is just what is meant by the contention that the sciences are solidly based on experience. In all of our opinion, the rule says, experience must play that same role.

What if experience has not yet delivered any relevant basis for judgment? Then the rule has at least negative import: believe only what is in accord with experience so far. Are there strictures against adding? We certainly can't live without opinion that outstrips our experience any more than without opinion going beyond the Scriptures. As an example, Augustine pointed out that he had never seen the ocean, yet was not irrational to believe in its reality. But there must be some constraints that we need for now to leave open. The empiricist rhetoric about allocating all one's belief in proportion to the evidence tends to suggest that some strong strictures along these lines may be available.[8] But here too, with this question we are already getting into the argument.

The argument against fundamentalism has three parts. First, it is not self-evident what is and what is not (genuine) Scripture. Second, the meaning of (putative) Scripture is not everywhere apodictically clear and hence requires interpretation. Third, in the attempt to settle whether some belief is in accordance with Scripture, we need to know how to draw out its implications. Each of these three points purports to refute the claim that belief could be based solely on, and be warranted solely by, Scripture. Each has its parallel for experience. That parallel then engenders a precisely analogous putative refutation of the claim that experience can be the sole basis and test of rational opinion.

I will state the three arguments as forcefully as I can. Of course, there will be points where the arguments are weak, or weaker than they sound. But we will pay due attention to the possibility that they can after all be dismissed out of hand. Despite their occasional weakness, they remain, even after three hundred years, very strong.

FIRST ARGUMENT: HOW DO WE IDENTIFY IT?

Let's begin with Scripture. Which texts are genuine Scripture, canonical rather than apocryphal? And of the texts in the canon, are any parts in the existing manuscripts errors or additions made in transcription?

According to the rule of faith, these questions are to be answered in accordance with Scripture. In fact, Scripture appears to say a good deal about it, when the text records that some speaker is a prophet or says of itself that it was recorded by an eyewitness. But this is not helpful. As long as the identity of Scripture is in question, we have—

by the rule of faith—no basis for determining what Scripture says. Therefore we cannot determine without circularity whether any putative identification of Scripture is acceptable.

Classical empiricism has a parallel problem with the idea of experience as a source of knowledge or rational opinion. The identification of experience, in the requisite sense, is already a problem. In a general sense, everything that happens to us, of which we are aware at the very least, is part of our experience. But when a basis for opinion is to be identified, that general notion is useless without certain distinctions. The *Merriam-Webster Collegiate Dictionary* gives the following as the first four entries for the noun "experience":

1a: direct observation of or participation in events as a basis of knowledge
  b: the fact or state of having been affected by or gained knowledge through direct observation or participation
2a: practical knowledge, skill, or practice derived from direct observation of or participation in events or in a particular activity
  b: the length of such participation ("has 10 years experience in the job")
3a: the conscious events that make up an individual life
  b: the events that make up the conscious past of a community or nation or mankind . . .
4: something personally encountered, undergone, or lived through

Note that this is a "success word"; in none of these senses does just anything count. Even for the fourth sense, if someone claims experience of something, we can doubt that claim. We can ask: Have you really personally lived through that? And we can ask ourselves, Did I really live through that?

Suppose I come in from the garden and report seeing a yellow flower. Perhaps what I actually saw was a candy wrapper, or perhaps I only saw grass but had a small hallucination or fainting spell. In all these cases my report was still presumably veridical in the minimal sense that indeed it seemed to me that I saw a yellow flower. As basis for knowledge claims, however, as evidence, or as test for opinion, that minimal sense is useless. For such a basis, we would need to identify experiences that are veridical in a further sense, namely, indicative of what it was that was actually seen, touched, or heard.

I'm not simply bringing in the dead Cartesian skeptical horse that we are all so tired of beating. The point is the parallel. On one side there are the believers and scholars, faced with all the texts inherited from the past. If they are to listen to Scripture, they need to be able to divide Scripture from not-Scripture. For this they would seem to need a criterion. But the rule of *Sola Scriptura* will now classify any such criterion as either circular or inadmissible. On the other side we see all of us experiencing, conscious agents. If we are to listen to experience, we need to be able to identify what our experience was and hence divide what we really lived through from what we only seemed to be living through. But there the rule of *Sola Experientia* will classify any criterion we use as either circular or inadmissible.

SECOND ARGUMENT: WHAT DOES IT MEAN?

Suppose we have identified Scripture, distinguishing it from the apocrypha. This genuine Scripture requires interpretation. Take the story of creation in Genesis. Saint Augustine interpreted this allegorically; fundamentalists see that as violating the rule of faith. But then what of the Song of Songs or Hosea? At the very least, the significance of these books lies largely in their associated meanings, when they are taken as allegories for certain aspects of human life in relation to God. In any case, the mere fact that competing interpretations are offered creates a question to be answered.

Again, the rule *Sola Scriptura* appears to be applicable. Scripture includes many directions to the reader by classifying some of its own parts as poetry or song, some as parables, some as history. But the same circularity threatens if we try to follow that rule. For the very passages that on one reading are directions to read something as history, biology, or astronomy are on another reading examples of familiar narrative devices common to many forms of fiction and dramatic literature. Thus, if a story begins with "Once upon a time there was . . ." or "In a galaxy far, far away and long, long ago . . .," its literal meaning includes the claim to be history, but we take that as part of its narrative structure.

Again, there is a parallel problem for the classical empiricist's notion of experience. Even after the identification of what is and what is not experience, in the requisite sense, there remains a dubitable element of interpretation. Two people who have looked into a furnace will report on, respectively, oxidation and phlogiston escape. The terms they have been taught at their mothers' knee are theory-laden, so the report is infested with theory. Again, this point remains even for the minimal fourth sense of personal encounter. If I report that I felt agitated, it may be unclear whether I was angry or afraid. A bit more hastily and less prudently I might just have said that I reacted in anger, or, alternatively, in fear. Can we let experience be the touchstone for what a given experience "really was"?

THIRD ARGUMENT: WHAT DOES IT IMPLY?

In the attempt to settle whether some belief is in accordance with Scripture, we need to know how to draw out its implications. Pure logic will not get us anywhere. It is not a matter of logic that all humans have hearts, kidneys, knees, and elbows—in fact, not all of them do. Yet Scripture surely need not say explicitly that Abraham was an ordinary human being with heart, kidneys, knees, and elbows for us to take it that he did. The point becomes more probative when we ask for implications of this ancient text for contemporary problems. What do its injunctions imply for our way of life today?

As my colleague David Lewis once said, the imitation of Christ does not mean trying to walk on water![9]

In assimilating ordinary descriptions we draw consequences via general background and default assumptions of our own. We can't, however, interpret the rule of faith as allowing us to add all our own opinions wherever, as far as pure logic is concerned, Scripture is silent. (This is especially evident in the case of miracle stories.) But again, we cannot use the rule without circularity to settle what is and what is not a genuine consequence or implication of Scripture.

Here too we find a parallel for the empiricist. Let's assume that identification and interpretation are complete and held fixed. Then the logical relations of compatibility, inconsistency, and consequence between the deliverances of experience and the opinions scrutinized remain a problem. An almost century-long, practically fruitless effort to codify evidential relations (so-called confirmation theory, a bit of bombast if anything is) should have convinced us that "in accord with experience" is not a simple, uncritically usable notion.

We have landed here in a problem ubiquitous in empiricist reflection on science: the problem of underdetermination. It is important to remind ourselves that this problem remains as a practical reality even after we have dismissed such radical variants as Putnam's paradox and Quine's ontological relativity, let alone all those boring old skeptical doubts. That even the most modest bit of theory goes beyond the experience we have so far, and our reports on our experience are infected with such theory—that point always remains. It is not a reason to be a skeptic, but it is also not negligible.

4. THE ARGUMENT HOIST ON ITS OWN PETARD?

We cannot apply the rule of *Sola Scriptura* or the parallel rule of *Sola Experientia* without identifying, interpreting, and extrapolating. But all three of these responses to texts admit of alternatives. Those rules then ask the impossible, namely, that choice between these alternatives should be on the basis of Scripture or experience itself. Hence the formulated epistemic positions are untenable. Their problems are in fact logical problems, having very little to do with what Scripture or experience is or is meant to be. That is important: the argument is based on absolutely minimal assumptions or information about what Scripture and experience are, and so it must generalize to foundationalist epistemic positions in general.

We cannot accept this conclusion too readily. What about that claimed parallel? Very little appears to be assumed about Scripture, but does even that little apply equally to experience? Apart from that, we also need to look more closely at the Jesuit argument itself. If it is too weak it may leave a loophole for the fundamentalist, if too strong it may turn into a general skepticism.

Finally, the Jesuit clearly counts on there being just two possible responses. The first is to say that the Jesuit's three problems don't arise at all and need no solution. The second is to say that he is right, but we have an additional source of information. Obviously he himself opts for the latter, with (church) tradition as the needed arbiter. Suppose we try to take the other tack and say that the three problems don't really arise:

   a. we don't need to try and identify Scripture because we already know what it is;
   b. we don't need to interpret it because its meaning is clear;
   c. we have no difficulty deriving its consequences, by the same rules as for any other text.

Feyerabend identifies this as the actual Protestant response. How could it be? Quite simply! For the Protestant the rule *Sola Scriptura* is heard and followed in a community where everyone already uses the word "Scripture" to refer to the same text and where everyone also already agrees in their reading of that text.

But we can at once also see the weakness of that response in a tug of war over converts. This response is possible only if given from within that sort of community. It would not be open to someone who first heard the rule, outside of such a context, and was then told to follow the rule. Therefore the Jesuit can maintain that the Protestants' decision to set aside church tradition on these matters deprives people of any way to identify, interpret, or extrapolate the Scriptures nonarbitrarily, unless they add a new tradition of their own. But if they do, then their source for belief is not Scripture alone but Scripture plus the new tradition. Hence they cannot very well charge—without indicting themselves as well—that the Catholic source for belief adds an extrascriptural source to Scripture.

There were in fact not two possible distinct responses at all. The first response, dismissing the argument, turns out on examination to reduce to the second, which admits an additional source for belief.

How would the parallel for classical empiricism go? As an example, also played up by Feyerabend, let us take Newton's famous fourth rule of reasoning in philosophy, which might be called the *"Sola Phenomena"* rule: "In experimental philosophy we are to look upon propositions collected by general induction from phenomena as accurately or very nearly true, notwithstanding any contrary hypotheses that may be imagined, until such time as other phenomena occur by which they may either be made more accurate, or liable to exception."[10] This is Newton's battle cry against the Cartesian "method of hypotheses" in his century's great methodological dispute.[11] We can easily see how the Jesuit's argument would raise parallel questions for it. How do we identify the phenomena? What do they mean (that is, how do we distinguish an accurate minimal description from one that amounts to a hypothesis by effectively adding an interpretative element)? Finally, what is this general induction, i.e. what are the implications of the phenomena? It would not help, or even make much sense, to suggest that the answers must themselves come by general induction from the phenomena!

Yet we doubt that these questions bothered Newton or his friends and admirers. They apparently understood quite well among themselves what were to count as the phenomena and what counted as a genuine induction as opposed to a hypothesis. From within their own scientific community they could so address the Cartesians. At the same time the Cartesians were quite within their rights to reject that English induction mongering as irreparably vague and ambiguous. For that is how it must seem to anyone outside that Newtonian community.

Thus the parallel between the theological and the scientific cases appears to hold, and the conclusion to be essentially the same in both cases. When the rule is putatively understood and followed there must in effect be a second authoritative source of information. That second source could be tacit within that community or could be designated there as "our" understanding—that is to say, its tradition. The existence or even the possibility of a differently constituted community prevents that tradition from having the force of pure logic. Therefore the first response reduces to the second.

We have now taken care of the suspicion that the Jesuit argument is too weak and leaves the fundamentalist or classical empiricist a loophole. Is it, on the other hand, too strong, and is the Jesuit hoist on his own petard? Doesn't the Jesuit argument work equally well against any putative foundation for knowledge? If so, it should apply to the view that correct opinion is opinion based solely on Scripture and tradition, or on Scripture identified and interpreted according to one particular tradition.

If that objection is cogent, then the Jesuit argument is more powerful than it looks, and it destroys even what we surmise to have been the Jesuit's own conclusion. At first blush, he gave us only the quite innocent-looking argument that belief can't be based on Scripture alone, at least not strictly speaking. Now it looks as if perhaps it can't be based on anything at all!

Consider this. Suppose that the Jesuit confronts the task of identifying, interpreting, and extrapolating from Scripture and for guidance decides to look to the accumulated interpretative experience of the past. This guidance is preserved in some of the many texts inherited from the past. Thus, by the lights of his own argument, he faces the precisely similar task of discerning the genuine church tradition within that welter of texts, determining its meaning, and reading off its implications for present concerns. But if he now imposes the rule of accepting guidance solely from Scripture plus church tradition, he is caught in the same trap. Any criterion he can bring to bear on the identification and reading of the tradition will by that rule be classified as either circular or inadmissible.

The issue becomes even more perplexing if we try to draw out the implications for classical empiricism and experience. At first blush the argument as adapted by Feyerabend shows us that we cannot be classical empiricists in his sense. But what would it be to forsake classical empiricism and be a nonclassical empiricist? Is there any recourse to be had at all from this devastating argument?

Consider this. Suppose that Bacon, Newton, Locke, or whoever these paradigm classical empiricists were had squarely faced the threefold task that Feyerabend says they ignored. That task consists of identifying the deliverances of experience in the relevant sense, determining their exact meaning with no overlay of hypotheses or assumptions, and singling out the precise rules of induction. There were certainly methodological texts regarded as canon in that English scientific community, including most especially Bacon's *Novum Organum* and Newton's *Rules of Reasoning in Philosophy*. But there was a reason why we see such a strong backlash against this tradition in the eighteenth century, with Hume's *reductio* to skepticism and Kant's massive infusion of contributions by the mind.[12]

That reason is precisely the near-vacuity and incurable ambiguity of those texts when read as directives to isolate the given and its implications. Those texts, no longer simply accepted as codes for an unquestioning common understanding of what counts as phenomena and how to read them, are at best part of the problem, not a solution. But how could anything be a solution?[13]

At this point we are threatened by a severe dilemma, of which one horn is a rank dogmatism and the other an entirely debilitating skepticism. How often have philosophers found themselves in this dilemma! For the empiricist it is a recurring and familiar charge that they, at least, can never escape it.

But let us not be too hasty. The Jesuit argument is indeed one of great and striking generality. Yet its initial and clearest application is still solely to foundationalist positions of a certain type: the type to seek a foundation in something formulable as a text. The deliverances of Scripture, of church tradition, of experience, of systematic observation and controlled testing, of theories accepted as rock-solid or even presupposed by the very possibility of true science: all of these candidates for foundations can be conceived of as formulable texts. But we stand before any text, in the first instance, as preschool children before the written word. Thus Bacon aptly exclaims that experience must become literate if we are to read the book of nature.[14] The exceedingly simple point on which we find ourselves caught is merely this: Yes, we are to become literate, but no one can become literate by means of book learning!

The proper conclusion is then: only non- or antifoundationalist positions can survive this critique. What we need to ask is: Are there such alternative possible positions? If so, are any of them open for empiricism as escape from the horns of its dilemma?

The Protestant undoubtedly thought of the Jesuit's conception of Scripture and of our dealings with Scripture as simplifyingly naïve. Without denying the faults of those classical empiricists, we must object to Feyerabend that it is not their turning back to experience that is the problem. The problem is naïveté about what experience is. So let us see if we can improve on that. Again I will try to start with the ostensibly simpler case of Jesuit versus Protestant and then go on to the much more complex issue of experience.

5. EXPERIENCE: UNDERMINING THE ANALOGY

The Protestants and the Jesuit in the above debate end up in much the same position. The Protestants had not forsworn all traditional understanding but only rejected the Catholic tradition. They can answer the argument, as I pointed out initially, from within the traditional understanding to which they still subscribe. Within a community that agrees in that pre-understanding, the rule simply eliminates much that others accept as authoritative. Fine; they rest their beliefs, based on Scripture, within a community tradition and not on thin air.

But the Jesuit must equally accede to this view of what it is that the reading of Scripture presupposes as prior and initially reliable. After adding a good deal of text accumulated as the wisdom of the church, he must make the same admission concerning his understanding of the totality. That understanding does not derive solely from the content of those texts. On the contrary, that understanding itself is the condition sine qua non for the text having content at all for him. Hence the Jesuit ends up saying much the same as Protestant defender.

Why did it seem at first that the Jesuit was in an entirely different epistemic situation from the Protestant? I suspect it is because the "tradition" response (which was depicted above as just another text-based foundationalism) can be taken as an antifoundationalist move. Let us explore that idea. The rule of faith itself is a (prescriptive) statement and has no meaning at all if regarded simply as a bit of syntax. Like any statement, it is meaningful only if heard as a statement in our language, with both sense and reference, therefore, fixed for us to some reasonable (or sufficient) extent. This is equally true of the questions that can be raised about it. We cannot think of our understanding or interpretation as a further text (belonging to a language with less semantic structure than our own?) that we could then believe or disbelieve, doubt or dispute.

In this way the objection is countered. The Jesuit argument applies to any foundation representable as a text in a language in which the sense and reference of that text are not already fully determined. Relying on tradition does not simply mean believing in an additional text that informs us of the meaning of all other texts, but must, rather, include our indispensable reliance on our understanding of our own language. That reliance is a precondition not only of the meaningfulness of the rule of faith but equally of any discussion thereof. Of course, our tradition, in this sense, has no power of legislation against other identifications and interpretations, offered from outside—except for us, whose tradition it is and who persevere in our adherence to that tradition!

In some respects this response has precisely the same weaknesses as were pointed out above. As a Protestant reply to the Jesuit, it would give up first of all on fundamentalism and second on the use of Scripture as an incontrovertible arbiter between them. Maintaining the rule of faith as understood would admittedly amount precisely to self-assertion, a matter of will, determined adherence to one's own tradition. As the Catholic alternative to fundamentalism it would amount, after explicit addition of the texts codifying their tradition, to an exactly similar stance. For this response would of course be neither more nor less than a determined maintenance of their own form of understanding of Scripture.

The two discussants can make their differences explicit and attempt to engage in a dialogue "on common basis" (that is to say, with those differences suspended). But there is no guarantee that, under such a suspension, either could demonstrate or sufficiently support his or her own side. The usual dilemmas of (even moderate) relativism appear: how to respect the coexistence and right to life of alternative beliefs and attitudes without giving up one's own.

Yet it is clear that we did not arrive at a debilitating form of relativism or skepticism here. Rather, from both an intellectual and (in a broad sense) political point of view, this is our actual situation. We cannot be rescued from this aspect of the human condition! The task for philosophy cannot be to execute the impossible rescue. That task is, rather, to account clearly for how, under these conditions, we can live and function epistemically perfectly well (as we sometimes do), and how changing one's mind remains rationally possible.

To summarize, then: the Jesuit argument does not lead to skepticism. It leads instead precisely to the rejection of any position that posits a foundation for all our knowledge and belief representable as a text. For we cannot draw on a text in any way without relying on something else, if only on our own language. This is true equally whether we regard the text as being in our own language or as translated into our language. But what we rely on in our understanding is not itself representable as a text or body of information, so the same questions do not arise. On the other hand, whatever we do rely on (whether our unstated tradition or the received meaning of our own language or any other effective source of information) clearly admits of alternatives. Therefore there can be nothing at all that could possibly play the sort of role that foundationalists or fundamentalists wanted a foundation to play.

Feyerabend extrapolated the Jesuit argument very quickly to apply to what he calls Baconian or classical empiricism, in which, he claims, experience plays the role of Scripture. It isn't really obvious that the analogy goes through that well, given that experience and texts are prima facie very different sorts of things. Even if we consider the conclusion of the previous section to be a stable resting point, the centrality of the notion of experience for empiricist thought requires us to look into this more closely. Isn't at least perceptual experience precisely (like) a sort of reading, and the deliverances of experience precisely (like) a sort of text?[15]

The disanalogies are not to be ignored. The analogy looks fine if we simply use the noun "experience"—a noun like "scripture," "source," "text." But this noun is a philosophical prop that we cannot afford to use naïvely. I want to make two distinctions so that we may disentangle ourselves here. One major historical confusion, for which you may blame empiricists if you like, conflates experience in the sense of events that happen to us of which we are aware with the judgments involved in this awareness.[16] For example, what happened to me was that I stepped on a garden hose, but I took it to be a snake. I jumped and screamed, so everyone noticed my mistake and laughed at me. Note the event (I stepped on the hose, and certainly noticed that happening) and note my response: the judgment that I was stepping on a snake. The two are by no means the same, nor inseparable, whether conceptually or in reality. This is clearest when the judgment is mistaken but equally correct when it is true.

It was the bane of modern empiricism to have ignored this special status of experience. Truly, this Janus-faced experience has a judgment side, and the content of that judgment can be represented as a text; in a way it *is* text. At the same time, the experience I had is not a text but a happening. It is not true that one of these two faces is the experience and the other something else; I'm pointing to the confusions that follow if we either conflate the two or ignore either. Indeed, even two-faced Janus is too simple an image. Our concept of experience is multifaceted, and the single word harbors a cluster of notions. For could we just take the intersection—what we experience is events which (a) happen to us, and (b) of which we are aware as they happen? Not at all, for at least two reasons.[17] The first is that, as

I said, "experience" is a success word.[18]I did not have the awesome experience of meeting a saint if I met him and was aware of meeting him but did not for one moment realize that he was a saint. Our ordinary usage is flexible here. If I am later asked to recount my experiences as a traveler, I may be right to mention that I met a saint. But the proper nuances would be ignored if I said "I had the experience of meeting a saint."

This first reason is intimately related to Francis Bacon's repeated insistence that experience must become literate.[19] We are to begin like a child before it learns to read, or a person faced with an inscription in a strange alphabet, or even (this is a lesser degree of illiteracy) someone who is faced with a highly technical text in his or her own language. The needed web of intellectual, emotional, and kinesthetic connections has not yet grown up, and we stand there nonplussed. But those connections can grow up in either a proper or a defective form: "literate" too is a success word.

The second reason adds to this requirement of accuracy that the judgment in question needs to be self-attributive.[20] An example will make this concrete and also introduce a crucial distinction.

> (1) Ric O., a mountaineer, returns to civilization and sees a newspaper for the first time in seventeen days. The headline proclaims, "Ric O. has won one million dollars in the state lottery." He exclaims, "Oh my God! I've won a million dollars!" Many years later he tells his grandchildren that he once had the experience of returning from the mountains to find that he had won a million dollars.
>
> (2) Ric O., a mountaineer, returns to civilization but has amnesia, as may happen after a sojourn above 17,000 feet. He sees a newspaper with the headline "Ric O. has won a million dollars." The name sounds familiar to him and he exclaims, "Look! Ric O. has won a million dollars!"

Unlike the example of the snake and the hose, this is a case of correct judgment. In these two scenarios, the same event happened to Ric

O., he was aware of this event happening to him, and his judgment was accurate and correct. But in the second scenario, it is deceptive or misleading to simply put it that way, for his response does not have the requisite first-person form. He does not have the experience of winning a prize, because he was not self-attributing the property in question, even though he does attribute it to the right person.[21]

With these distinctions in mind, how do the Jesuit arguments transpose? I have no problem of identification for the events that happen to me, at least not in the sense that I must find some criterion to isolate the events that happen to me among all the events that happen. On the other hand, I have in principle no problem of interpretation for the judgment I make in response. For when any such spontaneous judgment is explicit, it is made in my own language. And finally, for the same reason, I have no problem in principle about what does and does not follow from them, for logic derives from the structure of language, whatever it be. But those occurrences of "in principle" bear a heavy weight here!

The different puzzles must be kept disentangled from each other. None of this imperviousness in principle implies infallibility in my judgment or understanding; that is a different problem, to which we are in fact about to turn. The point now is that the three problems raised in the original Jesuit argument seem not to transpose and carry across to experience. Those arguments apply to a text whose meaning and status are in question, whereas here we have on one hand elements that are not text at all (what happens to me, my having the conceptual resources to frame judgments in response) and on the other hand texts that are mine, in my language, created by me in my own language. Therefore no such questions arise for them, either. Trying to step outside ourselves could only result in incoherence, in just the way that skepticism is so often just incoherence disguised as genuine doubt.[22]

Is that right? During the experience, or at the moment of the experience, no such questions arise, that is true. But if we were to conclude too much from this, we'd fall right back into an untenable "experience fundamentalism" to which those arguments would apply. So let us see what there lies beyond this "in principle" rescue of experience from the Jesuit's clutches.

6. FALLIBILITY: THE PROBLEM OF EPISTEMIC FRAILTY AND SIN

We need to amass three main points about experience and assimilate them to achieve a synoptic vision in which all three are seen in proper perspective. That is not easy since they seem at first blush to be at war with each other.

When I perceive something, a carriage return, say, that is because something happens to me of which I am aware and to which I respond in part with a perceptual judgment. This judgment identifies (classifies) the event in question. The identification may be correct or erroneous, accurate, imprecise, or mistaken. It also involves an element of interpretation, because it is couched in my own language, which I myself, on reflection, recognize to be heavily laden or infected with old beliefs and theories. But worse: the text may come shrouded in uncertainty, ambiguity, and inconsistency. I realize all this; despite my utter and inescapable reliance on my own language and judgment (consider the alternative!) I am able to doubt myself on many levels, to lesser and greater degrees.

So what does the rule of *Sola Experientia* prescribe? What I have experienced, in the sense of what has really happened to me, is the touchstone for all theory. But theory is, in me, confronted only with the text of my spontaneous judgments, that is, my immediate judgmental response to what befalls me. This text is already divided into dreaming, waking, thinking, musing, and so on. But it is also subject to a critique in which I isolate at least the first layer of interpretive raiment clothing experienced nature (to use Boltzmann's metaphor). What shall I take as guide for this task? In practice I will certainly trust in the reliability of my prior opinion and theoretical commitments. I'll do this equally in my critical self-scrutiny so as to police my own data. Nor is there any alternative: we can only start from where we are.

This self-reliance does not mean that I accept any immediate, spontaneous, unreflective responses as ultimate authority. On the contrary, what I rely on (my prior opinion, perceptual judgment theoretical commitments) I treat and regard as at once reliable and defeasible. So that is the second element. What we also saw in the preceding section (this is the third element to assimilate) is that this self-reliance has a sort of purely logical inescapability to it. An attempt to gauge it critically in our own case seems to precipitate us into incoherence.

So here is the puzzle when we recognize our own epistemic frailty and sin. It looks as if we are, practically speaking, forced into implicit reliance on something we know we do not have and moreover are unable to voice that knowledge coherently. We seem to be caught up in a dilemma: either blithely ignore our shortcomings, or land in incoherence if we don't!

That is how it seems, but it can't be that way. We know very well that all three elements are there to be understood and of course jointly understood, not just one at a time.[23] The predicament in which we find ourselves must derive from a faulty way of describing our epistemic situation. On one hand, coherence constrains the form of all our first-person judgment. On the other, we are able to stand back from ourselves sufficiently to see how we may need to change and can change.

We can suspend part of what we take for granted, as long as we are willing to rely on a sufficiently large part of our language and

prior opinion to describe the suspended part and its possible connections with the world. The philosopher's task at this point is to
show that this is coherently and rationally possible. We can change
our opinion, as well as our language, in the same way. We can
suspend some elements and then move on in a way for which there
can be no rule, blueprint, or recipe but for which we need no rule,
blueprint, or recipe, only the courage to go on, albeit in fear and
trembling. Here the philosopher's first task is precisely the same: to
show the coherence and rationality of such a way of life. There is
then still a further task: to elucidate precisely how we do so. Obviously we don't just make arbitrary, unpredictable, unaccountable
leaps into the unknown all the time!

Three. Tolerating Ambiguity: The Inexhaustible, Unfathomable Historical Self

> I conclude that the rules are ambiguous in the way in which certain
> drawings are ambiguous, that events can make them change face, that, in
> the heat of battle, the change often remains unnoticed so that we obtain a
> smooth changeover from one worldview . . . to another, and "incommen-
> surable," one.
>
> —FEYERABEND, *The Conquest of Abundance*, p. 39

We must accept that, like Neurath's mariner at sea, we are historically situated. We rely and must rely on our pre-understanding, our
own language, and our prior opinion as they are now and go on
from there. Rationality will consist not in having a specially good
starting point but in how well we criticize, amend, and update our
given condition. But even if we have succeeded in the first task (of
describing ourselves to ourselves in that way without incoherence),
there is still the question of just how we can go about this self-critical
pilgrim's progress. Worse: as we saw in the preceding lecture, the

transitions we must allow as rationally endorsable include transitions to ways of thinking that are literally absurd and senseless from the prior point of view.

The *Sola Scriptura* type of rule has now clearly met a devastating line of criticism, which raises deep suspicions about its actual role in the practice of communities that have this sort of rule. Yet Feyerabend suggests that we have something to learn from a practice that he manages to indict and praise at the same time. In fact, we have here a key to the problem of incommensurability ostensibly obstructing our understanding of conceptual and scientific revolutions. As we concluded earlier, we must admit into our epistemology a place for emotion, or analogues to emotion, in our description of rationally endorsable changes in view. That was as yet a very small step. Where does the emotion get its purchase? The answer we can now give draws on two loci of ambiguity: in the past understanding that will be modified and in the very rule that is meant to govern such modification.[24]

7. THE USES OF AN UNFOLLOWABLE RULE

The rule of *Sola Scriptura* plays two very effective but quite different roles in the community when it holds sway. First of all, because there is a tradition that identifies and interprets Scripture, the rule tells everyone who lives in that tradition not to depart from it. So it reinforces and maintains orthodoxy. This role is certainly exemplified by Newton's fourth rule of reasoning in philosophy, whose basic function was also quite clearly to stabilize opinions based on experience. Newton's rule tells us that no new or nontraditional interpretations of the source material are to be heeded. Only (new) source material can be consulted as a touchstone for our opinions. Thus seen, it is clearly of the *Sola Scriptura* type. Is the fourth rule a rationally compelling rule? Surely not. It is a counsel of epistemic conservatism, for which we may see some good practical reason.

But whereas the first and most obvious role is to strengthen and maintain tradition, the second, equally effective, role is as tool or weapon in the critique of accepted opinion. Indeed, it is a rule that (seen in a different way) seems precisely designed to allow the exploitation of ambiguities and vaguenesses in past understanding, of openings to change that a perceptive mind can grasp. Should the need arrive to revise our understanding, the means are then at hand. Suppose one of us advocates that we change our belief from A to B. There is exactly one acceptable form of argument in a community governed by this rule of faith:

(I) We admit that part of A was indeed solidly (but only solidly) based on Scripture (on experience, on experimental results, as the case may be).

(II) Then we point out interpretive elements in A, some extrapolation or generalization not logically implied by that source.

(III) Suspending the part of A that we have now acknowledged as interpretive, we are left with a weaker proposition A*, compatible with B.

(IV) As next and final step we point to another part of Scripture (of experience, of experimental results), which together with A* provides support for B.

The very first thing we must do is appreciate the element of false consciousness in this procedure if naïvely followed. But the second thing to do is to appropriate its good and useful purpose.

To begin, note the illusion traded on, namely, that the correct opinion is uniquely determined by the source. Given this illusion we can point to the interpretive elements in A as a mistake, an "unScriptural" or "unscientific" addition. This is how popular science texts now treat Newton, more or less as follows: "Newton did not arrive at Einstein's relativity because, enslaved by old ideas and seeing his own results with myopic eyes, he extrapolated his facts in a biased way. Einstein pointed out how Newton had gone beyond the deliverances of experience, removed Newton's metaphysical additions, and thus made way for the right theory, truly true to experience." This sort of indictment can always be leveled in retrospect. Earlier experience cannot logically imply what later experience will be like. Therefore if some opinion based on earlier experience does not fit the later appearances, it must have gone logically beyond what was given—of course! By its failure with respect to the future it stands convicted of overinterpretation. After all, experience (or Scripture) itself could not have been the source of error.

The pattern Feyerabend elicits here is familiar and convincing but also seems to be debunked when it is presented in this way. We observe the so-called rule as actually a dictum with two quite separate roles, unacknowledged if the practice is unreflective. In its first role, the rule enforces orthodoxy; in its second role it provides a vehicle for departures from orthodoxy. We are tempted to exclaim that in its two main roles, the rule of *Sola Scriptura* or *Sola Experientia* is at war with itself. In one role it maintains orthodoxy and forbids heeding the alternative interpretations ingenious minds can concoct. But in its other role it devalues any aspect of orthodoxy that can be identified as interpretive. This entails a permission that can successively peel off layer after layer, possibly leaving nothing intact in the end.

Happily it's only philosophers who take ideas to their logical extreme, and happily no one listens to philosophers when they do. In the hands of reasonable people, this dual-role rule is actually a great boon.[25] The rule will maintain the status quo as long as there are no serious anomalies or new situations that throw the tradition into crisis. When such crises do happen, that same rule shows the way to reasoned and proportionate change, providing a rational form for consensual revision. Happily reason, within a community, is a matter of politics in the broad sense of the term, of negotiation and dispute, strife and reconciliation, and not just of logic.

A member of a community would be missing something if, having perceived the possible other role for the rule, he or she were to simply start applying it ad libitem. The shift from one role to the other involves a change in value judgment. The new conviction might be, for example, that the stability of the status quo is no longer worth the cost, that its cost now outweighs the costs involved in advocating radical change. Such a change in values, as we found in the preceding lecture, we can only understand under the heading of emotion, not as factual or theoretical deliberation.

8. AN EXAMPLE: BOHM VERSUS THE COPENHAGEN SCHOOL

We have a striking recent illustration of this point in the development of quantum mechanics. In the 1950s David Bohm developed a new interpretation (or if you like, a new theory) that was designed to coincide with standard quantum mechanics in its empirical predictions. In this construction he followed some ideas earlier proposed by De Broglie that had been rejected by the physics community. In fact, Bohm's theory met with resistance when it was noted at all. But it found new and vigorous advocates about three decades later.[26]

The history of this episode is interesting in part because emotions sometimes run high in such debates, but also because the dismissal of Bohm's ideas (which contradicted a good deal of received wisdom about what quantum mechanics implies) was not generally based on any demonstration of their inadequacy. Instead we see there, one might say, Newton's fourth rule in action, in its status quo–maintaining role. If science were to be diverted each time a clever rival hypothesis is proposed, even one that also accounts for the empirical successes so far, theoretical stability would be in danger. Hence, the rule says, the standard line is to be maintained until there are rival empirical predictions, tests, or results at issue. The main physics community displayed thus precisely the value judgment signaled by this rule. Its Bohmian opponents were also quite right to see that this value judgment cannot have absolute hegemony. Purely theoretical developments can engender important changes in science; in any case, a value judgment is not a theoretical or experimental argument. Indeed, the Copenhagen orthodoxy (for example, the view that elementary particles cannot be ascribed continuous trajectories in space-time) was shown not to be implied by the experimental facts it cited for support. That was a new insight, a logical point, which should be acknowledged. It could indeed provide the fulcrum for an application of the rule in its second, innovation-guiding, role. But the point is again that the shift from the one role to the other, although logically possible at this point, would require a change in value judgment within the community. Such a change does not happen lightly.

Even if we grant all this, however, we may still have here the sense of a disturbing insinuation of double-think, bad faith, and self-deception. The mariners-at-sea image depicts our real situation, but can it sustain itself only through the illusion of foundations? Is authenticity possible? Are we dealing here merely with defense tactics, with the last defense of a waning orthodoxy? Or can we reframe this practice so that it involves at once a reasonable reliance on what we trust ourselves to have gained so far and also a sufficiently detached critical stance toward our past? Can we allow experience to play these two roles, which will alternately pull us in two different directions, making up our own minds without pretense that there is a further compelling rationale to be found behind those shifts?

These are not theoretical or even factual questions. These are calls for decision when they arise in the actual, practical context of a community in process of theoretical, cultural, or conceptual change.

For the liberal they are calls to a tolerance for ambiguity seen as key to a civilized life. The conservative sees the willful destruction of past values, and it all comes, he also says, from tolerance of ambiguity. But the choice between these two stances, each of which can be authentic, is not a theoretical choice.

Leaving polemics aside, we recognize that any systematic pursuit of knowledge or reliable opinion must involve a practice that has both features. There must be some assurance of stability and also leeway for far-reaching innovation. Once we recognize this uneasy tension, we can also see that although the format could be the form of self-deception if unconscious and of cynical manipulation if conscious, it need not be either.[27] Acknowledging that we need to settle on a policy that balances prudence and innovation, we can accept this form of stabilizing change consciously and without misleading rhetoric. The one thing that would defeat it altogether is the idea that rationality would require a recipe-like rule, with specified conditions under which alone the shift in roles is to happen!

9. AMBIGUITY AND VAGUENESS: OUR REDEEMING WEAKNESSES

There are two common misconceptions about ambiguity and vagueness. The first is that they are absent from our most precise discourse, exemplified by mathematics and the sciences. The second is that they are simply defects—not just sometimes defects or defects in some cases, but features that ought to be absent, that have no positive value at all even if their negative impact is sometimes negligible. Quite to the contrary, ambiguity and vagueness not only characterize also our most precise discourse at every stage of our history but are essential to the character of discourse.[28] Natural language, our language, is not a finished artifact. It is the locus of uncountable, so far unrealized possibilities, as well as of an inexhaustible historical identity whose archaeological investigation could not possibly be completed in finitely many steps.[29]

The distinctions I will introduce here are more commonly made for literature and art than for science.[30] But they pertain to every kind of representation. Science certainly provides us with representations of various kinds, such as texts, drawings, maps, diagrams, table-top models, graphs, and computer simulations. The first thing to ask about a representation is, What does it represent? What is it a representation of? The graph of an exponential curve may represent a bacterial population growing over time, for example. Then it is a representation of that bacteria colony, or if you like, of the colony's growth. The next question concerns the information stored and conveyed. That graph represents the colony as undergoing exponential growth. This answer concerns not representing *of* but representing *as*, and these two aspects of representation are to be kept distinct.

Third, we can then ask how accurate it is. This question is actually not as simple as it sounds to begin with. To put it colloquially, it is easy enough to say something true, impossible to say all that is true about a given subject. Selectivity in science is deliberate, purposeful, and subject to evaluation as well. We ask not only if a given science provides accurate information about what it selected for attention but whether it has selected well, whether it answers all or many important or relevant questions. So the evaluation of accuracy actually draws on values current or imposed in its context. What is important in the welter of data that assails us is not "written on the face of" the data, nor is it yet another datum among them. Only when the context is fixed and the relevant aspects and criteria are in place does the question of how accurate it is makes sense.

All of this sounds so prosaic that we might as well have been talking about a census, a railroad timetable, or a theater schedule.

Complexities come in when we look more deeply into representing as, where we encounter vast interpretive leeway. When do representations tend to invite interpretation? The most obvious answer is: precisely when a representation is vague or ambiguous.[31]

Views of science of the sort typically labeled "scientific realism" take the aim of science to be correct description, or accurate representation, of what there is. But there have been major shifts in even these views owing to the revolutionary upheavals in science. Compare the following sentiment from the middle of the nineteenth century:

> Now there do exist among us doctrines of solid and acknowledged certainty, and truths of which the discovery has been received with universal applause. These constitute what we commonly term Science.[32]

with a very conservative form of scientific realism in our time:

> Science aims at a literally true account of the physical world, and its success is to be reckoned by its progress toward achieving that aim.[33]

The two statements agree on truth as defining aim; the difference lies in the erosion of certainty, with its concordant disentangling of the two concepts of truth and of certainty. The end in view is still truth, but this no longer implies that we can have even potential certainty that this end has been attained. By mid-twentieth century scientific realists had come to see these two concepts as logically independent.

Apart from this erosion of certainty, there is the question whether we can speak here only of representation pure and simple, or whether interpretation also enters in. A relatively conservative philosopher of science might respond: "Precision, accuracy, univocity, invulnerability to deconstruction or alternative interpretation are evidently the very hallmarks of rigor in the sciences. That is perhaps the very reason why scientific texts won't be literary texts as well, and why science is not art." But let us scrutinize the sort of representation science provides.

Newton represented the solar system accurately in many respects (the respects that he selected for thematic presentation) but he represented it as (what we now call) a Newtonian mechanical system. Obviously he abstracted from the facts. But does abstraction consist simply in deletion of certain aspects, the ones not selected for representation? If so, abstraction can presumably introduce no inaccuracy or falsehood. In that case, what it produces is the truth remaining after we ignore some of the truth to be found. But this irenic account of Newton's induction, his rigorous derivation from the phenomena, is too simple and too comforting, too good to be true.

How the solar system appears to Newton's God, how it appears in the view from nowhere, is not how it appears to us. Attending to what does appear and has appeared to us, can we apply the interpretative adjective "Newtonian"? Newton showed us that we could, by constructing a mathematical model and showing that it provided an adequate representation of the solar system. God created the world, Newton represented it as a Newtonian mechanical system, and we saw that it was good. Later Einstein represented it as a relativistic mechanical system, and again we saw that it was good— this time even better. The conclusion to draw is that the phenomena, to the extent Newton knew them, admitted his sort of representation (nature could be represented as a Newtonian system) but did not dictate it. Those phenomena can equally be represented in an Einsteinian, relativistic system. We can draw a parallel here to the work of a portrait painter. The painting represents the subjects as arrogant or as complacent, and the fact is that their comportment, as displayed to the painter, allowed both interpretations.

So at the very least we must think of the representations of nature that science gives us as representations of nature as thus or so. The "as" indicates an interpretative element, and our example shows that the facts leave sufficient leeway to allow for representations as A or as B, where A and B are incompatible (in that nothing could at the same time be both A and B).

But that conservative philosopher might then still press a serious disanalogy between science and art here, after admitting to a minor analogy. By viewing the works of, for example, the Impressionists, or the Fauves, we might become enabled to see nature and humanity in a new way. Analogously, Newton showed us how to see nature in a new way. Certainly, the new way of seeing involves the application of an interpretative attribute. The phenomena (how nature had appeared to us so far) admitted of being classified as the appearances of Newtonian systems. Newton was wrong only in thinking that the interpretation was unique. Quite possibly Einstein's models fit the recorded phenomena prior to 1700 no better than do Newton's. The fact remains that, since they are a feasible alternative, the phenomena did not compel Newton's interpretation uniquely.

This admitted analogy (so the objection would go) must be followed by a much more important disanalogy. Unlike the case of art, the representation itself does not allow for different readings or viewings. The viewer may react to a particular painting, for example by seeing the men on the grass either as arrogant or as complacent. The painting admits both interpretative responses. Thus there are two levels at which non-univocal interpretation enters the scenario. The parallel between Newton's celestial mechanics and this painting would be as follows:

a. the real situation corresponds to the solar system,
b. the way the situation appeared to the painter corresponds to the recorded celestial phenomena (the data),
c. the painting corresponds to Newton's model.

So science, like art, interprets the phenomena, and not in a uniquely compelled way. Science itself, however, does not admit of alternative rival interpretations. Whereas there is ambiguity in the painting, and crucially so, there is no ambiguity in the scientific model. And so although the literary text is open, the scientific text remains a closed text.

The history of science put the lie to this story, and in successively more radical ways. Poincaré gave the following example. Gravitation, the only force treated successfully by Newton himself, is a central force, with the center supplied by the gravitating mass. In the eighteenth century, it was taken as a principle of mechanical modeling that all forces in nature are central forces. Was this an addition to Newton's science? We must first reflect on this question itself and ask what kind of answer it requires. Does it ask whether Newton deliberately omitted the principle from the principles of mechanics, or whether he indicated it tacitly, so that it was there for him but as a principle that had not risen to the level of explicit formulation? All Newton's explicitly constructed models are of the type admitted in the eighteenth century; it is as if he already had that principle as well. But "as if" is all we can say.

Should we instead take Newton's science to be defined solely by what was explicitly stated? That is not such an easy alternative, either. For in that case all the Newtonians would appear to have misunderstood Newton's mechanics. To take one example, Laplace only formulated the common understanding when he used the dramatic device of an omniscient genie to convey that the Newtonian world picture is entirely deterministic. But if we look only to explicitly formulated principles, we must say that this science was not deterministic. The law of conservation of energy was not recognized as an independent and needed addition until the nineteenth century and the science allows for indeterminism before the addition is made.[34]

What retrenchment could come next? Newtonian physics managed to create in this audience (the physicists and educated lay public of the modern era) the impression of total determinism. In consequence their own view of science began to include it as a criterion;

the telos of science was representation as deterministic. This conviction was not shared by all (Charles Sanders Peirce being one honorable exception), and indeed it was compelled neither by the phenomena, nor by the science, nor by the success of science. Science itself admitted of different interpretations, even if at each stage one interpretation seemed to be dominant.[35]

So in science too, we find interpretation at two different levels. The theory represents the phenomena as thus or so, and that representation itself is subject to more than one tenable but significantly different interpretation. As in art, we find the persons involved (those who create the work, those who peruse or appreciate it) often unconscious of the non-uniqueness of their interpretations and of the creative element in their response as readers. The texts of science too are open texts.

SCIENTIFIC REVOLUTION/CONVERSION IN PERSPECTIVE

What happens in a scientific revolution? From the prior point of view, the received scientific opinion of the day, the new theories are absurd or unintelligible. The transition to the new view of nature, the conversion to that view, does not admit of justification within prior understanding or standards of acceptability. The beliefs, values, criteria, assumptions, presuppositions, claims to knowledge may become weighed down by anomalies and diminishing returns, disappointed expectations. But they are never defeated in open battle. Hence the change that makes change possible goes so deep that it foregoes any prior rationale. It is a change through (some analogue of) emotion, playing the role Sartre described, in which old values and views are let go.

But from the posterior point of view, the transition was eminently rational. Vagueness, incompleteness, ambiguities all came to light, interpretative elements and assumptions were made explicit. By being made explicit, they were made to lose their grip on the scientific imagination. The story of how the scientific representation of nature was changed, with reason and in an eminently rational way, can then be told. That story is part of the justification the new status quo can give as its credentials and as reason to demand commitment. Not to mention, of course, that nothing succeeds like success.

The empirical sciences do live by the rule of *Sola Experientia:* nothing trumps experience. The bottom line is agreement with experimental and observational fact. But in this rule there is a true and redeeming ambiguity. For the main part, it plays the role of maintaining the hegemony of the ruling paradigm, the accepted theories in the scientific community. Thus normal science's steady progress is not allowed to be derailed by every Velikowski (or Bohm or Einstein) to come along. New theories are not worth much attention until there are new, telling experimental findings. In this role the rule rightly plays on the substantive empirical success that the accepted theories have to their credit. We should also honor those who work on solutions even to persistent anomalies in the prior accepted framework, from Galileo's rivals to Poisson (when he famously resisted the wave theory of light) to Lorentz.

But if the emotional situation changes, we suddenly see that the scientist is a warrior, not a bookkeeper. Then the same rule can play its second role. In that role it provides a form for critique of the older theory as involving assumptions that go beyond the prior deliverances of experience. That allows for a critical examination of how the older experimental and observational results were presented and for the partial suspension of the older theories. For that too can be done in the name of *Sola Experientia.* The tension between these two roles is felt only at certain disturbed and disturbing moments in history, but is in fact its final redeeming value.[36] For the empiricist, the way in which scientific practice thus shows how we can let go of our beliefs, as opposed to how it dictates belief, is the more inspiring lesson.

What Is Science—and
What Is It to Be Secular?

I am part of all that I have met;
Yet all experience is an arch wherethrough
Gleams that untravelled world, whose margin fades
For ever and for ever when I move.
—TENNYSON, *Ulysses*

The empiricist tradition was in the past thoroughly entangled with the materialism from which I dissociated it. Empiricists have also by and large, in the past, displayed a specifically secular orientation, often enough with reason to think of the religious as allied with superstition and opposition to science. Does the empirical stance allow for anything other than a secular orientation?

Given that the natural sciences loom so large in empiricist thinking, the answer might be thought to turn on the relation between science and religion. I think that is a mistake, at least as the subject is commonly understood and discussed. Studies targeting "science and religion"—the code for a certain academic region—strike me as mainly irrelevant to empiricist concerns. You may also know a document the engineers circulated when I was a student, called "Stress Analysis of a Strapless Evening Gown." I am struck by the similarities to certain science-and-religion studies. Classical stress analysis is a beautiful subject in applied physical science. I don't doubt that it has as much intrinsic interest as any bit of science you could mention. But the reason it was so avidly circulated was quite obviously its topic of application. Since the study was conducted with notable scientific integrity, however, it answered only questions within the parameters of physical stress and so had no bearing (saving titillated prurience) on anything that gave its topic such independent human interest. Somehow the two sources of fascination, physics and the female body, combined to hide the irrelevance.

To my mind, the questions of what science is and what it is to be secular are only historically and culturally related, not by any internal necessity. So what would I like to do, when setting these topics side by side? Well, let us try to say precisely what it is to be secular, and what relation that orientation has in fact, however incidentally from the logical point of view, to science. The religious may have some condescending answer to this, and the secular themselves a self-congratulatory reply, but the real challenge is to find an answer that each can accept as both intelligible and correct. This requirement would practically condemn us to failure if we meant to have a complete answer. If we look for necessary and sufficient conditions for the secular orientation that can be understood without presuppositions, concepts, or forms of discourse peculiar to either the secular or the religious, we seem bound to fail. What I hope to find instead is something recognized by each, the secular and the nonsecular, of which both can say: "There is something that divides us, of which I can understand both sides, if only by analogy to something that I know and value in my own world."[1]

To begin I will contrast two forms of inquiry, two cognitive approaches to ourselves and the world we live in. Science certainly provides a paradigm example of one of these, which I will call objectifying inquiry. But we also have concrete examples of the other. For our purpose, however, the more important contrast will be between two attitudes that one can have toward the scientific form of inquiry.

One is to be content with the scientific form as exclusively sufficient, so to speak. The other is a discontent, an "abiding wonder," though (as I see it) a discontent in possible peaceful coexistence with science and every form of practical cognition. Central examples of secularism display that contentment, and central examples of religious life exemplify the discontent: an abiding astonishment not allayed by the fruits of scientific inquiry. I must hasten to add that this point of difference is not nearly enough to demarcate a boundary between the two. There are secular artists who display such discontent and abiding wonder; there may well be religious scholars who do not. But perhaps we can, as scientists do, count some success if we arrive at an imperfect approximation to what it is (not) to be secular.

One. What Is Science?

1. THE SENSES OF "SCIENCE"

"What is science?" quite obviously divides into several questions. The word "science" displays a typical ambiguity between activity and product. We say that science tells us that smoking is unhealthy: this refers to the product—findings, well-confirmed theories accepted in the scientific community. We also say that science investigates such structures as links between smoking and health or between background radiation and the history of the universe. Here we refer to the activity in which scientists are engaged.

This product-activity ambiguity is ubiquitous in English. Recall Aristotle's answer to the question "What is tragedy?" The word "tragedy" also has that typical ambiguity between activity and product. When Aristotle begins "Tragedy is the representation of an action . . . .," he is referring to the dramatists' art and the craft they exercise, but also to the tragedies (their product) performed on stage. Thus he is using a third word with that typical ambiguity, "representation," which also stands equivocally for an activity and the product of such activity. Aristotle continues: "Tragedy is a representation of a serious, complete action which has magnitude, in embellished speech . . . by people acting, and not by narration; accomplishing by means of pity and terror the catharsis of such emotions" (*Poetics*, 49b25). Thus to identify just what sort of representation tragedy is, he specifies the object, manner, medium, and aim of tragedy. Aiming for Aristotelian completeness, one could try to do the same for science.[2] For today, however, I propose to focus solely on the manner. What form does scientific inquiry characteristically take?

No pretense of a complete answer to the question, therefore! I am focusing here on just one aspect of one half of the question.

2. OBJECTIFICATION AS CHARACTERISTIC OF SCIENCE

Scientific inquiry is an objectifying procedure. What can be meant by this? As usual, many things are meant. I will try to isolate a cluster of intentions that seem to go together in this context. They concern specifically how a scientific inquiry is delimited in a certain way beforehand.[3] That is most easily seen in what Kuhn called "normal science," but we will pay equal attention to the "revolutionary" stages as well.

SENSES OF "OBJECTIFY": 1

The first sense in which objectification appears as a feature of scientific inquiry is well illustrated by the progress of science in the seventeenth and eighteenth centuries as described in Catherine Wilson's study of microscopy, *The Invisible World:*

> We need to distinguish between the objectivity of reductive ontologies or metaphysics and the objectivity of modern science.

The former is not constitutive of and is largely irrelevant to the latter. The experimental and observational sciences of the seventeenth and eighteenth centuries . . . began to make themselves objective in their constitution of a scientific object: an object that is collected, labeled, put in a museum, that is sliced, dissected, solidified, dyed, and put under a microscope. (p. 37)

We are reminded here of the sense in which the surgeon needs to see or treat his patient as an object. Let us call this "objective distancing."[4]

This is definitely a sense in which inquiries are said to be objective, a way of "taking ourselves out of the picture," so to speak, with both positive and negative connotations. Wilson illustrates the attitude toward what is studied in this way with the very concrete operations of preparing an object for microscopic inspection. The surgeon's nurses similarly prepare the patient for surgical inspection and treatment, thus constituting, one might say, a medical object. While applauding the necessity of this procedure and the surgeon's objectivity, we may be uncomfortably reminded of more negative connotations, relating even to the "objectivity" in the way in which a pornographer, slave master, or sexist spouse relates to another human being in his or her power.[5] We should not let these negative connotations overwhelm us. What would we do without the surgeon's objectivity?

SENSES OF "OBJECTIFY": 2

There is in fact a second initial sense in which one sees science as objectifying. We see science as giving a new shape to the world we experience, a shape at once enriched and impoverished. Again I prefer to quote the philosopher and historian of science Wilson rather than any literary or "merely" philosophical writer: "In summary, there were two facets to the objectification of nature. Exact natural history encouraged its contemplation as a system: as forming in itself a unity, a plenitude, and a harmony, independent of human interests. It also encouraged the subtraction of moral attributes and purposes: the new discourse of nature was as impoverished in cultural terms as it was enriched in observational terms" (p. 212). Again we may relate this to, for example, the period early in the twentieth century when Max Weber gained respect for sociology as a discipline by defining a value-free methodology. The scientists who heeded his message—as the entire profession learned to do, until it was thrown into skeptical self-doubts by a new generation—constructed an ostensibly value-neutral world. So let us call this process "objective neutralization." Whatever doubts we may have come to have about this, there was much need for an effort in this direction. Quite apart from sociology, there were the sexism, racism, and national chauvinism that we can now, in retrospect, see so clearly displayed in psychology, paleontology, and evolutionary biology when pointed out graphically by new generations of scientists conscious of their pasts.

SENSES OF "OBJECTIFY": 3

Finally, what can be meant by saying that a scientific investigation is an objectifying inquiry? Let's begin with a reminder of why it is scientifically important to delimit an inquiry beforehand. Certain studies of astrology and parapsychology have been taken to task specifically for violating this requirement. For example, in one study no important correlations were found between astrological sun signs and the professions traditionally associated with them. But a further look into the data showed strong correlations of an unexpected sort between some astrologically significant patterns and other professions. The questions asked before the study began, for which the study was designed, received negative answers. Is there any significance to the correlations that were then found instead?

Not as research results! They may be helpful as pointers toward new studies to be designed for the questions they suggest. But they do not confirm anything about the symptomatic significance of astrological signs. In any data, some correlations can be found if all you are looking for is correlations! This was of course also the criticism of the early Royal Society, which had not yet learned the lesson that, as Kant had it, made modern science possible: "When Galileo caused balls, the weights of which he has himself previously determined, to roll down an inclined plane; when Torricelli made the air carry a weight which he had calculated beforehand to be equal to that of a definite volume of water . . ., a light broke upon all students of nature. They learned that reason has insight only into that which it produces after a plan of its own, and that it must [constrain] nature to give answer to questions of reason's own determining." (*Critique of Pure Reason,* B xii–xiii). I cannot emphasize this too much: to point out these forms of objectification in science is by no means an indictment or critique. On the contrary, as Kant points out, they are among the very keys to success of our modern science. Somewhere along the long way of Western civilization we realized how much we could accomplish cognitively by taking ourselves out of the picture.[6] We see this happening in the "first relativity revolution" of ancient astronomy: relativizing the zenith, losing the cosmic up/down asymmetry, was a first step on a very long path that still needed Weber in about 1900 to bring us back to it in the social sciences. Science is one paradigm of rational inquiry, a shining example of what human reason can accomplish. The characteristic form it takes, and the specificity of that form, does not diminish this achievement by one iota. The keys to empirical success may consist in these nontrivial limits voluntarily accepted. The very specificity of the form of scientific inquiry implies that there must be alternative approaches to nature to be seen in contrast. Let us try to sharpen that contrast.

3. OBJECTIFYING INQUIRY: PRE-DEMARCATION

Of the three forms of objectification (or senses of "objectify") we have noted, I will devote our discussion mainly to the third: objectifying inquiry. We must be careful to distinguish this and to view it separately from objective distancing and objective neutralization.[7] I will list five of its salient aspects, all of them readily illustrated in science. The topic is so large that I can only offer thumbnail sketches of each. Indeed, as a description of scientific inquiry, this will at best be simplifying, not to say superficial. But I hope it will throw light on the precise factors that we need for our contrast.

THE DOMAIN

A science, or a research project within a science, has a domain. It is tempting to think of its initial delimiting as specifying a set of things, for example, "this will be a study of frogs." But that is not accurate, since the central subject matter will inevitably have to be connected with other things. Even an anatomical study of frogs will inquire into, for example, the rate of coagulation of frog blood when exposed to air, and the air is not part of a frog.

It is more accurate to delimit such a domain in terms of the quantities or parameters allowed to figure in the description of the phenomena to be studied. Under quantities I include properties and relations.[8] Think of students who have to write reports on some field work (or lab experiment) done as part of this study of frogs. They will have been taught beforehand the proper form to report the results, including the proper characteristics on which to report and the terms in which to write the observed characteristics.

INDEPENDENCE

The constraint of objectivity for the domain goes beyond its prior specification in terms of a set of relevant parameters. The parameters chosen must be, in a certain sense, independent of who is doing the research. The student of my example will have learned to write such reports in a purely impersonal way; no first-person pronouns, for example!

But that requirement of independence is not so easy to make precise. Obviously, this constraint does not mean ruling out quantities that pertain to humans. That would rule out weight and size! We may very well happen to be in the very domain we are studying. Not when we are studying frogs; but it seems only proper that brains should be studied by people with brains, and intelligence by the intelligent, even if not psychopathology by psychopaths.

So what does this mean, "independent of us"? Certain kinds of anthropocentrism, or observer-centrism, are obviously to be ruled out. If, for example, we divide the frogs into small, medium, or large, that should be short for a classification relative to the frog population, not relative to us. This constraint is sometimes assimilated to the requirement that all those quantities be measurable. But (regardless of whether that is indeed a requirement) these constraints are not the same. It would not help, for example, if observers had a good way of measuring how much they personally like frogs; that quantity has no place in the study of frogs (as opposed to frog-observer relations, which would be a different domain).

In the twentieth century this constraint of objectivity saw some controversy. In the initial receptions first of relativity and then of the new quantum theory it was suspected (and even asserted) that this constraint is violated. We still hear it said sometimes that the great lesson was precisely that this observer independence is violated in the new physics. For philosophy of science this is now an old controversy; I think we have managed to separate the genuine conceptual puzzles from the appearances. Relativity is not relativity to the observer but to frames of reference that may or may not be connected with observers. The measurement problem in quantum mechanics takes precisely the same form for inanimate instruments as for conscious observers. The ways in which the observer is present and nonnegligible in observation is now more salient but not in principle different from before.

RESTRICTIONS ON THE RELEVANT PARAMETERS

So the first step in setting up the scientific inquiry is to select the "relevant" quantities. All questions to be broached must be questions formulable in terms of these quantities.

The paradigm example of this procedure was Galileo's list of primary qualities for physics. Physical description was to proceed solely in terms of these qualities; no others were to be admitted. Modern physics accepted this discipline with the salutary effect that kinematics could be isolated for initial study, and dynamics did not—as in the Aristotelian tradition—run ahead of kinematics. This sort of theoretical discipline would prevent empty verbiage of the "dormative virtue" type.

But the discipline was one thing; the ontology preached in Galileo's evangelical mood was another. The conviction that this is not merely a discipline in praxis but the proper new ontology was not part of science itself. That conviction did have its consequences for science, for better and worse. It inspired Descartes to look for a deterministic physics written entirely in kinematic terms. That was not possible, as Leibniz and Newton quickly established. We must carefully distinguish, in Catherine Wilson's terms, the objectivity proclaimed by a reductive ontology and the objectivity proper to scientific procedures. Despite the philosophical propaganda of the time (then as now), there is little connection between the two. We must distinguish Galileo's requirement as methodological discipline from his insistence that these are the basic parameters of reality. The methodological requirement shaped modern science even while the list of "primary qualities" kept changing.

NATURE PUT TO THE QUESTION

We come now to the Inquisitorial "putting nature to the question," in which the phenomena in the domain are observed under both natural and artificial (experimental) conditions. This is never observation, pure and simple. The disciplined relevant acts of observation must register precisely what happens in the previously delimited terms. That is, the phenomena are to be described in the observation reports solely in terms of those "relevant" quantities. This description must be systematic; the result will be a "data model," which can be studied to discern patterns in the phenomena.[9] The theoretician's responsibility to the data is paralleled at this level by the experimenter's responsibility both to the phenomena and to the background theory within which the experimental or observational conditions are designed.

THEORETICAL MODELS; INTRODUCTION OF NEW QUANTITIES

The framing and investigating of hypotheses, which will stand or fall depending on their fit (in various ways) to these data models, will be equally constrained in terms of admissible quantities. But these hypotheses may include quantities not used in the construction of the data models.

Is there more to this than a simple addition? The newly introduced theoretical quantities soon begin to affect the very structure and content of observation reports. Perhaps the terms in which the phenomena were reported in the past remain syntactically the same, but they no longer function logically in the same way. Nevertheless, it is equally shallow to depict this as simply a change in the "observation language." The measurement of theoretically defined quantities has a rather special form, which presupposes the model (thus the measurement result really takes the form "If this is a system of such and such a kind then its F has value f"). Clearly we have here an exceedingly subtle subject for philosophical study.[10] To put it very briefly: the theoretical models (proffered, by means of those hypotheses, as candidates for the representation of the phenomena) are confronted by the data models. Here nature, indeed, natural selection, takes its rightful toll, for fit to those data models is ultimately the bottom line.[11]

What are the constraints on the introduction of new parameters when theoretical models (or in general, explanations of phenomena) are constructed? At the most fundamental level (introduction of a new fundamental physical theory) I really do not know how to characterize them. That there must be such constraints closely tied to the immediately preceding history of the subject, and to connections between the new models and the older ones, I am convinced. Quarks and superstrings are admissible at stages where demonic intervention would not be. Closer to home, in the less fundamental sciences, we see one obvious constraint: the new parameters should belong to an accepted theory with a wider domain. Thus the physiology of frogs in the eighteenth century came to draw on chemistry and physics to explain the twitching produced in frog legs by means of electricity. At that point the "shell structure" of the sciences comes into play.[12]

4. OBJECTIFICATION: SCIENCE IN THE WIDEST SENSE?

Actual scientific work does not fit the above description all that well. Does that mean that actual scientific inquiry is after all not an objectifying inquiry in this sense? Well, not necessarily; that depends on how it departs from the above format. After all, no actual human work fits its own design all that well, no matter how carefully spelled out beforehand. There are two more interesting questions to ask about the above description. The first is whether, on a broader look, scientific inquiry itself must escape this sort of confinement, which admittedly generalizes the quite special format of experiments and experimental result reports. The second is whether, on the contrary, our generalization is really so broad that any rationally acceptable form of inquiry must automatically fall under it. As I see it, with some minor adjustments the pattern of objectifying inquiry is certainly general enough to include the sciences and in fact all disciplines pursued with academic discipline. But it certainly does not cover every cognitive or inquisitive stance that a rational person can reasonably have.

IS GENUINE NOVELTY POSSIBLE?

One challenge takes this form: if science is simply as so described, then no genuine novelty can ever possibly come out of scientific inquiry. But we do see such genuine novelty; hence science cannot be as so described.

That objectifying inquiry does not at all allow for genuine novelty is suggested, for example, by the philosophical theologian Rudolf Bultmann. What he reports is an effect perhaps endemic in the scientifically literate public and perhaps among scientists and scholars generally: "[O]bjectifying thinking . . . understands its object in the context of the domain of objects to which it belongs. Thus, for objectifying thinking a phenomenon is not understood and is a mere *x* or enigma until it can be located in some definite place in the order proper to some domain of objects. Nothing can be new here in a radical sense; each individual thing is to some extent already foreseen in the outline that always guides the study of objects in a particular domain."[13] There seem to be two parts to what he suggests. The first is that he sees this sort of study (as do some philosophers of science) as automatically involving completeness claims with respect to its family of "relevant" parameters. This is part of Bultmann's characterization of "objectifying." But I have not made it part of what is meant here by "objectifying inquiry." The second part is that radically novel results are precluded by the requirement that the domain and family of relevant parameters must be specified beforehand. The reason would be that the answers found can only fit the subject studied into one of the predefined pigeonholes.

Well, I think that is a good point. In the theory of questions that logicians have presented, a question is typically identified through its set of possible direct answers (leaving aside which are the true answers). On this conception, you have not posed a well-defined question at all unless you have an explicit characterization of the range of possible answers. That is, to have a meaningful question you must be able to tell us what would count as a real answer. That conception of question does seem to be involved in what I outlined as characteristic of objectifying inquiry.

Is that how it always is in science? The main counterexamples typically offered are the great scientific revolutions: the Copernican-Galilean, the Darwinian, the Einsteinian. Above I used Thomas Kuhn's term "normal science." In his picture the long periods of normal science (which perhaps do fit my description of objectifying inquiry) are punctuated by conceptual revolutions (which do not). That picture is not uncontroversial (recall, for example, Steven Weinberg's "The Revolution That Did Not Happen," discussed in the previous lecture). But in Kuhn's picture genuine novelty appears in science precisely because objectifying inquiry can come into a crisis and will then be interrupted by a very different sort of theoretical development. Does science then escape those disciplinary constraints of objectifying inquiry?

ABNORMAL ENDINGS: CRISIS

So let us look at how such a clearly delimited inquiry can face failure when questions formulated in its own terms cannot be answered in its own terms. Bultmann continues:

If something appears that cannot be made understandable on the basis of the possibilities previously known (or assumed), objectifying science cannot be content simply to accept this fact or to assume the encroachment of some transcendent power. The upshot, rather, is what is called a "crisis in the foundations" of the particular science. This means that the science in question revises its presuppositions; it recognizes that the guiding outline by which its field of objects was previously circumscribed is no longer adequate, and it develops a new outline in which the phenomenon that proved enigmatic in the old one now becomes understandable. (p. 142)

The range of responses is actually more diverse than Bultmann indicates.[14] If, for instance, it is asked how current values of a certain quantity depend functionally on its preceding values or on current or preceding values of other quantities, there may be no answer. Then the modifications introduced to escape this crisis may indeed revise or extend the list of admissible relevant quantities. But the science may alternatively admit statistical modes of description that still utilize only the "old" quantities.

Be that as it may, the point remains that in the response to crisis, in both Kuhn's and Bultmann's (earlier) description we find genuine novelty, attained through a different sort of inquiry. But that is followed immediately by a return to objectifying inquiry to test that novelty before it can be accepted as a revision of the body of accepted science. Crises and revolutions in science do not take us out of science, and specifically not outside this enterprise of objectifying inquiry.

DOES SCIENCE AUTOMATICALLY INVOLVE COMPLETENESS CLAIMS?

When a theory can introduce new parameters, does that show that the initial list was never proposed as complete? Or is every such novelty the rejection of a previous completeness claim? Familiar examples suggest the latter. Galileo certainly makes a completeness claim for his list of primary qualities. When Newton brings in his forces and masses, the Cartesians object strongly to this introduction of nonkinematic quantities. The findings are not preordained; in that sense there is plenty of novelty. But the terms in which new findings must come, in order to be admissible within the inquiry, are preordained (to determine the scope of the inquiry and its exact character and telos).

Nevertheless, the prior selection of quantities admissible in the description of the phenomena—hence in the formulation of questions to be asked and answers to be given—does not by itself entail such completeness claims. We do not have to think of this objectifying as necessarily linked to a thesis of reduction or supervenience. It need not be assumed that all other qualities will be explicable in terms of the initial list. Such an assumption will only appear as a completeness claim for a certain theory, produced as science-as-product by the inquiry. In the case of theories of frogs, such a claim will be less likely to come along than in the case of fundamental physics, of course. But it is never a necessary accompaniment. Another paradigm example is the methodological innovation attempted by behaviorism in psychology. There too we may distinguish the attempt to set up a well-delimited and well-defined scientific inquiry from the short-lived completeness claims associated with it.

HOW GENERAL IS THIS CONCEPT OF OBJECTIFYING INQUIRY?

All three forms of objectification—objectifying inquiry, objective distancing, and objective neutralization—may be recognized as important aspects of normal science and as ingredients in revolutionary theoretical developments as well. A well-designed scientific inquiry pre-demarcates its domain, its relevant questions, and the parameters within which they can be answered, putting strict limits on the extent to which it can "multiply entities" (not beyond necessity!) while acknowledging, at the very heart of its methodology, the possibility of instructive defeat. But such inquiry will still generally be thought of as not objective (even biased and subverted) if the practitioners ignore the strict discipline required by objective distancing and the production of a factual, value-neutral representation. So much and so harsh a light has been cast in other literature on these latter two forms that I am content to concentrate on the first.

If we attempt to look beyond objectifying inquiry, we must face two doubts about whether there is a "beyond" at all. First of all, is all true, genuine, cognitively significant inquiry (saving its incidental defects and shortcomings) necessarily of this type? And if not, can we find any genuine examples that instantiate the remaining possibilities? Or is all that just a romantic fancy?

The aspects of objectifying inquiry that I listed above derive in part from the empirical character of science. But they characterize features that science shares with other sorts of academic study, including ones to be found in the humanities.[15] In English, the word "science" has taken on as its central meaning a reference to the natural sciences, with a secondary application to the social sciences, and is not used to refer to the humanities. The German *Wissenschaft* still retains the wider meaning. So we could perhaps list those aspects of objectifying inquiry, with minor amendments, as characterizing Wissenschaft in general.

Words and meanings aside, the demand for a scientific approach is not simply or even at all a request for sophisticated instrumentation or even experimental procedures. When the demand is made for a scientific study of history, Scripture, literature, or the realm of aesthetic or religious experience, by far the largest part of the demand is the call for the process to be objectifying in the above three senses. Or so I submit.

In view of this generality, we may wonder whether the demands to conform to this pattern of objectifying inquiry are at all substantive. Won't any systematic, conscientiously conducted inquiry be like that? The answer is no. When it seems otherwise, that is because this question is easily confused with other questions in the neighborhood. These neighboring questions include the following:

a. Can the results be lasting, communicable, or valuable at all unless the inquiry was objectifying?
b. Can't the same topics of concern also be investigated scientifically?

I will leave the first aside for now. The second, I think, hinges on ambiguity. Describe or point out any subject, and you have a candidate target for objectifying inquiry. In that sense literally everything falls within the domain of science, in principle. It does not follow that what one gets to study in that way is precisely what one knew initially. The product of science is a model that fits the target within the specified relevant parameters, that is, a theoretical model that fits the data model derived from observation within those parameters. These models, which "reason . . . produces after a plan of its own," are what one gets to understand so well. To paraphrase our earlier citation from Kant: we get to understand nature precisely to the extent of seeing how those well-understood models selectively and approximately represent nature.

ARE THERE NONOBJECTIFYING FORMS OF INQUIRY?

Nevertheless, we do have concrete, recognizable instances of other cognitively significant approaches. The first example I would mention of a sustained argument to this effect is Aristotle's *Poetics*. To answer Plato's charge that poetry is all lies, Aristotle develops the view that on the contrary the fictions depicted in tragedy are more revealing of deeper truths than is history and that proper viewing of tragedy is a learning experience. The action on the stage is described in cognitive terms, and so is, in a parallel fashion, the experience of the viewing public. The characters viewed and the audience equally move through suffering and reversal to recognition. To be a viewer is in part to open yourself to be led by the hand through an inquiry into a side of human nature that will be newly revealed to you. And we can add to this that the poet, in the writing, was also involved in such an inquiry of which we here see the fruits.

As the second example I still want to point to art, but in a more general way. The first reaction to radically new art is typically: "This is not art!" The public or the critics are scathing in their denunciation of the realistic novel, impressionist painting, Queneau and Warhol, . . . you may provide your own examples. The sustained contemplation of the new art is a learning experience. In retrospect we see the artist too as having explored the art in such a way that afterward we say: he or she did something no one had ever been able to do before and achieved an insight no one had achieved before. As the third example we have the many religious texts that either depict or give instructions for a spiritual journey of discovery. These range from Bunyan's *Pilgrim's Progress* and Lewis's *Pilgrim's Regress* to Augustine's *Confessions* and Loyola's *Spiritual Exercises.*

We need not stop with these paradigm examples. Not only in meditation and aesthetic experience but also in empathetic exploration of someone else's feelings or predicaments there is indeed systematic, conscientiously conducted inquiry.[16] This process is cognitive and can be sustained and systematic, and yet is not objectifying in our sense.

Although we can see some of the features of objectifying inquiry in each, we also see a lack of such features that we cannot classify as defects. Generally the domain is not pre-defined, the parameters within which one is to respond are not pre-set, there is no demand for new postulated factors to fill the gaps in explanation. But moreover, the developments that throw normal objectifying inquiry into crisis ("something appears that cannot be made understandable on the basis of the possibilities previously known . . . or assumed") are precisely the best outcome such inquiry can have. When the other person appears as a mystery, when the encounter is apprehended as contact with another world only overlapping one's own, when experience no longer fits the everyday pigeonholes, that is the dawn of true understanding. When the artwork that at first appears dismissable and "simply not art" reveals its own inner necessity, and one sees how it goes beyond past art by breaking yet fulfilling past demands, we break through to aesthetic cognition.

THE RECURRING REALIST-ANTIREALIST BREAK

I can easily imagine dissatisfaction with what I have just asserted. On one hand it may seem like sheer romanticism and an invitation to *Schwaermerei*. Am I suggesting that we set out on just any kind of inquiry with merely a receptive attitude, with no blueprint of any kind? Of course not. Admittedly, the above negative description ("the domain is not pre-defined") cannot indicate sufficient conditions for anything of significance. It will undoubtedly apply as well to aimless self-indulgent daydreaming and to much else that also is not objective inquiry. Obviously.

On the other hand, you may complain that to situate the form of creative inquiry pointed out above in the realms of feeling and to deny it to science overlooks forms of creativity in science. Well, let's simply not locate nonobjectifying ways of approaching ourselves and our world in realms of feeling. In fact, I did not mean to do so at all. To understand the examples above as pertaining simply to feelings ("mere feelings," "inner" occurrences) would already be dismissive and deny their significance.

Let us agree that certain creative moments of discovery in science appear precisely where objectifying inquiry, its normal everyday business, ends or falls into crisis. To follow the strict blueprint of objectifying inquiry in science (or in the humanities or anywhere else) is a tactic for success precisely until we encounter phenomena that break the bounds of our given concepts. Those moments are the occasion, the condition of possibility, for high moments of creation in science as well. But there is still a difference between this and the cognitive activity we see in art, religion, and empathy. In science, the good outcome then largely consists in the possible definition of new designs for objectifying inquiry (even if less limited than or even radically different from the preceding ones that fell into crisis) to again enjoy "normal" success for a while.

The concept of objectifying inquiry neither includes the whole of empirical science nor is peculiar to it. And yet it is both typical of the empirical sciences in their normal stage and constitutes the content of familiar demands for objective, scientific inquiry. The empiricist sees it as a paradigm of rational inquiry. But now it should be abundantly clear that I wish to emphasize the indefinite article: a paradigm of inquiry. And here we may feel the pressures of the secular orientation toward disagreement with this emphasis. All the examples I gave above of nonobjectifying inquiry could by that very feature be classified as defective. The secular may insist that in such cases we gain understanding in spite of the very different nonscientific way of approaching the subject. Are not also art, moral insight, and human understanding—even religion—found within the limits of reason alone? Did we not learn in the Enlightenment and its nineteenth-century aftermath to at least demarcate the bounds of sense, to delimit what can be expected beyond objectifying inquiry, to resist any claims of art, religion, and emotion to be revealing something that such inquiry cannot bring to light?

I wanted to give voice here to all these demurrals, queries, and misgivings precisely in order to carry us through to our second major question. Having reflected to this extent on what science is, do we now have a clue to what it is to be secular?

Two. So What Is It to Be Secular?

Science is strongly associated with secularism. On some understandings of science, science itself is betrayed by any departure from the secular. On some understandings of religion, we can even identify the secular through a certain satisfaction with science all by itself alone.

These two rather different views have something in common, something we may be delighted to see: they approach the relation between science and the secular-religious divide on the level of attitude, orientation, and stance. But they are both too simplistic; neither of these views can be quite right. The first I reject outright, at least as thus baldly stated. If science is an enterprise with clearly discernible criteria of success, it has no need of a secular or any other loyalty oath. The value of any individual's contribution to science will be appropriately gauged by those criteria alone, not by the place given to science in his or her own life. The second fails to do justice to the varieties of human understanding and experience. The line between the religious and the secular is blurred in aesthetic and moral thinking, in philosophies of life, and in nontheistic religions. The idea that the objectifying study proper to scientific inquiry may by no means suffice as total guide to life is not exclusively religious.

So we have still no answer to the question of what it is to be secular. Yet I hope to illuminate this to some extent by focusing on those two, in themselves unsatisfactory, views. Remember, from the outset we have to face our ultimate failure: to speak at once to the religious and the secular; we must content ourselves with aiming for an imperfect approximation.

5. THE OBJECTIFYING ATTITUDE

Just as objectifying inquiry is centrally important to the characterization of science but not definitive of it, so, I submit, is a certain attitude, the objectifying attitude, central and crucial to, while not definitive of, the secular. It will take some doing to make this plausible, I realize. But I'm sure we all had intimations of what that attitude involves as I was trying to demarcate objectifying inquiry above.

When I suggested that it is in departures from objectifying inquiry or in its failures that true understanding dawns of another person, what did you think? Did you not imagine someone in the audience laughing or grimacing, ruefully, cynically, scornfully, or just sadly, to witness such a wildly, unrealistically romantic notion? Wouldn't many retort that there is only one real kind of understanding, and that it consists precisely in finding the right pigeonhole, the proper classification? And that this applies equally to understanding a natural process, a novel, a performance, a person, a tragedy? And furthermore that there is only one secure way to achieve such understanding, namely, through what I have detailed as objectifying inquiry—and that there is nothing more to be understood? That reaction is precisely what I mean to refer to as the objectifying attitude. Below I will introduce other terms in which religious thinkers have pointed this out, rather better and more illuminatingly than in any words I can supply.

As I said, this attitude is not definitive of the secular. It is possible to be secular and not have that attitude. The many who achieve an empathetic understanding of each other as well as the few who show us ourselves in art and literature exemplify contrary attitudes no less than do the saints. Equally, the many religious who don't escape the grip of an objectifying attitude on our—so deeply culturally conditioned—thought patterns are not thereby to be reckoned among the secular. For the objectifying attitude manifests itself in responses to experience, to what happens to us. Grace may be real and tangible even if followed by an essentially theoretical or even debunking response when recollected in tranquillity. So, as I must again repeat,

I can offer no more than an imperfect approximation, but one that I still hope will throw some light on the difference. For I do see this attitude as a central feature of the secularization of our culture throughout its history.

6. SECULARIZATION OF THE WORLD PICTURE

We should be skeptical of any history of ideas or of the Zeitgeist that purports to show profound differences between ourselves and our ancestors. Whether seeing us as dwarfs standing on the shoulders of giants or as newly born into an Age of Aquarius and free from history's oppression, such visions tend to dissolve upon scrutiny. Yet those ideas seem often to become part of the common wisdom; then they gain some importance, namely, as themselves symptoms of the times. So it is, I think, with the general conviction that Western society has been increasingly secularized during the modern era.

The tension between the secular and the religious orientations is perennial. We can see the same tension already in ancient Greece, and undoubtedly we can trace similar tensions elsewhere. To see just how secular officially pious Romans were, a few brief looks at Cicero's *On the Gods,* Ovid's irony, or Lucilius' or Horace's satire will suffice. In fact it is hard for me to imagine anyone more secular than the officially pious Roman gentleman. One period of transition, just before our modern era, is perhaps especially important for us. In the early Renaissance, when ancient learning was both newly appreciated and explored in unforeseen ways, artistic representation was revolutionized by the techniques of perspective and chiaroscuro. The result was an art that—whether as symptom or as contributing cause or both—reflected a sort of secularization of the spiritual. Even while the cosmology depicted was still Aristotelian-Ptolemaic, the personages divine and earthly were now all set in the same space and interacting in essentially earthly ways, however miraculous. (In

Raphael's *Disputa,* "saintly feet in paradise cast earthly shadows on heavenly clouds.")[17] When the finite, spherical cosmos was replaced in Galileo's time by a translation-invariant infinite space, the more symbolic medieval rendering did not come back, as perhaps it should and could have done. Instead the divine was thereafter depicted simply through scrupulously observed and intricately rendered earthly effects. The sense of the wholly Other, the felt but uncomprehended mystic presences pointing beyond themselves to a world not of this world, and not located with respect to our world, was lacking in such mundane perspective.

The word "secular," meaning "worldly" and used in contrast with "spiritual" or "religious," is old, but "secularism" at least is a new word dating from the mid-nineteenth century.[18] For some, this word connotes a melancholy or painful sense of loss and for some a feeling of genuine liberation.

We begin with this sense of loss, and its absence. At the roots of philosophy, of religion, and of poetry and art, this sense of loss is not ignored. Philosophy is in some ways similar to the scientific enterprise. Its telos is not the same, but it is for the most part an academic enterprise, that is, also objectifying. Yet it can clarify and bring to light the sense of loss that comes with objectification, including its own. For philosophy is not only the owl who flies at dusk but also the snake always attempting to bite its own tail. So there that sense of loss is also taken seriously but in a specific way that produces a constant tension in philosophy—inevitably as it constantly or at least recurrently comes face to face with the limitations that it itself uncovers and then recognizes as being its own as well.

What about ways of taking this sense of loss seriously? Is there a loss to be taken seriously at all? Or is it possible to be content with objectification and its fruits?

I am inclined to see here in philosophy that temperamental divide that gives rise as well to the realist-antirealist debates. For the antirealist, a theory can at best replace real life by a phantasm, even if it is of a particularly useful and survival-adaptive sort. For the realist quite the opposite is the case! The newly accepted scientific theory replaces a previously fictionalized life with a more realistic one. So we see here a sense of satisfaction with the objectification: that objectifying inquiry was the microscope that revealed the real things we live among. Ranged against this realism we see a contrary attitude: dissatisfaction with the objectification, in a general way, a continuing sense of wonder not alleviated by the successes of that putative replacement.

If we give weight to this discontent, what follows? What should we do? Quite clearly the answer is not to insistently save the older conceptions in the face of their difficulties and anomalies, against the empirically and practically victorious new theories. Authentic response to our discontent means struggling with a simultaneous sense of loss and sense of liberating gain in the new world we are entering. The romantic movement in the nineteenth century appeared as a reaction against Enlightenment materialism on one hand (exemplified in Goethe's reaction to d'Holbach)[19] and against the industrialization and compartmentalization of society on the other. As this movement saw it, industrialization and secularization have a common intellectual component. Industrialization won't work unless the population, from worker to head of state, is by and large content with a predominantly materialistic orientation, in both senses of "materialistic." At least to the romantic mind—as again in the 1960s reaction in Western countries—the two materialisms are intimately connected.

Such reactions are of course followed by counterreactions, classifying romanticism as reactionary in a pejorative sense and saying "Enough; no more fictionalizing!" For it seems that reactions against what is seen as destructive objectification, the replacement of real life by an impoverished fiction, tend to lead to new fictions, deficient or distorting in other ways, which then need a new remedy of their own. And each reaction in turn comes with the rhetoric of bringing us out of fiction into reality.

So perhaps the one moment of truth is the insight into how some accepted or proposed representation fails, how it is defective, deficient, flawed, imperfect; and that moment is not a moment of propositional formulation but of startled awareness. Can we find some way to progress prior to the sudden, startled insight? Perhaps we can, if we pay attention to the ways in which the new diagnosis is not being evaluated in its own context. But perhaps I'm overreaching: this may be counsel to transcend our own historical situation, something that can *ex hypothesi* not be part of our craft or sullen art but can only come through chance or grace.

7. EXISTENTIAL RESPONSE

I have gone as far as I can now with purely abstract, general reflections. It is time to listen to some other thinkers in the twentieth century who struggled with the confrontation between our religions and the modern secular spirit. As briefly as I can I will introduce three: Emil Fackenheim, Martin Buber, and Rudolf Bultmann. The first two are Jewish philosophers; the third, whom I mentioned before, a Christian theologian. All three have been, with some justice, classified as existentialists. Their approach to the very idea of science and how we should relate to science certainly draws on the existentialist tradition from Pascal through Kierkegaard to Sartre. These thinkers took a position radically different from the so-called neo-orthodox view of Karl Barth, who refused a dialogue with scientists, because theologians' and scientists' topics of concern are disjoint and unrelated to each other. For the existentialists, dialogue between the religious and the secular is, on the contrary, inescapable as well as imperative. On the other hand, none of the three makes the opposite mistake, so well exemplified in our days, of thinking that such a dialogue just has to be endless variations on Genesis and the Big Bang.

EMIL FACKENHEIM, *GOD'S PRESENCE IN HISTORY*

Fackenheim's second Deems lecture addressed the challenge of modern secularism.[20] I'll begin with his conclusion and work backward from there. Faith and secularism cannot refute one another; in dispute they can only beg the question. Yet they do not confront each other on even terms: "By the terms of its own self-understanding, modern secularism can afford to ignore faith. . . . By the terms of its own self-understanding, however, modern faith (Jewish or Christian) cannot afford to ignore secularism. Religious immediacy must expose itself to the threat of subjectivist-reductionist reflection."[21] He continues:

> What inspires this necessity? *The fact is that, in modern times, the secular world is "where the action is," and that a God of history must be where the action is.* Yet self-exposure to secularity involves self-exposure to secularism—the critical dissipation of the very possibility of the presence of God.
>
> Jewish no more than Christian faith can avoid this self-exposure. For a Christian to do so would be to seek flight into a worldless church. For a Jew it would mean flight into the premodern Ghetto. But if God is a God of history He must be a God of contemporary secular history also. Either flight is impossible. (p. 46, emphasis in original)

This is relevant to our discussion only if there is some significant relationship with secularism as here understood and with the perception of an essentially secular methodological naturalism in science. But that appears to be exactly how Fackenheim understands it.

As illustration he asks us to imagine a modern secular person present at some of the great shaping events of the Jewish religion. At the Red Sea crossing even the maidservants saw what no scholar or even prophet of later times has seen. At Mount Sinai the Israelites heard with their own ears and saw with their eyes; these were historic moments of immediacy, of divine presence in the world. But what are these moments to the secular critic? To the secular mind, what is alone immediate is that the maidservants thought they saw, that the Israelites thought they heard, that it seemed to them that they perceived, and that they had the feeling of immediacy and presence, that they had the experiences described: "And while those gripped by this feeling may have been overwhelmed by 'abiding astonishment'—by a wonder only 'deepened' by causal explanations—these conditions do not hold true of the modern critic when he reflects on these facts. For that critic is filled not with abiding astonishment but only with scientific or historical curiosity; and the curiosity ceases to abide when the facts are explained" (pp. 41–42). So, whatever the protestations of the religious, the secular critic continues to see God solely as a hypothesis. The secular inquirer has preset the parameters, the terms of description for the phenomena that are (or can be) there to be investigated. It is already presupposed in the inquiry that the data to be had are characteristics of subjective experience. Thus, for the secular inquirer, the idea of God can only come in as a hypothesis (as part of a theoretical model), originally perhaps introduced to explain mysterious natural events, now unconsciously inferred or posited to account for those mysterious subjective experiences. As explanatory hypothesis, of course, it is a rival to the causal explanation, and the more satisfactory the latter, the less needed is the former. So, very soon and inevitably one must reach the conclusion of Laplace's quip to Napoleon: Je n'ai aucun besoin de cette hypothèse.[22]

The secular critic so depicted is not the scientist, although he or she may be a scientist, incidentally. To classify the idea of God as a hypothesis is to interpret history. To speak seriously of unconsciously inferred hypotheses, postulating a subconscious addicted to inference to the best explanation, is to engage in pseudo science, unscientific armchair psychology. None of that is to the main point. The main point is prior to any issues about how an inquiry into the religious phenomena can be followed by such diagnoses. This critic is satisfied with the scientific inquiry and its products, that is the end of the matter, there are no other questions that need be asked. As Fackenheim said, such a critic's "curiosity ceases to abide when the facts are explained." Imagining the critic present at the Red Sea, Fackenheim writes, "He would see what the maidservants saw— nothing less than the presence of God. Indeed, while the experience lasted, he would partake, like the maidservants, of an abiding as- tonishment. Unlike the maidservants, however, he would cease to abide in this state of astonishment once immediacy had yielded to critical, scientifically inspired reflection" (p. 43). This satisfaction is not part of science as science. Neither is the attitude that the experi- ence does not have the meaning it purports to have, nor any signifi- cance other than that attaching to unusual subjective experiences in general. That is not science; it is the secular standpoint, which is merely one possible orientation for the participants in science.

One analogy that comes to mind here is a certain philosophical stance with respect to values. Wilfrid Sellars argued that we will not even feel a temptation in the naturalistic fallacy but will maintain our naturalism quite comfortably while countenancing the irre- ducibility of value judgment, if we reflect on one simple point. To prediction and explanation of what happens in history, all informa- tion about values is irrelevant, once we are given the fact that the humans involved had certain values and made certain value judg- ments. For then it is clear that not values but only humans' having values is what really matters to the course of history.

Sellars can maintain this point of view only in a question- begging way, by restricting what is to be predicted and explained. He is assuming that we are not to predict whether slavery will be wrong under the economic conditions of the twenty-first century or explain why slavery was wrong in nineteenth-century America, but only whether and why there can be slavery and how it is evaluated by values held, past, present, or to come.

His response to this charge of question-begging in his argument—surely a grave charge in philosophy—would undoubtedly have been: But what else is there to predict or explain? and what could possibly remain as question when those questions have been answered? This is precisely similar to the characteristic form of secular detachment with respect to religious affirmation. It is the objectifying attitude exemplified.

MARTIN BUBER, *THE ECLIPSE OF GOD*

Fackenheim's diagnosis of the confrontation with the secular was, as he explains, deeply indebted to Martin Buber's analysis of the human condition. When he equates secularism with "subjectivist reductionism," he follows Buber's thought in *The Eclipse of God:*

> In some periods, that which men "believe in" as something absolutely independent of themselves is a reality with which they are in a living relation. . . . In other periods, on the contrary, this reality is replaced by a varying representation that men "have" and therefore can handle. . . .
>
> Men who are still "religious" in such times usually fail to realize that the relation conceived of as religious no longer exists between them and a reality independent of them, but has existence only within the mind—a mind which at the same time contains hypostatized images, hypostatized "ideas."
>
> Concomitantly there appears, more or less clearly, a certain type of person, who thinks that this is as it should be: in the opinion of this person, religion has never been anything but an intra-psychic process whose products are "projected" on a place in itself fictitious but vested with reality by the soul. (p. 13)

It is not clear to what extent Buber's picture of history is meant to be an illuminating myth and to what extent a literal division of historical epochs. The point that remains is that significance is already lost if we think of the *experience* of God's presence as what is immediate to us, rather than God.

Let me try to make this clear in several ways. Buber speaks of the eclipse of God to point to a change that may take place at the very heart of a religion. That would happen precisely if faith comes to appear even to its adherents solely in terms of public representations and private, subjective experience. This is a phenomenon we can identify in other areas of life, for example if love comes to be understood solely in terms of the public and private theater of love supplemented by the feelings, pangs, and rushes that we read about in Harlequin novels. Within the public arena there may indeed be no difference between hypocrisy and sincerity beyond bad acting. In that case the feelings, pangs, and rushes come to bear the burden of private verification of sincerity. But if really nothing more is left of the concept, then kitsch, the penny dreadful, and bad art have indeed succeeded in taking their toll, and love does not exist anymore. So it could go with a religion, most especially with an established, institutionalized religion, which has accrued all the necessary preconditions for alienation. And quite possibly, in both cases, it's not only kitsch and bad art that is to blame: the *soi-disant* "scientific attitude"—that is, the objectifying attitude—plays a central part in this degeneracy.

Let's not for one moment ignore the rightful place of objectifying inquiry in our intellectual life. It is a poor love, and a poor sense of the sacred, that cannot live in a world infused by science. Certainly there is a subjective aspect to both love and religious experience, to be uncovered and studied by those who wish to focus on that aspect. So there is to perception, to walking and climbing mountains, to swimming the Channel or crossing the Sahara. There is a subjective aspect to art, and we can assent to Plato's "dreams for the waking" and even, I suppose, to the Freudian "dreams that money can buy." But there is a fallacy lurking in them thar bushes for philosophy to fall into.

Consider an analogy. When I drive a car, I am in touch with the road through my feet, without any consciousness of my feet. As soon as I start to skid on an icy patch, however, this experience changes; now I am no longer in touch with the road but only with my feet or at best with the accelerator and the brake. If we try to analyze the normal experience of driving a car, we must take into account the phenomenology of skidding but not let it overwhelm the account of driving itself.

The idea that "really" my sensation is all along of my feet, where the nerve endings are (or that what I see is the image on my retina, or worse yet, a sense datum floating in ghostly grimace between me and what is out there) is of course a philosophical mistake we are not likely to make again. We can now appreciate the confusion in which it is engendered. But that confusion is a natural concomitant of objectifying study, if engaged in unself-critically. In such study we analyze the total phenomenon by "slicing" it into parts each of which could have occurred, in some way or other, in the absence of other parts. Within that analysis, the distinction I drew here becomes, rather, a distinction entirely on the subjective side: there is only a residue of subjective qualities. This may in fact be a good way to learn something about the phenomenon; what is peculiar to the objectifying attitude is the total satisfaction with simply learning that.

RUDOLF BULTMANN, *NEW TESTAMENT AND MYTHOLOGY*

The understanding of secularism that Buber and Fackenheim give us is, to my mind, the best context in which to read Rudolf Bultmann. It is Bultmann who asks us to confront the inroads of science on religion in the most graphic and uncompromising terms. But when he turns from problem to solution, he proposes an understanding of science that makes it independent of secularism. That is the crucial step, and it allows an understanding of the Gospel compatible with science as thus understood.

Bultmann is a quite unfashionable theologian and appears not to be in fashion today even as a topic of study. Specifically, his proffered solution is apparently not of much interest. I do not see how anyone can deny the problem he poses:

> The world picture of the New Testament is a mythical world picture. The world is a three-story structure, with earth in the middle, heaven above it, and hell below. Heaven is the dwelling place of God and of heavenly figures, the angels; the world below is hell, the place of torment. But even the earth is not simply the scene of natural day-to- day occurrences, of foresight and work that reckon with order and regularity; rather, it, too, is a theater for the working of supernatural powers, God and his angels, Satan and his demons. These supernatural powers intervene in natural occurrences and in the thinking, willing, and acting of human beings; wonders are nothing unusual. (p. 1)

To this extent the Gospel is unbelievable today. (Indeed, to this extent the Gospel would have been unbelievable to most of the educated in most intervening centuries, including the Middle Ages. The same goes, of course, for other ancient sacred scriptures.) If we think of this mythology, current in the first century A.D., as an inextricable part of the Gospel, then the Gospel cannot speak to those educated in the twentieth century. So here are our choices: reject the Gospel, reject our contemporary scientific world picture, or find some way to modify our understanding of our past.

Bultmann was presumably addressing the European intellectuals of his acquaintance, as one of them. The Enlightenment has not in fact taken such hold everywhere. Yet the problem he raises arises for everyone, mutatis mutandis. Details aside, every one of us stares at the first century across a vast cultural and historical chasm. Mostly we ignore that, because we have made our peace with so much that it is easy to forget our teething pains. When Aristotelianism first

reached the Latin West, it was seen as a vanguard of resurgent pagan-
ism attempting to seduce the church; a few centuries later it was the
starting point for Aquinas's *Summa Theologiae*.[23] When Copernicus's theory became viable it was by no means the Roman Catholic
Church alone that condemned it as contrary to Scripture; Luther,
Melanchton, and Calvin were in vehement agreement.[24] But of
course the educated Christian knew how to adjust, and rightly so.
Within a century of the painstaking chronology dating Creation to
4004 B.C., scientific geology was replacing scriptural studies of the
age of the earth. During the past hundred years most Christians have
assimilated Darwinian evolutionary theory, somewhat more quickly
though not with less difficulty than their ancestors adapted to Copernican cosmology.

We do not need to apologize for these *crises de conscience*. But if
we are at all inclined to think that Bultmann's problem is spurious or
artificially concocted, it must be because we ignore all that we have
long since discarded or discounted in scriptural descriptions of the
natural and organic world, concentrating on what we can retain.

There are two simplistic solutions. To Bultmann's great credit, he
did not allow us either of them. The simplistic solutions are either to
maintain the mythological picture yoked to instrumentalism about
science or to render the Gospel hygienic by simply filtering out the
unscientific factual claims. To suggest the former would be both
pointless and impossible. Pointless because there is nothing specifically Christian about that mythical world picture dominant in first-
century Palestine. Impossible because no one can appropriate a
world picture by sheer resolve.[25]

But to suggest the latter, to continue the nineteenth-century hu-
manistic evisceration of the Gospel, is also a mistake, according to
Bultmann. It may not look like a mistake to the secular, sympathet-
ically watching as the religious struggle with continual loss of mythic
elements, but it is a mistake to the Christian: "The question, then, is

how demythologizing is to be carried out. . . . [T]he demythologizing undertaken by the critical theology of the nineteenth century
was carried out in an inappropriate way—namely, in such a way that
with the elimination of the mythology the kerygma itself was also
eliminated" (p. 11). That is, the Gospel was not so much interpreted
as replaced by certain basic religious and moral ideas, an idealistic
ethic that is religiously motivated. Can there be an interpretation
that demythologizes in the sense of disclosing "the truth of the
kerygma as kerygma" for those who do not think mythologically?

Bultmann's own answer was to take on the task of interpreting
the mythology of the New Testament in existentialist terms.[26] This
will strike as insightful only those already educated in, or to some
extent convinced of, the existentialist understanding of our condition in general. But there is an element of his project that we
can examine independently thereof, for his demythologizing project relates, in this respect, directly to the objectifying character
of science.

The possibility of understanding ourselves through the New
Testament cannot very well be—so Bultmann argues—that of finding there a new scientific anthropology, rival to secular anthropologies, "whose correctness could be disputed and whose general
validity could be demonstrated by certain facts" (p. 15). Is there an
alternative to the sort of understanding that science can provide?
"Science" is to be taken here in its broadest (but still academic)
sense. Hence the question concerns objectifying inquiry in general
and is linked to his characterization of scientific inquiry in those
terms. Like Buber and Fackenheim, he points to an abiding wonder
that does not cease with the conclusion of such inquiry. But in
addition Bultmann points to another sphere of life, other aspects of
existence, in the way that existentialism has typically continued voluntarist traditions in epistemology.[27] "[T]he issue is whether the
New Testament offers us an understanding of ourselves that con-

stitutes for us a genuine question of decision" (p. 15). First John the Baptist and then Jesus issued a call to decision to their contemporaries: can this be understood in our century and our society as a call to decision, mutatis mutandis? The very same question may be raised about the call of the Jewish prophets or the call of the Buddha. In the end it is the question whether there is a possibility, not of leaving the world behind, but of living differently within the world, of being within the divine presence in the world, of hearing and understanding from within the world, across every and any cultural context, within human existence.

8. PERSONS; ENCOUNTER WITH THE DIVINE

dust thou art, and unto dust shalt thou return.

—GENESIS 3:19

Science, whether understood with the scientific realist or with the empiricist, provides us with a world picture, the world picture Fackenheim and Bultmann point to as sufficing for the secular. Accepted in either sense, it can be our entire world picture. But if it is, we ourselves don't seem to fit into our own world picture. This was an acute problem from the very beginning of modern science. It was the problem that engendered Descartes's dualism, Malebranche's mind-body occasionalism, and Leibniz's monads reconciled by preestablished harmony, as well as a panoply of contemporary metaphysical positions on the mind-body problem. If Bultmann or any of the others is to complete the religious response to secularism, this problem must not remain a problem. For if it does, then their response will always be written off as mere capitulation to materialism by one side and as a mixture of mutually incoherent parts by the other.

   As I argued in the second lecture, this is a problem area beset by illusions and false philosophical consciousness. There is no factual thesis of materialism to confront. Materialism and naturalism as embraced in contemporary analytic philosophy have nothing to them but a certain attitude, a spirit of deference to the content of physics. That is a sort of deference to science not shared by empiricism in general. (As far as I can see it is also quite foreign to the physicists themselves, who playfully and adventurously alter that content in their explorations of theory and nature.) Nevertheless, we still face the question of how to think about persons, especially because that topic covers the, for religion, all-important subject of personal encounter with the divine, of the presence of God in human history.

We can dispense with mind-body dualism at once, or so it seems to me. There is a mystery about consciousness, a mystery about how it is possible for flesh and bones to think, feel, and communicate. But how could that mystery be dispelled by postulating a special mental substance as bearer of consciousness? Drop the rhetorically chosen persuasive name of "mental substance," call it "ectoplasm," say, and you see at once that the mystery remains unchanged. It is just as difficult to understand how ectoplasm can think as how flesh and blood can think.

But neither does it help to postulate that there are special parameters, so far unknown or at least left outside the scope of science until now, that characterize persons among things in the world. That philosophical move may have initially represented a tactical advance; for as we saw, identifying a domain of inquiry takes in general the form of specifying a set of "relevant" parameters instead of things. David Chalmers brought this move into special salience, and as he clearly recognizes, any such newly postulated parameters can then appear in the domain of future science.[28] Despite their present near-total obscurity, such putative parameters already have names such as "qualia."

But no objectifying inquiry can reveal what persons are or who the persons are among things in the world.[29] Consider how that question arises in a concrete setting: the question whether black slaves, descendants of blacks sold on the open market, belong to the domain of discourse of the Constitution of the United States of America. This question arose in the middle of the nineteenth century, when some blacks sued for that status, and was settled in the negative by the Supreme Court of that day. Was this a factual question concerning the parameters pertaining to these organisms? I imagine that essentially the same question arose in history for other races and ethnic groups. Perversely enough, it arose all over again in recent history for Slavs, Jews, Gypsies, but perhaps the question first arose between Neanderthal and Cro-Magnon, long before Greek and barbarian. We must entertain the possibility that in the future it will arise for other species, whether some already known, such as dolphins, or presently unknown. The question is not a theoretical but a moral and existential question, and it is not settled, unless relative to a prior moral decision, by factual inquiry. What counts as thinking counts as consciousness, and what counts as conscious counts as a person, with the rights of a person—that is the crucial point. In an encounter with a different being, group, or species in which this question arises we are called to decision, called to take a stand. That is also, of course, why the traditional philosophical "problem of other minds" is a pseudo problem.

Were these beings already persons before we accepted them as such? Yes, of course; our opinion that they are persons implies that they were persons all along. Equally, we would have faced the same tribunal before them; we can only hope that we were recognized as persons there. Could we make a mistake in reaching such a judgment? Of course; there are conditions under which we will revise a judgment. That revision would then imply the belief that they were never persons at all. I am not oblivious to the problems in philosophy of language in this neighborhood; for now I merely want to focus on what I see as more important problems.[30] The point here is only that acceptance of something as a person, although it involves an element of decision, does not make that being a person. Nor was it required for that being to be a person; to say so would also involve a conceptual mistake. Nor does our finding about the limits of objectifying inquiry here entail that it is all "just subjective," and least of all that it is "objectively unimportant."

The question of personhood and the decision it calls for are significant. When I come face to face with you, it is of crucial importance to me whether you are a person. The question whether you are a "you" coincides with the demand that I take a certain attitude toward you. Hegel, Marx, and Sartre speak perhaps all too simplistically of lordship and bondage, Heidegger of more nuanced forms of care. For much contemporary philosophy this domain of interpersonal knowledge and interaction is simply terra incognita.[31] It is easier to escape into theoretical-sounding, quasi- (if not blatantly pseudo-) scientific questions of fact about "mental states" and evade the element of choice.

We are indeed beings of flesh and blood. This is a simple truism; it is not materialism, and there is no reductionist claim involved (even if any such claim really makes sense at all). It means simply that we persons manifest ourselves in the first instance through our bodies and bodily movements and equally, in a seamlessly woven fabric, by how we choose and arrange our clothes, environments, rooms, houses, the paths we take to work and the work itself, all the incarnate activities and processes into which we enter.

There is one special case of personhood: God. The God of Abraham, Isaac, and Jacob is a person. (If you like, bracket the question whether God exists. What follows will, I hope, be the right thing to say whether or not it has any application in the real world.)[32] I shall not even mention in the same breath such naïve simulacra as Descartes' God, let alone a ruler of the universe located somewhere in space or space outside of space, or some other pseudoscientific miscreant. Encounter with the divine does not mean seeing the ghost in the world machine, nor contemplation of a theoretically postulated hypothesis of which neither science nor we ourselves have any need. The great myth in which we live and breathe and have our being has long since broken our anthropocentric categories.[33]

But an encounter with the divine is a personal encounter. As we human persons do, so God too manifests himself to us only through the familiar materials among which we live; how else? There is no similar localizing constraint; God's work goes on everywhere and every-when, throughout history. Sacred places are where we encounter God, or perhaps a sacred place is precisely a place where God was encountered. The sacraments, as we are taught, are but the outward signs of inward grace. An encounter with God does not involve solving a theoretical equation or answering a factual query; its searing question is an existential demand we face in fear and trembling. As with a human person, the encounter coincides with a call to decision: possible stances toward ourselves and to our world come to the fore and ask for choice. The choice is momentous and sometimes, in some ways, inescapable, for it pertains to our ultimate concerns.

We would indeed land in a but slightly disguised materialism if we added that the objectifying inquiry, brought to perfection in the sciences, suffices to understand all there is to understand about persons. If, moreover, we added this about God, the result would be rhetorically embellished pantheism.[34] Then, indeed, persons and God would be best studied as objectified "scientific objects" in the sense we saw displayed by Catherine Wilson in her study of the microscope. Such additions are also, we note, precisely what characterize the typical core of secularism, the salient necessary condition in what it is to be secular. But we make no such addition.

9. STRANGER IN A STRANGE LAND

> . . . one of the things writing does is wipe things out. Replace them.
> —MARGUERITE DURAS, *Emily L.*

There is much to fault the three philosophical theologians I discussed. Fackenheim's contrast between the secular and the religious actually goes no further than the objectifying attitude, which is at best typical but certainly not definitive of the secular. Buber falls into the all-too-easy fiction of golden ages and ages on feet of clay. The fact is that each one of us, and every one of the many centuries we have lived through, is an incoherent superposition of alternate realities. Bultmann wanders somewhat negligently, almost blithely, into the modern myth of the stranger and the call to authenticity of existentialism. Yet each of these weaknesses is but the other side of a genuine coin, the blindness that accompanies true insight.

In this lecture, too, as I did earlier, I placed all the weight of change on stance or attitude rather than on theory. If I am right, then what distinguishes the secular from the religious is not the theories they hold, or beliefs about what the world is like, although those too are often found among the differences. The crucial distinction lies in a certain attitude, in how we approach the world and relate to our own experience. We can theorize about that, of course, but having a theory about a stance is no substitute for having it, and rejecting it won't consist in disbelieving a theory. I have argued this now for empiricism, for materialism and naturalism, and finally for the secularism that relegates all religion to subjectivity and illusion.

Each of the "isms" I mention here has at some time appropriated for itself all the credit for the advances of science, in order to claim its liberating power and moral authority. Each has at some point intimated that it consists in nothing more than full-fledged acceptance of what science tells us about the world. Coupled with this, a little paradoxically, comes the insistence that science would die if it weren't for the scientists' conscious or unconscious adherence to this philosophical position. All of this is false; in fact, it is in philosophy that we see the most glaring examples of false consciousness, and they occur precisely at this point.

I am an empiricist, or at least I try to be, while trying to discern what empiricism can be after all we have learned during the demise of modern philosophy. As an empiricist, I see the empirical sciences as a paradigm of rationality in a largely irrational and often antirational world. I see objectifying inquiry as the sine qua non of the development of modern science and its incredible, breathtaking achievements in our increasing knowledge of nature. At the same time, while this objectifying inquiry has brought us untold riches, what does it profit us to gain the whole world and lose our own soul? Riches come with a temptation, a tempting fallacy, namely, to have us view them as all there is to be had, when they are so much. This is true of all riches, and it is true of the riches of objective knowledge. Poor are the rich who succumb to this fallacy.

So now, how shall we go on? Philosophy may already have suffered too much from its perennial revolutions for us to ask for yet another revolution. And I certainly do not think we need new theories in philosophy. But I do think that we must change, or change back, the way we do philosophy. Technical work is required; there are many problems to be solved, but this work should be in aid of an authentic, engaged project in the world, self-conscious and conscious of what sort of enterprise it is. That means, in the first place, consciousness of its own limits.

Not exactly a new message to bring you—it is precisely what Socrates tries to tell Cratylus at the end of their dialogue. They have been discussing language, words, images, and representations. Socrates says about the different theories:

[B]ut if this is a battle of words, some claiming to be true and others contending that they are, must there not be a criterion by which to judge their truth? And if we can learn about things both from the words about them and from those things themselves, which is likely to be the clearer and nobler way?[35]

Appendix A. Scientific Cosmology

In Lecture 1 I confronted analytic philosophy with the simple question "Does the world exist?" and argued that it fails the confrontation. Certainly, there are metaphysical theories that give apparent sense (or least grammatical respectability) to the question. But metaphysical theory-writing lacks the credentials for what it purports to be, that is, for factual inquiry into what there is. Analytic ontology sports also an apparently more modest program, that of excavating the ontic commitments buried deep inside the empirical sciences. Like the more ambitious program, it rests on a presupposed philosophy of science that is at best controversial and controvertible. To show that, let us stay with the question of whether the world exists and have a look at the relevant part of the physical sciences.

There is indeed and always has been a scientific discipline that deals with the world as a whole: cosmology. Aristotle's *De Caelo* describes the universe; so does Descartes's *The World, or Treatise on Light,* and so does Newton's *System of the World.* But it is only in the past century that we see this discipline blossoming into a lively area of physics research. The crucial step in modeling totalities as opposed to aggregates is precisely the introduction of global attributes not reducible to local properties. That crucial step was taken in general relativity. From that point on the global geometry of space-time is a truly autonomous aspect of the scientific world picture.

So doesn't this part of science, scientific cosmology, imply that the world exists? Here is a sample statement from an early introduction to the subject: "Our direct knowledge of the universe is confined to a limited region of space and time. In order to obtain some idea of the universe as a whole we must extrapolate and construct a world-model which will reproduce satisfactorily the principal features of the observable region."[1] This captures, I think, the common understanding of what cosmology is about. The statement clearly presupposes that there is such a thing as the world or universe as a whole. Indeed, it is a simple truism that scientific cosmology is at first blush simply the theory of what the world is like and more generally a theory of (physically) possible universes (worlds). But is this the only or even the best way to understand the science? Let us take a look at its history, aim, and structure and reflect on how we can relate to this scientific enterprise.

To construct his *System of the World*, Newton added to the three laws of motion of his *Principia* the single law that there is just one force: attractive, between any two bodies, proportional directly to their mass and inversely to the square of the distance between them. This does not govern simply the stars and planets but every part of the material universe no matter how large or how small. We may therefore say, using Whitrow's term, that a Newtonian world-model is any system of entities subject to exactly those four laws.

Is the real world (exactly like) one of these Newtonian world-models, or is it meant to be? Even Newton would not have asserted this without qualification. Although the laws of motion may be correct, there are presumably additional forces connecting the various bodies and their parts. So what are these world-models that are in effect constructed in the writing of the *Principia*? The world-models themselves are mathematical structures. In constructing them Newton was happy enough to work with simplifying assumptions, so as to save the phenomena of planetary motion. In addition, of course, he also points to a richer cosmology in which the world-models contain other forces as well, but all in accord with his dynamics.

Enter here, however, a fundamental divide in philosophy of science. I have, in effect, been taking the liberty of describing Newton's theory in the terms of the so-called semantic approach. According to this approach, we are using only a very shallow concept of science if we think of its theories as consisting of axioms and theorems. Instead, to present a theory is to present a family of models, augmented with hypotheses about the extent to which the real things studied are adequately represented by these models. Philosophers willing to discuss science in these terms today differ nevertheless in what they see as the aim pursued in science and consequently in what they think counts as scientific success. One benefit of the semantic approach is that it allows us to describe these philosophical differences effectively and conveniently. According to constructive empiricism, the aim is only to construct models in which the observable phenomena can be embedded. (Slogan: The aim is empirical adequacy.) Even given perfect success, then, not all elements of the models need have corresponding elements in reality. Rival positions going by the name of scientific realism imply that if the model is to count as entirely successful, then every significant element of the model must correspond to something real. Thus elements purporting to represent unobservable structure must have corresponding elements in reality as well.

The difference between these two philosophical views of science concerns in part how theory-acceptance in science is portrayed. In practice, there is of course qualified acceptance only. But this acceptance-in-practice derives its meaning from what is understood to be included in unqualified acceptance, namely, belief in the empirical adequacy of the theory (constructive empiricism) or belief in its truth (scientific realism).[2]

The different sorts of positions sketched here can be accompanied by varying understanding of physical cosmology. If a world-model need only save the phenomena then it need not as a whole correspond to anything at all. Its success is quite independent of whether all the phenomena are part of one thing, the world. For scientific realism the situation is a little more complex. The first realist suggestion will certainly be that there must be "physical space-time" to correspond to the space-time found in the cosmological models.[3]

Michael Friedman discussed space-time theories and general relativistic cosmology in his *Foundations of Space-Time Theories* with explicit reference to the debate over scientific realism. In relativistic cosmology, a world-model (to continue with Whitrow's terminology) is a space-time, which is a four-dimensional differentiable manifold M with certain geometrical objects defined in terms of M. These geometric objects are designated as absolute or dynamic objects, the latter depending on the distribution of matter-energy and the former independent thereof. They must satisfy the field equations of the theory while certain further equations, the equations of motion, specify the possible trajectories followed by material particles.

In such a cosmological model there is therefore one salient whole: the space-time itself. In Newton's case, the question whether the world exists is the question whether there is one Newtonian system of bodies of which all bodies are part (with major worries attaching only to the case of infinitely many bodies). In relativistic cosmology, mass and energy are quantities defined in terms of space-time, and so the question seems to become whether space-time itself is real, a "substance." At least, that is what the question seems to become in the philosophical literature. More recently John Earman examined various precise purported equivalents of this graphically phrased question in his *World Enough and Space-Time*.[4] In relativistic cosmology there is indeed an obvious candidate for a "totality," namely space-time itself.[5] But does the mathematical space-time correspond to a real entity, real space-time? That it does so is a philosophical position, manifold substantivalism. It is a philosophical position, not a conclusion to be read off the physics. It is an interpretation that may or may not be a tenable addition to the bare theory. Earman's book ends on a distinctly uncomfortable note. Although manifold substantivalism was in a much better position in classical physics than Leibniz or Mach appreciated, and perhaps even in a better position after the advent of general relativity, it has recently been placed on the defensive, and Earman sees not much hope in any of its defenses.

Whereas Earman appears to broach these issues entirely from within a scientific realist perspective, Friedman considered also constructive empiricism while arguing for realism with respect to space-time. His main argument was a version of what Putnam called the conjunction objection: if two theories are both true then so is their conjunction, but if they are both empirically adequate their conjunction may not even be consistent, let alone adequate. The logical point is correct, of course, but its importance depends on how scientists go about combining theories that they accept. A typical pattern to be found in the history of science is that simultaneously accepted theories are used very gingerly in combination. Their successor theory is typically inconsistent with both while accounting for their success, namely, by saving the phenomena that they saved.[6] This is exactly what constructive empiricism would lead one to expect.

There is, as far as I can see, no "indispensability argument" (of the sort that Putnam gave for realism about mathematical entities, for example) for the reality of the world. Such an argument would have to show that the existence of the world as a whole, whether as system of bodies or as space-time, is required for the success of cosmology. It appears that this is at most relative to certain philosophical views about science, to wit, that the embeddability of all actual phenomena in such a model is not sufficient for success.

To conclude, then: whether the world exists is not settled by the success or acceptance of physical cosmology, except relative to certain philosophical points of view. The disturbing corollary for analytic ontology is that it is never a simple bringing to light of existential commitments in our theories. At best it does so relative to some more basic philosophical stance that is taken for granted. Ontic commitments of science are there only in the eye of the philosophical beholder.

Appendix B. A History of the Name "Empiricism"

This appendix elaborates on the brief remarks in the body of the text; there is some overlap, so the reader need not page back and forth between the two.

1. Not a Simple Historical Question

There are two obvious ways to take the question of what empiricism is. First of all we can take it to be a straightforward historical question. That is, we can undertake to inquire into its distinctive characteristics, assuming that we already know which philosophers and philosophies belong to the tradition.[7] But unless we have a general idea about how to identify what belongs to the tradition, we can't be sure that our list is either accurate or complete. Therefore the common characteristics of the members of that list might not at all be what identifies the tradition.

Second, we can ask for the origin of the classification. Was it perhaps introduced by a particular person or group, in a specific historical context? Does our use of the name derive from a traceable act of baptism or dubbing, for example? That has indeed been suggested for our current academic use of the term "empiricism." Roger Woolhouse writes about the textbook classification of the "British empiricists" Locke, Berkeley, and Hume in opposition to the "Continental rationalists":

> Berkeley and Hume were indeed both British, but they would not have seen themselves as falling, along with Locke, into a school diametrically opposed to Descartes and Leibniz on the Continent. . . . Nor would these philosophers have characterized themselves or others primarily by these labels. They would have spoken first of Cartesians, Platonists, or Aristotelians, not of rationalists or empiricists.

The fact is that the systematic use of the labels "empiricist" and "rationalist" is a product of nineteenth-century histories of philosophy, which saw seventeenth- (and eighteenth-) century philosophy in idealized terms, as a conflict between two opposing schools which reached some sort of resolution in the philosophy of Kant.[8]

There are indeed reasons for Woolhouse's diagnosis. (We will note a similar diagnosis by Loeb below.) The British empiricists, now so called, of the seventeenth and eighteenth centuries did not refer to themselves or identify themselves as empiricists.[9] Indeed, as we shall see, in the first half of the nineteenth century it was still terminologically possible to deny of some of the British empiricists that they were empiricists.

Yet Woolhouse's verdict needs to be qualified, it seems to me, for those histories did follow at any rate one way in which Kant himself had identified empiricists (as we shall see below). Moreover, they reflected a view of a major division in philosophy that was also current among those who were not triumphalist admirers of Kant or of the Kantian turn in philosophy. Nevertheless, granting these qualifications, this point about the nineteenth-century historians and their new professionalism helps to explain why the use of "empiricism" became stabilized in the way and to the extent it did.

Even if it were not so, and Woolhouse's remark could stand entirely without qualification, it would be necessary at this point to inquire into precisely what happened. What criteria were in fact established by nineteenth-century historians, explicitly or implicitly, for the systematic use of "empiricist" as a classifier of philosophical positions? What were or could have been their reasons for choosing the particular criteria associated with that particular term? It is (and would be) equally necessary to inquire into the extent to which the philosophers who subsequently officially termed themselves empiricists followed the usage established by the historians.

2. Early Modern Use: Scientific Methodologies

Latin derived its *empiricus* from the Greek: *peira* ("trial, experiment"), *empeiros* ("skilled"), *empeiria* ("experience"). The earliest use appears to refer to a school of physicians: empirici, as opposed to dogmatici or methodoci. The empirici professed to base their practice entirely on experience (that is, on the accumulated experience of the medical profession) and not on theories drawn from more general philosophies or cosmologies. The term "empiric(k)" acquired in English a pejorative use, still easily accessible today in Shakespeare: "We must not corrupt our hope, To prostitute our past-cure malladie To empiricks" (*All's*

Well That Ends Well, II.i). One imagines that this was due to the pre-eminence of physicians who did rely on theory rather than observation.

Historians can cite a clear and early precedent for the use of "empiricist" and "rationalist" as classification by Francis Bacon: "Those who have practised the sciences have been either empiricists or dogmatists. The empiricists, like the ants, merely collect and use: the rationalists, like spiders, spin webs out of themselves. But the way of the bees lies in between: she gathers materials from the flowers of the garden and the field and then by her own powers transforms and digests them; and the real work of philosophy is similar."[10] Bacon's use is surprising to our ears in two ways. First, this discussion predates the separation of philosophy and natural science, and from our current vantage point is more easily interpreted as a remark on scientific method than on philosophy. Second, Bacon, whom we now place naturally at the beginning of British empiricism, here classifies himself as neither rationalist nor empiricist (in his sense of these terms).

Leibniz simply followed Bacon's usage, I think, in his *New Essays on Human Understanding*, written as critical response to Locke. Leibniz's use occurs here in a classic debate over a thesis later sometimes taken to identify the empiricist-rationalist opposition.[11]

> [B]easts are sheer empirics and are guided entirely by instances. While men are capable of demonstrative knowledge (science), beasts, so far as one can judge, never manage to form necessary propositions, since the faculty by which they make [inferences] is something lower than the reason which is to be found in men. The [inferences] of beasts are just like those of simple empirics who maintain that what happened once will happen again in a case which is similar in the respects that they are impressed by. . . . That is what makes it so easy for men to ensnare beasts, and so easy for simple empirics to make mistakes.[12]

Although Locke never responded to these essays, there is no reason to think that he would have demurred on this point. The term "empiricism" seems to be solidly associated at this time (and we will see more of this later) with overly simplistic use of inductive procedures in the empirical sciences.

3. Kant: Classifying Philosophical Currents

In Kant we find, to my knowledge, the first indisputable use of "empiricism" as a classification of philosophies as opposed to scientific methodologies.[13] His usage is as usual somewhat idiosyncratic, or perhaps I should say creative. Kant's division into empiricists and dogmatists appears in two places in the

Critique of Pure Reason, in the section on the Antinomies of Pure Reason, and in the last chapter, "The History of Pure Reason." As far as the use in the Antinomies is concerned, the interpretation is somewhat controversial.[14]

Kant introduces the term "empiricist" early on in his discussion of the antinomies of pure reason (A466; B494). I will quickly outline his use in the antinomies (A426–A461; B454–B489) and then the (not obviously the same) use in the later passage on empiricism (A466–A476; B494–B504).

The antinomies are four pairs of contrary assertions, each of which is a "transcendental assertion," in the sense of "lay[ing] claim to insight into what is beyond the field of all possible experiences" (A425; B453). Here we find Kant's most graphic polemics against this sort of metaphysics (a polemics that, ironically, later became the hallmark of what we now call empiricism): "If in employing the principles of understanding we do not merely apply our reason to objects of experience, but venture to extend these principles beyond the limits of experience, there arise pseudo-rational doctrines which can neither hope for confirmation in experience nor fear refutation by it" (A421; B448–9). The four pairs of assertions, labeled "Thesis" and "Antithesis" in each case, are:

> *First Antinomy*
> *Thesis.* The world has a beginning in time, and is also limited as regards space.
> *Antithesis.* The world has no beginning and no limits in space; it is infinite as regards both time and space.
> *Second Antinomy*
> *Thesis.* Every composite substance in the world is made up of simple parts. . . .
> *Antithesis.* No composite thing in the world is made up of simple parts, and there nowhere exists in the world anything simple.
> *Third Antinomy*
> *Thesis.* Causality in accordance with laws of nature is not the only causality . . . there is also another causality, that of freedom.
> *Antithesis.* There is no freedom, everything in the world takes place solely in accordance with laws of nature.
> *Fourth Antinomy*
> *Thesis.* There belongs to the world, either as its part or as its cause, a being that is absolutely necessary.
> *Antithesis.* An absolutely necessary being nowhere exists in the world, nor does it exist outside the world as its cause.

The order in which the pairs are arranged is not arbitrary. According to Kant, the four theses together constitute a perennial, ever-popular philosophy, dogmatism, and the four antitheses make up a perennially recurring academic philosophy, empiricism. The latter, he says, is perhaps surprisingly unpopular (A472; B500), but once we understand the reason for this, we realize that "there is no need to fear that it [empiricism] will ever pass the limits of the Schools, and acquire any considerable influence in the general life or any real favour among the multitude" (A474; B502). His reasons for these sociological reflections may at first sound a little parochial; more likely he is writing with a little touch of irony to irritate his Enlightenment colleagues.

The three advantages of dogmatism he lists are as follows. First of all, there is the practical interest deriving from the facts (according to the theses) "[t]hat the world has a beginning, that my thinking self is of simple and therefore indestructible nature, that it is free in its voluntary actions and raised above the compulsion of nature, and finally that all order in the things constituting the world is due to a primordial being." These putative facts are, he writes, the very "foundation stones of morals and religion" (A466; B494). The second advantage is the satisfaction of reason's speculative interest: the theses imply that the entire cosmic structure can be grasped a priori. The third advantage, for the dogmatic philosopher, is that above-noted perennial popularity, in which the philosophical dogmatist makes common cause with the mass of mankind.

But actually, as Kant sees it, with respect to the speculative interest it is really the empiricist who enjoys a considerable advantage. Empiricism is completely unsatisfactory from a practical point of view, because if the antitheses are accepted, then "moral ideas and principles lose all validity, and share in the fate of the transcendental ideas which served as their theoretical support."[15] But speculatively, "according to empiricism the understanding is always on its own proper ground, namely, the field of genuinely possible experiences, investigating their laws, and by means of these laws affording indefinite expression to the sure and comprehensible knowledge which it supplies" (A468; B496). Empiricism is in other words a manifesto of the autonomy and self-sufficiency of natural reason: "The empiricist will never allow, therefore, that any epoch of nature is to be taken as the absolutely first, or that any limit of his insight into the extent of nature is to be regarded as the widest possible. Nor does he permit any transition from the objects of nature—which he can analyze through observation and mathematics . . .—to those which neither sense nor imagination can ever represent *in concreto*." (A469; B497). This is followed by a surprisingly positive passage, in which the authorial voice momentarily seems to lose this faintly ironic tone. Kant comments that if the empiricist were to restrict himself to this intellectual attitude and to debunking the presumptions of those who pretend a greater reach for the intellect, it would leave us a good deal of leeway for extrascientific intellectual presuppositions and faith. But, he adds, empiricism itself frequently "becomes dogmatic in its attitude towards ideas, and confidently denies whatever lies beyond the sphere of its intuitive knowledge." Such dogmatism offends in exactly the same way as its dogmatist opponents do, by engaging in the very sort of metaphysics that Kant is here destroying.[16]

Kant's own solution to the antinomies begins with the introduction of the notion of presupposition, in the methodological sense in which this concept came to play a crucial role in subsequent philosophical reasoning:

> If our question is directed simply to a yes or a no, we are well advised to leave aside the supposed grounds of the answer, and first consider what we should gain according as the answer is in the affirmative or in the negative. Should we then find that in both cases the outcome is mere nonsense, there will be good reason for instituting a critical examination of our question, to determine whether the question does not itself rest on a groundless presupposition. (A485; B513)

But I do not intend to go further into the Kantian critical philosophy's deconstruction of the concepts of world, space, and time. This much should suffice to explain how he sees the empiricist tradition in philosophy (up to his own time).

Kant's second discussion of empiricism in the first critique, partly but not wholly in line with the above, occurs in a different contrast class. The last chapter, titled "The History of Pure Reason," sketches "three issues in regard to which the most noteworthy changes [in metaphysical theory] in the course of the resulting controversies" have occurred in the history of philosophy. The first concerns the object of our knowledge through reason (the contrast is between sensualists such as Epicurus and intellectualists such as Plato). The third concerns method (the contrast is between the naturalistic, such as Bacon's ants, and the scientific; the latter divides into dogmatic, such as Wolff, and the skeptical, such as Hume). The empiricists are once more encountered in the discussion of the second issue:

> In respect of the origin of the modes of "knowledge through pure reason," the question is as to whether they are derived from experience, or whether in independence of experience they have their origin in reason. Aristotle may be regarded as the chief of the empiricists, and Plato as the chief of the noologists. Locke, who in modern times followed Aristotle, and Leibniz, who followed Plato . . . have not been able to bring this conflict to any definitive conclusion. (A854; B882)

If taking sides on the antinomies in one way (namely, holding to the four antitheses) was meant to define empiricism, this later passage, near the end of the first critique, is very puzzling. Here the division between empiricists and the contrasting school, in terms of an issue in epistemology, is much more like the later "standard" contrast between empiricists and rationalists. So either the two uses of "empiricist" in the first critique are not the same or the true empiricists are only those who satisfy both criteria. We should probably conclude that Kant did not regard either feature as defining the term. We could instead take it that in his usage, empiricism is what we would now call a "cluster concept" with a cluster of associated features rather than a precise definition.

4. Mill: An Alternative Classification of Philosophies

Mill did not like Kant, and it is to be doubted that he read Kant very carefully. But Mill too uses the term "empiricism" to classify philosophies. We can summarize his usage roughly as follows: Mill extends Bacon's use by including among the empiricists philosophers who take it that the ants are right, so to speak, that is, philosophers who endorse the methodology of those whom Bacon called empiricists.

Instructive here is Mill's discussion of the similar division in both politics and philosophy and his insistence that he himself is not an empiricist (in the sense in which he uses the term). In his early essays on Coleridge and Bentham he places them on opposite sides of a great divide, while in many respects sharing a common ground derived from earlier British philosophy.

They agreed, as Mill presents the matter, on the need for a very skeptical, critical inquiry into our presumed knowledge. They agreed also on the need for a basis for this inquiry in psychology, that is, in a theory concerning the sources of human knowledge and the objects accessible to human faculties. But they disagreed on that theory. The great precedent was Locke's view, according to which all knowledge consists of generalizations from experience. This has as a consequence that there is no (nontrivial) knowledge a priori. Bentham does side with Locke; Coleridge takes the opposite view. Aligned with German philosophy after Kant, Coleridge admits that no knowledge is possible without experience but holds that some of this knowledge is nevertheless not derived from experience. Among a priori knowledge, accessible through what he calls intuition rather than the senses, Coleridge lists fundamental principles of religion, morals, mathematics, and physical science. Mill refers to the two schools of thought as the school of experience and the school of intuition.

But Mill does not allow the term "empiricism" to be used for this school of experience, to which he proclaims himself to belong. On the contrary, he reserves that term for a more radical position (occupied, as he sees it, neither by himself nor by Locke) that he attributes to the Whigs Burke, Macintosh, and

Macaulay. Mill's use here is continuous with the use by Bacon, as cited above, and with the common pejorative usage referring to an antitheoretical approach in medicine. Thus he writes in his monumental *A System of Logic Ratiocinative and Inductive* of 1843:

> In these examples we see bad generalization a posteriori, or empiricism properly so called: causation inferred from casual conjunction. [V. v.5; p. 792][17]
>
> [I]f . . . "the proper study of mankind" is not destined to remain the only subject which Philosophy cannot succeed in rescuing from Empiricism; the same process through which the laws of many simpler phenomena have by general acknowledgment been placed beyond dispute, must be consciously and deliberately applied to those more difficult inquiries. [VI.i.12; p. 834]
>
> When this time shall come, no important branch of human affairs will be any longer abandoned to empiricism and unscientific surmise.(VI.x. 8; p. 930)

And in his essay *Auguste Comte and Positivism* we still find "direct induction [is] usually no better than empiricism."[18] But induction took central place in Mill's epistemology, though in a form that he considered vastly more sophisticated than simple, "direct" empiricist induction. In fact, because of the use that term had enjoyed in British intellectual history, from Bacon through Newton to Mill's adversary Whewell, it would have been hard to use "induction" as a pejorative term.

Indeed, Mill placed induction on a pedestal to such an extent that it seemed to some that he was coming dangerously close to the rationalism he decried. Thus John Venn explains in the preface to his *Empirical Logic* that he chose his title explicitly to show his disagreement with Mill:[19] "By the introduction of the term Empirical into the title, I wish to emphasize my belief that no ultimate objective certainty, such as Mill for instance seemed to attribute to the results of Induction, is attainable by any exercise of human reason." Venn clearly accepts Mill's self-classification as a non-empiricist, and Venn sees this non-empiricism instantiated in a certain overblown view of what induction can do for us.

But in Mill's own view, Mill does not come even close to ranging himself against Locke with what he calls the German or a priori thesis (which he attributes as well to Coleridge and Whewell) that there is also knowledge independent of experience. That thesis he rejects vociferously in many places.[20] So what is this distinction between "experientialist" and empiricist, in Mill's usage? The distinction concerns the methods that lead from the deliverances of experience (apart from which we have no other source of information) to knowledge, or views about such methods. In contrast with the so-called empiricists, Mill holds that there is indeed knowledge based on experience that has a much better epistemic status than "mere" generalization on experience.[21]

This is a difficult position to hold, for we (as well as nineteenth-century respondents to Mill) wish immediately to ask: What is the status of the claim that this method leads us to such knowledge? Mill replies to this with his own special solution of Hume's problem: this claim is itself shown by induction properly construed and is therefore knowledge with that privileged status.[22]

However this may be, we see here distinguished two views that may indeed be held separately. The first is that all knowledge and rational opinion derive from experience, the second, that there is no nontrivial absolute certainty to be had. They are both views to be found in the history of epistemology, both associated with empiricism, both held by those whom Mill called empiricists. Mill, along with Aristotle, Saint Thomas, and Kant, holds the first view, too: all knowledge begins with experience. If we now call Mill himself an empiricist, it is presumably because historians of philosophy did not (always) employ adherence to the second view as (partial) criterion for the use of "empiricist." Yet it is equally clear that holding the first view is not a sufficient condition for the name "empiricist" at any stage in this long history.

5. Emergence of the Textbook Classification

The main criterion that has governed the use of "empiricism" since its introduction is the thesis that all knowledge derives from experience. Mill used this as one criterion but added another to distinguish the empiricists among those who hold this thesis. In this he was not followed by later writers. It is possible that the standardizing of the division in the mid- to late nineteenth century drew mainly on the passage I cited above from Kant's chapter "The History of Pure Reason."

There is a short but careful discussion of this standardizing in L. E. Loeb's introduction to early modern philosophy.[23] Loeb describes a "standard theory" of the history of modern philosophy that has a strong hold on philosophers and historians of philosophy. It has three principal components. The first is a division into major and lesser philosophers. The second is a division, among the major figures, between Continental rationalists and British empiricists, identified through supposedly central epistemological theses, notably the rejection of innate ideas as source of knowledge. The third is the claim that there is within each of these two schools a certain dialectical development that follows the chronological order in the major figures. According to Loeb, who is drawing also on a number of other recent historical studies, this "standard" theory can be found very clearly in such important contemporary histories as Copleston's, with Kuno Fisher and the British idealist T. H. Green as possible nineteenth-century major proponents of the theory.[24]

This "official" criterion (experience as foundation for knowledge) did not in fact properly fix the use of the term, even after Mill and even within the remainder of the nineteenth century. It was very well known that in their own way both the Aristotelian Schoolmen, against which the seventeenth century railed, and Kant, who was meant to have superseded both empiricists and rationalists, held to versions of the view that "there is nothing in the mind which is not first in the senses." Mill had correctly noted that this does not help, all by itself, to distinguish among all the philosophies in question.

Two major questions come up at once. What counts as experience, and what is involved in the transition from experience to knowledge? (Unfortunately, these questions were themselves heavily flavored with aspects of modern philosophy, notably its psychologism, that were really on the way out by the end of the nineteenth century but reappeared in later stages of analytic philosophy. We will have to leave discussion of that obstacle for now.) I want to cite three sources here to bring out the difficulties, one from the end of that century and two from the next, to explain how these questions give difficulty.

In 1898 the Stuart Professor of Logic at Princeton University, John Grier Hibben, published an introductory philosophy text.[25] Its sixth chapter is devoted to the "problem of knowledge," which he said was introduced by Locke and comprised two parts: the source of knowledge and its nature. With respect to the former part, he distinguished two schools. The first is rationalism: the source is primarily in the mind itself, which is immediately aware of certain fundamental principles that give form to the material supplied by sensation. The second, which includes preeminently Locke, Condillac, Hume, and Mill, is "the theory which refers all knowledge to experience as its source, namely, empiricism" (p. 97). These two schools were followed by the critical school of Kant, sloganized by Kant's dictum that the understanding makes nature but does not create it, thus giving proper due both to the mind's work and to something foreign for it to work on.

This way of presenting the history of modern philosophy was presumably standard by this date. But when Hibben then introduced August Comte's positivism as a new and modified form of empiricism, the benefit of our hindsight shows a subtle and by him apparently unnoticed difficulty. On the face of it, his classification is correct, given that Comte "insisted on the positive facts of experience, the facts which form the subject matter of science, as the sole basis of our knowledge" (p. 100). But when, on the preceding pages, Hibben enlarged on just what Locke, Condillac, Hume, and Mill had meant by the view that experience is the source of knowledge, he had outlined the sensationalist-associationist psychology by which they described experience. Look at how different this is from even the nutshell presentation of Comte's view:

> Comte regards all knowledge as circumscribed by the general laws of science which have been experimentally determined, and which account for the sequence of phenomena, the measurement of their intensity, and all their quantitative relations, but which, however, are silent concerning the underlying ground of these phenomena, and their significance. . . . The end of knowledge, according to Comte, is the more perfect systematization of the sciences, in which task all metaphysical presuppositions must be strenuously avoided. (p. 101)

This sounds much more like what empiricists say in the twentieth century than anything we have come across yet. It is not psychology, and it does not relate to sensations, associations, and other operations of the mind. It concerns, rather, methodology and the questions of epistemology that can be separated from psychology.[26] The terms "experience" and "source," used in both contexts, confer a mostly verbal unity that may be quite deceptive.

Two views are being conflated here. Empiricism is identified as the view that experience is the sole source of knowledge. Positivism is the view that knowledge can be acquired only through the particular, empirical sciences, not, for example, through philosophy or any of its branches. It is an equivocation to state this by saying that science is the only source of knowledge. Science obtains information in the sense that the process of scientific investigation does. Scientific investigation includes and indeed centers on constrained forms of experience (systematic observation in controlled conditions), reports of that experience that are constrained to take a certain form, and certain kinds of theoretical activity pertaining to those reports. There is, however, a great deal of experience, and of course a great deal of intellectual activity (not to mention human activity not falling under either heading) that does not belong to the process. Positivism, therefore, appears to be an amendment to the empiricist thesis, to the effect that only a certain kind of experience is a source of information, and then only if followed by a certain kind of intellectual activity. One can imagine this accompanied either with a simple qualification (all experience is a source of information, but you get little or nothing of value from it outside the context of scientific inquiry; you can to some extent improve your own life by importing and adapting scientific method into daily life) or else with a wholesale dismissal (a severe skepticism that leaves us knowing little or nothing about ourselves and the world until we reach the end of the scientific rainbow). In either case the classification of positivism as a type or subspecies of empiricism appears to be supportable, but not the conflation of positivism with empiricism.[27]

Around the end of the nineteenth century some philosophers consciously classified themselves as empiricists. William James, for example, called his position "radical empiricism," and various European philosophers associated themselves in one way or another with Comte's positivism or with Mach's phenomenalism. But they lived in a time of rapid philosophical change, and it was not always clear whether they were (a) ignoring the Kantian and post-Kantian critique of the earlier empiricism, (b) answering and overcoming that critique, or (c) developing a significantly different position under the same name. James's position is worth a separate discussion in this context, but I'll add here just a few remarks on two others in America.

There were many revolts against modern philosophy going on in the latter part of the nineteenth century. Most of them included attempts to recast philosophical issues in a quite different idiom. The turn away from "psychologism" in particular was not always equally conscious, explicit, or successful. There are many interesting transitional figures in this period in whom we can trace this change. Thus Charles Sanders Peirce, for example, appears to embrace a basic doctrine of empiricism: "Our perceptual judgments are the first premisses of all our reasonings. . . . All our other judgments are so many theories whose only justification is that they have been and will be bourne out by perceptual judgments" (5.116). Note that although the judgments and theories could be taken to be psychic entities, the terminology is basically that familiar to us from contemporary logic and epistemology. "Premisses," "theories," "justification" need not have a primarily psychological significance. But when Peirce develops this account of judgment (opinion, knowledge) he considers his first task to be to clarify what perceptual judgment is and enters upon introspective psychology.[28]

Peirce, of course, was a bit of a maverick even in American thought, although now he is referred to more than almost any of his contemporaries. More mainstream at that time, as perceived by their contemporaries, were the personalists or personal idealists, among whom Borden Parker Bowne (active roughly 1880 to 1910) described his own position as transcendental empiricism.[29] It is quite interesting to note the overlap with Comte's positivism, despite the avowed metaphysical starting point. According to Bowne, there is no causality in nature, although there are plenty of regularities. The self, the person, is the only cause; all causation is volitional. Science only describes how things happen and does not explain why they happen, at least not in any fundamental sense.

Science explains in the (possibly quite common) sense that it exhibits phenomena as instances of empirically discovered regularities, which is all that the so-called "laws" of nature are.[30]

Not that Bowne took himself to be causing the natural phenomena or their regularities: "the alternative is supernatural explanation or none." In other words, Comte was right about science but there is a level of explanation quite outside science, in terms of personal action foreign to science but proper to metaphysics.

6. William James: "Radical Empiricism"

James is an example of a philosopher who laid claim to a philosophical position, explicitly calling it a form of empiricism, which he characterizes as an attitude rather than a thesis about what the world is like. This is of course of importance to my proposal, in the body of the text, to regard empiricist philosophical positions as stances rather than theories. We cannot, however, maintain that he is uncontroversially a (pure) example of this sort of philosophizing. The evidence for what precisely James was taking as a position tends to be a bit mixed, perhaps due at least in part to the fact that his writing is often addressed to general audiences.

James presents his position of "radical empiricism" first in the preface to *The Will to Believe* (1897) and develops it further in subsequent books. He begins at once, quite unself-consciously, by describing his position as an attitude. The book is a collection of addresses to student philosophy clubs around the country and "taken together express a tolerably definite philosophic attitude in a very untechnical way." He continues: "Were I obliged to give a short name to the attitude in question, I should call it that of radical empiricism," and adds, "I say 'empiricism' because it is contented to regard its most assured conclusions concerning matters of fact as hypotheses liable to modification in the course of future experience."[31] This is a crucial statement; such sentiments do lie at the heart of the newer forms of empiricism.

Yet even this simple beginning is full of potential perplexities when we examine it. I will outline the main one briefly (see below for reference to its further discussion elsewhere). The word "its" in the passage just quoted is not easy to construe: an attitude is not something that has conclusions. Taking this passage perhaps a bit too literally, one might be tempted to conclude that any philosopher who is contented to regard his own thinking as fallible is a radical empiricist, regardless of what views he has. That would trivialize the position.

Being a little more cautious, we can interpret James as follows: it is part of empiricism to both have and admire the attitude described in the passage, to regard it as an intellectual virtue, and to denigrate more dogmatic attitudes as in some way at odds with the ideals of rational inquiry. This may not be quite as trivial, although it is the sort of thing that quite often is given mere lip service paid to it in scientific contexts. Whether it is trivial depends on what the attitude amounts to if spelled out in detail. In fact, this idea encounters some serious difficulties of its own when we attempt to spell it out precisely.

It emerges at once, when we continue reading the preface, that James subscribes also to something one is tempted to call a metaphysical thesis. He begins with a negative addition: his empiricism is to be called "radical" exactly because "it treats the doctrine of monism itself as an hypothesis, and, unlike so much of the half-way empiricism that is current under the name of positivism or agnosticism or naturalism, it does not dogmatically affirm monism as something with which all experience has got to square" (p. viii). He does not immediately say what monism is; we think at once of substance monism, in contrast to, for example, Descartes's dualism. The explanation of pluralism as rival to monism that follows in this preface does not bear this out. But whatever monism is, it is a hypothesis.

Terminologically, the quoted passage is very curious. If the first passage gives the proper use of "empiricist," then among those who hold to this hypothesis of monism there is no empiricism other than radical empiricism. For according to the foregoing, the attitude in question is part of what it is to be an empiricist, whereas to maintain monism with the proper attitude would seem to be permissible for an empiricist, at least as far as the preceding passage goes. Yet this is not satisfactory, if we think of metaphysics as antithetical to empiricism.

I take it that the passage just cited is meant to imply that radical empiricists do not maintain the thesis of monism but rather take it to be at best a hypothesis that a philosopher (including an empiricist?) could hold.[32] The next few paragraphs of the preface include advocacy of "pluralism," introduced as rival to monism. If that is a real rival, then it too appears to be a metaphysical thesis, and one has to presume that it too is "not dogmatically affirm[ed] . . . as something with which all experience has got to square." We should conclude presumably that the radical empiricist does assert or maintain this pluralist thesis (whatever it is, if it is a thesis) but with the proper nondogmatic attitude.

Later the position began to sound still more metaphysical. In the preface to *The Meaning of Truth* (1909) James says that radical empiricism consists of "a postulate, . . . a statement of fact, and . . . a generalized conclusion." The first is not a postulate but a norm proposed for philosophical practice: to discuss only matters definable in terms drawn from experience. (Perhaps again we can say that a radical empiricist is, among other things, a philosopher who follows this norm, or is determined to follow it, or admires those who do, and so on.) The statement of fact is that relations are real. That appears to have a corollary or possibly sibling, to the effect that singular causal connections are directly perceived (in more or less the sense later to be found in Whitehead, Armstrong, and Nancy Cartwright). The general conclusion appears to be about the world but is even more metaphysical than the statement of fact, and to me quite unintelligible; I will not bother to reproduce it here.[33]

Curiously, radical empiricism does explicitly include some statements about what the world is like, although they are not of the "experience is the source of knowledge" type. (In *The Will to Believe* we do find such statements, however.) Also noteworthy, and important for later developments, is the emphasis on attitudes and norms as part of the position. But an earlier "typical" empiricist element, skepticism with respect to causation (its reality doubted by Hume and banished from science by Comte and by Bowne), is explicitly removed in favor of a bit of realist metaphysics.[34]

It appears, then, that in the end radical empiricism is a mixture of attitudes, norms, and empirical beliefs (or rather metaphysical statements that James took to have some empirical content). Pragmatism, on the other hand, is said to have "no doctrines save its method."[35] It does, however, include a certain theory of truth, which is therefore presumably not a doctrine, but I am not sure what it might be instead. Possibly there is no theory of truth there but only a method of determining whether something is true or false, in which case being a radical empiricist might consist (apart from the noted contentment) in a belief that this method would, if applied to the statement of fact and generalized conclusion, lead to a determination that they are true.

In the title essay, "The Will to Believe," we find further explanations of what James understands empiricism to be. The first (in section 5) is an elaboration of the epistemic attitude described as definitive of empiricism in the preface. The empiricist is not a skeptic, James says, for he believes that there is truth to be discovered and we can discover it. "But the faith that truth exists, and that our minds can find it, may be held in two ways. We may talk of the *empiricist* way and the *absolutist* way of believing in truth. The absolutists in this matter say that we not only can attain to knowing truth, but we can *know when* we have attained to knowing it; while the empiricists think that although we may attain it, we cannot infallibly know when" (p. 12, emphasis in original). I think this is just a corollary to the point that empiricists regard all their own claims as fallible. They know and know that they know, but do not infallibly know that they know, and do not think ever that they infallibly know something. Fine. The contrary is surely at best a philosophical conceit. James adds that if we look at the history of opinions, we see that the empiricist tendency has largely prevailed in science, whereas in philosophy the absolutist tendency has had everything its own way.

Unfortunately for us, this is no longer a point on which philosophers are much divided; they rush to claim to feel each more fallible than the next. We can't use this as a criterion to single out empiricists.

A more interesting elaboration occurs in section 7. James has quoted Clifford's famous dictum that "It is wrong always, everywhere, and for every one, to believe anything upon insufficient evidence." This was clearly written in the belief that rationality prescribes some correct method for weighing evidence and establishing the threshold of sufficiency. By that method Clifford, who had a touchingly uncritical faith in the science of his day, could and did form all his beliefs on sufficient evidence alone.

James's view of our epistemic situation is not as sanguine. As explained in Lecture 3, we labor, according to James, with two dictates from rationality: believe truth, shun error. How to weigh evidence, and where to set the threshold, James claims to be not a theoretically decidable matter; this is where our "passional nature" plays an inevitable role. Clifford's exhortation has "a thoroughly fantastical sound" under these conditions and reveals at best something about his particular passions, not about rationality:

> [H]e who says, "Better go without belief forever than believe a lie!" merely shows his own preponderant private horror of becoming a dupe. He may be critical of many of his desires and fears, but this fear he slavishly obeys. . . . Our errors are surely not such awfully solemn things. In a world where we are so certain to incur them in spite of all our caution, a certain lightness of heart seems healthier than this excessive nervousness on their behalf. At any rate, it seems the fittest thing for the empiricist philosopher. (pp. 18–19)

This is voluntarist epistemology plus advocacy of a certain attitude for which there is room within this epistemology. Again the attitude is what is explicitly ascribed to the empiricist. In this case it is an attitude of less caution, whereas the earlier one (to keep regarding all one's conclusions as hypotheses only) was an attitude of greater caution. It appears that in toto the advocated or at least admired attitude is one of lesser caution in believing putative conclusions but doing so with a cautious attitude. To put it differently: to be audacious in adopting hypotheses but to keep regarding them as hypotheses vulnerable to the fortunes of future experience.

The final passage about empiricism in this essay occurs on the second-to-last page. It elaborates on the critique of Clifford and adds a new element to the picture of the empiricist: tolerance of rival opinions. Indeed this characteristic (I don't know whether to call it an attitude, but it is of that order) is given preeminent status in this philosophical position:

> if we are empiricists, if we believe that no bell in us tolls to let us know for certain when truth is in our grasp, then it seems a piece of idle fantasticality to preach so solemnly our duty of waiting for the bell. Indeed we *may* wait if we will . . . but if we do so, we do so at our peril as much as if we believed. In either case we *act*, taking our life in our hands. No one of us ought to issue vetoes to the other. . . . We ought, on the contrary, delicately and profoundly to respect one another's mental freedom; . . . then only shall we have that spirit of inner tolerance . . . which is empiricism's glory. (p. 30, emphasis in original)

It is not at all clear to me that James did develop a coherent philosophical position. But it is clear that a very large part of the position he attempted to develop as his own consisted in attitudes rather than in theses about what the world and we ourselves are like.

7. Critique: The Difficulties About Experience (Husserl, Dewey)

Husserl's criticism of the empiricists in his *Ideas* was, however severe, not in my opinion unfair. He begins with a sympathetic statement concerning its philosophical motives, but follows that with the criticism that experience, as empiricists conceive it, does not extend far enough for what even they themselves claim as knowledge. He identifies their motives as essentially the same as his own:

> Empiricistic Naturalism springs, as we must recognize, from the most praiseworthy motives. It is an intellectually practical radicalism, which in opposition to all "idols," to the powers of tradition and superstition, to crude and refined prejudices of every kind, seeks to establish the right of self-governing Reason to be the only authority in matters that concern truth. Now to pass rational or scientific judgements upon facts (Sachen) means being guided by the facts themselves, getting away from talk and opinion back to the facts. . . . It is only another way of expressing the very same thing—so the empiricist thinks—to say that all science must spring from experience, that its mediated knowledge must be grounded in immediate experience.[36]

(Note that this is written well before the Vienna Circle began; we must take its reference to be to those who aligned themselves with, for example, Comte and

Mach. The sentence about Reason echoes Kant's discussion of empiricism in connection with the antinomies.) This initial sympathy is then quickly followed by the crucial criticism that the claims made about this relation of "grounding" cannot themselves have that same status. Therefore the empiricist is implicitly claiming knowledge beyond what he "officially" admits:

> It is sufficient to question empiricists concerning the source of the validity of their general thesis (e. g., that "all valid thought has its ground in experience as the sole object-giving intuition") to get them involved in demonstrable absurdities. Direct experience gives only singular elements and no generalities, and is thus insufficient. It can make no appeal to intuition of essences, since it denies such intuition; it must clearly rely on induction, and so generally on the system of mediate modes of inference through which the science of experience wins its general propositions. How fares it now, we ask, with the truth of mediated conclusions, be these deductively or inductively inferred? Is this truth . . . itself something experientiable . . . ? . . . Empiricists appear to have overlooked the fact that the scientific demands which in their own theses they exact from all knowledge are equally addressed to these theses themselves.[37]

Husserl diagnoses the empiricists' difficulties as resulting from their uncritical identification of five distinct items in the philosophical inventory: (a) judgments and intuitions playing a primary role in the individual building up of opinion, (b) ground or warrant in immediate evidence, (c) psychic events known by introspection, (d) sensation, and (e) perceptual experience.

It was part of Husserl's critique that despite their emphasis and preoccupation, empiricists do not identify this all-important matter of experience. This is also the main import of John Dewey's essay "An Empirical Survey of Empiricisms."

According to Dewey there are three basic conceptions of experience, found in different periods of the history of philosophy and giving rise to three distinct forms of empiricism. The first is that of antiquity, used, for example, to distinguish the several schools of medicine and persisting until the seventeenth century. We might add that as he characterizes it, it is still probably the common notion of experience found outside philosophical contexts: "It denotes the accumulated information of the past, not merely the individual's own past but the social past, transmitted through language and even more through apprenticeship in the various crafts, so far as this information was condensed in matter-of-fact generalizations about how to do certain things like building a house, making a statue, leading an army, or knowing what to expect under certain circumstances."[38] But in modern philosophy, when views are characterized by the slogan "Identification of experience as the source of knowledge," the second conception is in play: that of experience as consisting of psychic events that are (a) individual (events that happen to one individual and involve only one individual) and (b) logically speaking, entirely uninformative (in that the information that such an event happens to the individual does not logically imply anything about his surroundings, condition, or circumstances). These psychic experiences are indeed described and classified as experiences of this or that, but they can be had (logically speaking) without there being any this or that. They are the peculiar subject matter of psychology.

Now it would be quite a tour de force to ground our science, common sense, and received wisdom on experience—even if they were the deliverances solely of experience in the first sense—if experience is taken in the latter sense. Indeed it is so heroic, not to say quixotic, a task that it could occupy philosophers uselessly for centuries. Dewey sees exactly the same internal incoherence in empiricism so understood as Husserl did:

> It is a fact, or seems to be a fact, that the natural sciences . . . depend upon experience. At the same time, it is unanswerable that if experience were what a sensational-associationist said it was, it could not possibly produce science. Therefore there is a mistake somewhere. Either the natural sciences do not have the intimate dependence on experience that the enthusiasts on this subject think they have, or experience is a different sort of thing from what it had been analyzed as being. (pp. 19–20)

The sciences do depend, in some significant sense, on systematic observation and experimentation. Those activities are not the simple receiving of impressions by Locke's tabula rasa. Moreover, even being the outcome of that process does not give a datum absolute authority. Indeed, nothing about where the datum comes from makes it so privileged that it cannot be discounted on the basis of later data. Following this line of thought, Dewey says, "one would deduce at least one phase of the philosophy of William James, namely, that validity is not a matter of origin nor of antecedents, but of consequents . . . [:] that the value of ideas is independent of their origin, that it is a matter of their outcome as they are used in directing new observation and new experiment" (pp. 20–21). Whereas James calls himself a radical empiricist, Dewey is certainly right in regarding this contention of James's as directed as much against Locke and Mill as against the rationalists. *Soi-disant* empiricism has entered a new stage, with a new understanding of experience to inform its slogans about the source of all information about the world.

Dewey only points to the concept of experience that he discerns, claiming that it is still inchoate, that it regards a "fundamental transformation in the concept of experience now in the process of developing" (p. 21). One cannot help but recall the ants and bees of Bacon's *Novum Organum* and think that modern empiricist thought had come full circle to its own origin. Hard not to suspect that the seducing motive in the meanwhile had lain in the false hopes for foundationalism in epistemology. Systematic observation and experimentation is a complex and social rather than a simple and individual process. So it needed something behind it if the science it leads to is to rest on secure foundations. What could that be but its building blocks, and what could those be but the psychic events happening to the individuals involved? Then we have a story of philosophers led astray by their own hopes and by convictions about what had to be so if the world was to be intelligible to them at all.

8. Reichenbach's View of the History of Empiricism

We must not blame William James too much for the imprecision of his popular presentations of his views; the same may be said for Reichenbach. From their popular presentations we can glean quite a bit about their conception of empiricism—and the direction into which they were attempting to steer the use of the word "empiricism." Reichenbach's work as a whole was indeed crucial in the shaping of a truer contemporary empiricism.

REICHENBACH'S POPULAR WRITINGS

In Chapter 5 of *The Rise of Scientific Philosophy* Hans Reichenbach gives us a capsule, cartoon-like history of empiricism. He presents it as a tradition, going back to ancient Greece, of opposition to philosophical attempts to construct systems based on claims of esoteric knowledge (through means other than sense perception plus deductive reasoning).[39] To begin he appears to identify one attitude (they "regard empirical science, and not mathematics, as the ideal form of knowledge") and one belief ("they insist that sense observation is the primary source and the ultimate judge of knowledge") as hallmarks of the empiricists.

When Reichenbach goes on to present his list of empiricists, however, it is not clear that they are selected by means of these criteria, or even that he has not at once forgotten all about those criteria. As early members of the empiricist tradition he lists the Greek atomists. This may be one of many instances of confusion between what it is to be an empiricist in philosophy and what it is to be an empirical scientist, as if the mere fact that one admires the other's form of pursuit of knowledge suffices to eradicate the distinction. No better warranted (in view of his own criteria) are Reichenbach's next entries of the skeptics Carneades and Sextus Empiricus. One can only wonder, under these circumstances, at his description of Roger Bacon, Peter Aureoli, and William of Ockham, "who courageously attempted to defend the empiricist position, [but were] too deeply imbued with theological modes of thought to be comparable with the empiricists of an earlier or later time" (p. 77). As paradigm examples of modern empiricism he then lists Francis Bacon, John Locke, and David Hume. In their case it is indeed true that they admired empirical science and that their view of factual knowledge does not by and large give it the same status as mathematics. But it is only with serious qualification (as Reichenbach himself notes) that we can attribute to them the view that sense observation is the primary source and ultimate judge of all knowledge.

So what exactly is Reichenbach doing? He calls his own position logical empiricism, and he is telling us *ex cathedra,* as a logical empiricist, where his sympathies lie. He admires the more empirical natural philosophers, in proportion to their empirical bent, and he is in sympathy with philosophers who criticize claims to knowledge that avowedly go beyond knowledge based on experience. He agrees with the skeptical arguments that demolish claims to certainty concerning matters that are logically contingent. He regards as his allies all critics of what he calls rationalists, that is, of metaphysical system builders. We had best view his list of members of the empiricist tradition as conveying to us in part what he takes empiricism to be, in addition to the "official" criteria he lists, rather than the dubious assertion that they meet those criteria.

Reichenbach is, moreover, in total agreement with the conclusion of Green, Husserl, Dewey, and other writers, noted above, that modern empiricism ended in disaster.

The disaster, as Reichenbach sees it, is that Hume reduced to absurdity the view that all knowledge, as conceived by the modern empiricist, derives entirely from experience. This point stands no matter how much leeway we give the empiricists with respect to the operations of the mind that lead from "raw" experience to scientific knowledge.

The argument is simple: we do know that the planets move in ellipses, but the senses do not tell us that they do so. For what we know by sense observation is only single facts about what is and has been so far, whereas this piece of knowledge is general and gives information also about the future. Thus we have acquired this bit of knowledge by some ampliative procedure. Following Bacon, we may call this procedure (whatever it may be) induction. Any statement to the effect that this procedure leads from knowledge that we have by sense observation to knowledge (or even to information that is reliable to whatever small degree you like) not logically implied by the former is itself ampliative. Therefore it is not known by sense observation, either. The conclusion appears to be inevitable: we have knowledge that does not derive, in any nontrivial sense, from knowledge had by sense observation. This is so at least if our premise about what we know about planetary orbits is correct; and who would want to deny that? In close parallel with my earlier quotations from Husserl and Dewey on the breakdown of empiricism, Reichenbach displays "the dilemma of the empiricist": either be a radical empiricist and admit no results other than what can be logically derived from experience, or admit the inductive inference. On the first horn, empiricists "cannot make inductions and must renounce any statement about the future"; on the second they have "admitted a nonanalytic principle not derivable from experience and [have] abandoned empiricism" (p. 89).

Yet we must remember that Reichenbach is an empiricist, calls himself an empiricist, and aligns himself with philosophers in the tradition that he here clearly says broke down. Hence the criteria which entail that empiricism is caught on this dilemma do not after all define empiricism for Reichenbach. When he comments on this himself, he says that the earlier empiricists had an inadequate concept of knowledge. But the reductio argument did not explicitly invoke any criteria of knowledge. On this diagnosis, then, some hidden premise about knowledge must be driving that argument.

The fact is that epistemology was radically transformed between the times of Hume and of Reichenbach. What twentieth-century empiricists can have in common with the earlier modern empiricists must be something quite abstruse. I think we will not be able to appreciate it without first looking at this transformation, in which Reichenbach himself played a crucial role.

REICHENBACH'S THIRD WAY

So what is the proper project for empiricism, according to Reichenbach? He knew very well that there had been a second sequel to the seventeenth-century confrontation. Starting with Kant, the new idealist tradition had attempted to finesse the problem. Philosophy should give us a theory of what there is but cannot demonstrate its correctness without circularity. It may, however, be able to demonstrate that theory's status as indubitable for us; it may be able to convict any disagreements with that theory of subjective incoherence.

There are important points of contact between modern empiricism and modern idealism. Kant defined a "transcendental assertion" as a "claim to insight into what is beyond the field of all possible experience" (A425; B453). Transcendental idealism rejects all transcendental assertions as necessarily baseless. Foundationalist epistemologies of the sort we now identify with modern empiricism are thereby rejected, for they involve claims about how experience—as a whole—is related to what there is, independent of and separate from experience. But this rejection is entirely of a piece with the empiricist critique of rationalist metaphysics. As we might say: transcendental empiricism is a project totally at odds with its inspiration, is hoist on its own petard by its own insight, and is to be rejected on its own ground.

In retrospect we can see both projects, foundationalist and empiricist, confusedly started in Descartes. Foundationalism was the project to construct all knowledge on a foundation that cannot be false, by a method that cannot introduce falsity. Idealism, on the other hand, is the project to find a story of the world that is indubitable by uncovering the logical preconditions of a coherent epistemic life, coherent meaningful experience, and thought. The nagging question whether what is indubitable must also be true is then to be properly treated in the same way, of course: what is indubitable is indubitably true, for the supposition that something incoherent might still be true is itself incoherent.

Now Reichenbach rejected explicitly not only the modern empiricists' foundational project but also the Kantian idealist project. He did not simply reject them. He submitted each to a thoroughgoing critique and he argued that both pursued impossibilities. His main reason for this is that logic is empty. It may be very illuminating to delve into what is certain, indubitable, coherent, and incoherent. But a genuinely contentfull theory of the world must be logically contingent and therefore unreachable in this way. On the positive side, Reichenbach appropriated impartially many of the real achievements of all sides in modern philosophy, and he showed by shining example how to do philosophy instead. There are three major points to this effort.

The first point is to allocate the aim of theorizing about what there is to empirical science. That is not the philosopher's part. The nearest project to foundationalist epistemology that makes sense is to be found in the empirical sciences: biology, ecology, psychology, sociology, cognitive science. A philosopher who engages in cognitive science is not doing philosophy. If the choice is between doing that discredited sort of epistemology and leaving philosophy, then better to leave! Reichenbach, however, does not see this as the only choice.

The second point is to reclassify much of those traditionally attempted stories of the world, with their putative universal and necessary principles. As a quick example, look at what happened to the principle of causality at Reichenbach's hands. This principle is demoted from thesis of determinism to methodological rule. Acceptance of this rule is a matter of decision vulnerable to future data, namely, a decision to portray the world as a "normal system" free from causal anomalies. Eventually the principle of causality undergoes the further demotion from methodological rule to useful tactic, one that we could decide (or not) to pursue first when modeling phenomena, defeasibly.[40]

The third point—the theme of voluntarism in the new epistemology— emerges from this. Reichenbach's conceptual resources for epistemology in a new key were not as yet very refined. It would be easy to criticize the specific terms he used, such as "decision," "rule," "convention," and "definition." Still, a fairly clear picture emerges. You cannot theorize about the world without making decisions and choices about how to theorize. Your decisions and choices may be vindicated or not vindicated, no matter how careful, reasonable, prudent, or humanly justified you are. To say this is not to detract from reason but to shift our focus from the limited security of reason to the limitless caprice of nature and history. For the security reason gives us is only enough to keep us from making fools of ourselves, from sabotaging ourselves, from discernible incoherence. Even that gift is not exactly foolproof. We can't even prove the logical consistency of any reasonably powerful theory, and there is no decision procedure guaranteed to keep us out of logical self-contradiction. Even if we are lucky enough not to contradict ourselves, all we can say logically speaking is that our expectations will either be satisfied or not be satisfied in future experience— *que sera, sera.* . . .

DRAWING ON SCIENCE, THE RIGHT WAY

Reichenbach was a great if not exactly subtle evangelist for science. I take it to be a hallmark of the empiricist tradition that empirical science is placed on a sort of pedestal, as paradigm for rational inquiry. What follows from this is not unequivocal. We are clearly exhorted to follow science's example throughout our lives, in all inquiry and thought. But it is easy to come away with the wrong lesson. So what does it mean? What lesson should we draw from science?

The lesson is not the rationalists', that we should write axiomatic theories of ever greater certainty and generality about what there is. By the same token, I think, it is not the lesson of today's naturalism, that we should value only factual scientific inquiry into science and cognition. That would be the same lesson as the rationalists drew, minus the axioms, the certainty, and the generality. The question of what lesson we should draw from science, what it is to adhere to this paradigm, is an invitation to the new empiricists to describe how they see science, or rather, what they take to be the ideal exemplified, however imperfectly, in science. To paraphrase a remark of Adolf Grünbaum's in another context: the lessons of science are not to be read off from it like numbers and addresses from a telephone book.

With this conclusion we see a philosophical task, in which Reichenbach was certainly engaged, which is neither metaphysics, nor traditional epistemology, nor itself one of empirical inquiry. He presents us with a view of what science is, its point, its aims, its goals, its avowed criteria of adequacy and of self-evaluation, and its reflective attitudes toward its own procedures and results. He arrives at this view within the historical context of the upheavals that created contemporary physics, and he asserts that this actual science exemplifies his articulated concept of science. True to his own insight, he must admit the limitations of his historical perspective and the precarious character of his claims. But that is part of following the example of science as he described it.

I had better emphasize this. There is no unequivocal, context-independent sense to imitation of anything. Reichenbach selects and interprets, he extrapolates—as he must, if he is to present us with an example to follow. Fine; another place where we should not criticize a philosopher for not doing the impossible. My main point is that Reichenbach is engaged in a philosophical activity, a genuine heir to traditional epistemology, which is not identifiable with writing theories about what there is or what the world is like. The point is delicate, for he cannot do this without some theorizing. He is asserting apparently factual claims: science is this or that. He accepts responsibility for their accuracy: some of the assertions were in fact false.[41] But we lose the point of what he is doing if that is all we see. For Reichenbach is articulating a paradigm for rational inquiry and advocates it as one to be followed. It is important (but only important) that the articulated view of science is exemplified by real science to some significant (but only significant) extent and that it succeeds well (but only well) in "rationalizing" real scientific practice.

I hold up this example of Reichenbach, as I have described him, as one to be emulated in developing new empiricism(s). The example I so present is of Reichenbach as I described him, not, perhaps, of the real, historical Reichenbach. Certainly it is important for my presentation that this view of Reichenbach is exemplified in his writings to some reasonable approximation. But the more important question is whether the example is worthy of emulation.

Appendix C. Bultmann's Theology Is Not a Philosophy

One misconstrual of Bultmann's project should be prevented, and I think that some quotations from his work will suffice for this. Demythologizing in Bultmann's sense does not consist in retaining the universal moral or spiritual message of the Gospel in a scientific-secular dress. The Gospel is not telling us a way to improve the quality of life understood no differently from the way the secular understand that. But neither is Bultmann reducing the Gospel to a certain philosophy, as if to follow Christ means becoming an existentialist. Philosophy can only provide a "pre-understanding" within which the Gospel can make sense to us in a certain way.

This is spelled out quite clearly in his *New Testament and Mythology,* where he addresses the charge that his view entails that "the Christian understanding of being can be realized without Christ, that what we find in the New Testament is simply an understanding of being that is discovered for the first time and more or less clearly expressed" (p. 21). He concedes that there is some basis for this and that for example Heidegger's existentialist analysis of human existence, on which he clearly draws, may very well look like a profane version of the New Testament view of who we are. On that analysis, after all, we are "beings existing historically in care for ourselves on the basis of anxiety, ever in the moment of decision between the past and the future, whether we will lose ourselves in the world of [everydayness], or whether we will attain our authenticity by surrendering all securities and being unreservedly free for the future. Is this not how we are also understood in the New Testament?" (p. 23).

But there is one great difference. This philosophy comes with the implied conviction that all that is needed to bring about the realization of our "nature" is that it be shown to us, all we need for the decision is to see clearly this character of the human condition. The New Testament rejects any such confidence. There we find instead the conviction that "we can in no way free our-selves from our factual fallenness in the world but are freed from it only by an act of God." The Gospel is not a doctrine about our "nature" but the proclama-tion of this liberating act of God. "The New Testament says, then, that without this saving act of God the human situation is desperate, while philosophy by no means does or can look upon it as a desperate situation" (p. 25–26).

The New Testament and existentialism speak to us in very similar terms: the kingdom of God is among us; an authentic life is open to us because we are already in it and it is already ours.

> But the New Testament speaks this way only to believers who have allowed God's liberating act to take place in their existence, not to all human beings as such. It disputes the claim that life already belongs to all men and women, and it holds the human situation in general to be desperate.
>
> Why? Precisely because it knows that we can only be and become what we already are and because human beings as such, before and outside of Christ, are not already in their authentic being—in life—but are rather in death. (p. 26)

For existentialism, at least in the secular form of Heidegger and Sartre, our authenticity is something that we can realize at any time. Ought implies can! On the New Testament understanding, as Bultmann sees it, human beings generally have lost the possibility in fact. Indeed, this conviction of autonomy and ability to choose and construct an authentic existence by their own hands, so to speak, is part of the self-deception that prevents authenticity. "If genuine life is a life of submission, it is missed not only by those who live by disposing of what can be disposed of instead of by submitting but also by those who understand even submission to be an aim that they can dispose of and do not see that their authentic life can only be an absolute gift" (p. 28).

But given all that, there is of course still quite a bit of philosophy to be found in Bultmann's writings; they are not simply devotional reading. Espe-cially interesting in connection with our inquiry into what science is like is his discussion of myth in relation to objectifying inquiry. What precisely myth is, is itself a question of considerable philosophical interest.[42] Like most words of any importance, "myth" has a continuum of meanings. There is the great myth in which an entire culture lives, moves, breathes, and has its being. There are also the uncountable small myths that momentarily smooth this life with explana-tion. No single simple theory would fit all, though of course simple theories have been proposed. One such simple theory made myths out to be proto-science, early attempts at scientific explanation. That fits quite a few of those small myths rather well. We imagine primitive cultures and uneducated, unsophisticated yet intelligent beings making up elementary if fanciful explanations of natural phenomena and human affairs, and producing myths as a result. But if Bultmann is right (and not only Bultmann, but Cassirer and Susanne Langer, to name only some associated with Yale), it is not at all just primitive unsophisticates who produce myth.

In his essay "On the Problem of Demythologizing" (found in *New Testament*), Bultmann characterizes myth as an objectifying kind of thinking like that of science. But it is as it were mistakenly what it turns out to be: myth talks about transcendent powers or persons as though they were immanent and worldly. By doing so, it manages at the same time to serve and defeat its own end. The myths depict our human condition as subject to demons and gods "as powers on which we know ourselves to be dependent, of which we do not dispose, whose favor we need and whose wrath we fear. It thus makes apparent our knowledge that the world in which we live as human beings is full of enigmas and mysteries, and that we are not lords over the world and our own life. In this way myth gives expression to a certain understanding of human existence." But by taking this form, "myth objectifies the transcendent into the immanent, and thus also into the disposable, as becomes evident when cult more and more becomes action calculated to influence the attitude of the deity."[43]

Bultmann's critique definitely does not do justice to all the roles of myth in our thinking and life. His notion of myth fits a multitude of small myths but is quite inadequate as a general concept. But it may characterize precisely anthropocentric theological theories of the sort that could be produced by the kind of objectifying inquiry that I described above.

I would go further and say that myth produced in such a way is essentially secular, or at least entirely accessible to the secular. The collaborators in such an objectifying study of religion need not themselves be in any way religious, certainly not in any way gripped by religion. For this is a crucial thing about objectifying thinking: it is equally open to all and remains on a level where participation requires no sort of engagement. Even when it comes to devising explanatory theories, showing how the phenomena could possibly be what given sacred scriptures say they are can in principle be done equally well by secular scholars with no stake in the outcome. For it is crucial to objectifying thinking that it can be engaged in without any stake in the outcome. I emphasize "can," and may have to mean this in a rather weak sense; such impartiality may not be always be possible. But it is recognized that objective study may be willy-nilly obstructed by any related commitment on the part of the participants.

So what shall we locate at the borderline between religious and secular? Perhaps that is where we find most typically confusion over the status of objectifying, scientific, or quasi-scientific study. It seems to me a sad delusion when there are books by scientists ostensibly about God or the divine mysteries and in actual fact about the Big Bang, black holes, and quantum mechanical paradoxes. Here the religious mysteries are equated with mysteries of a different category, exactly as Bultmann explains. For the natural scientist, engaged in empirical research, there are of course many mysteries, and always new mysteries arise continually. "But these mysteries are completely irrelevant to existential self-understanding—at least directly—and have nothing to do with the mystery of God's act. It is sadly misleading when such mysteries are set forth in edifying discourses as the mysteries of God; for this can only lead to concealing the real mystery of God" (*New Testament*, pp. 104–5). As one philosophy student explained it to me: sometimes popular science writers seem to think that if something is only big enough or small enough, it must have to do with the meaning of life. That is, in a nutshell, Bultmann's quarrel with one distinctive contemporary form of (small) myth-making.

Notes

Preface

1. This is how Joseph Kockelmans (one of my teachers when I was a graduate student) framed the challenge in his 1986 presidential address to the American Philosophical Association.

2. The Terry Lectures consist of a series of four presentations at Yale University over the course of two weeks. The fourth of my five lectures was omitted from that series in October 1999 but delivered as part of the Cardinal Mercier Lectures at Louvain-la-Neuve two months later.

3. It has done so specifically in "The World of Empiricism" and "The Peculiar Effects of Love and Desire."

4. See the introduction to her French translation of my *Laws and Symmetry*.

Lecture 1. Against Analytic Metaphysics

1. The type of metaphysics to which I refer, and which I take to be the enterprise engaged in by, for example, Descartes and Leibniz, is characterized by the attempted construction of a theory of the world, of the same form as a fundamental science and continuous with (as extension or foundation of) the natural sciences. I will characterize this sort of metaphysics further below and in Lecture 2.

2. Of course, that is one of the things Kant did, and he did show that seventeenth-century metaphysics (indeed, theoretical reason as he knew it) is powerless to deal even with that simple question.

3. For sections 2–7 I am drawing mainly on my " 'World' is not a count noun." The main drawback of the example I am choosing instead of issues such as God, freedom, or personal identity is that it does not have a large associated body of literature. Because of its very simplicity it may be dismissed as a "don't

care." But of course I take it to be illustrative in that respect as well; I hold that all the issues, as construed in analytic metaphysics, end up as don't cares.

4. Think, for example, of Kant's scathing response to the British empiricists' atomistic view of perception. We don't simply have a stream of sense data; my perception is always of myself in a world of such and such form. Nothing short of that rings phenomenologically true to our experience.

5. I cannot resist mentioning my experience when I first arrived to teach at Yale and came to know my greatly valued colleague Frederick Fitch, a truly original as well as wonderfully human logician. He told me that in his course on metaphysics he always ended with the latest version of his proof of God's existence. At that time he was not satisfied with the proof because God was a relation; he was more satisfied by the time I left for God had turned out to be a proposition.

6. I mean standard (Zermelo-Fraenkel) set theory. Even in elementary math we can find relevant analogies: a series of increasing sizes may increase without limit, but its size is not a natural number greater than all natural numbers, which is impossible. But that example is less telling because of course there are cardinal numbers greater than the natural numbers. The same point might then be made by asking how many cardinals there are; is the answer a number greater than all cardinal numbers?

7. We are tempted to ask: Is this the world of Abraham, Isaac, and Jacob we are speaking of, or the world of the philosophers?

8. For a careful study of Kant's pre-Critical notion of world, see Friedman, *Kant and the Exact Sciences*, pp. 5, 7, 13–14, 25, 32 n. 54, 33–34.

9. Or perhaps he created a few more. The consequence—that there is only one material world—if thus combined with some basic principles of Newton's science (read as of unrestricted application) has some strange further consequences. Absolute space and its parts are real according to Newton, but massless, and they do not interact with material bodies. So on Kant's concept of a world, and Newton's view of space, it follows that there are real entities (e.g., space) that are not part of this world! Or perhaps that space is, or is part of, a second world.

10. Is that really possible? Is it possible that some things are neither far nor near, at literally no distance at all from us, and yet not here? One example is provided by quantum mechanics on the orthodox interpretation, which lets particles have a velocity but no position—unfortunately, those are meant to be part of our world! In any case, this seems to be a question for the philosophy of space and time, and we have to leave it aside for now.

11. Mereology was created by Lesniewski early in the twentieth century, developed by, among others, Tarski, Leonard, and Goodman, and further by David Lewis in *Parts of Classes*. It is a theory of the part-whole relation. Axioms that imply the reality of sums are not pure logic, however; they are existence postulates.

12. Quine himself was, it seems to me, left farthest behind; see my review of his *Pursuit of Truth*. But I have argued elsewhere that even such a sophisticated writer as David Lewis displays unconfronted conflicts with the major putative insights into science generally credited to Kuhn and Feyerabend (see my "Putnam's Paradox").

13. I can cite many examples, but one that I have explicitly discussed elsewhere is central to David Armstrong's *What Is a Law of Nature?* See my *Laws and Symmetry*, ch. 6, sec. 3.

14. I am referring here to the views of science, acceptance, and explanation developed in my *Scientific Image*. Those views are disputable and certainly disputed, but although the analytic metaphysician may disagree, the point remains that there is a certain specific philosophical view of science at the basis of that metaphysical enterprise.

15. This is correct even if we take the aim for science to be empirical adequacy, rather than truth over all, for empirical adequacy is truth or accuracy with respect to the empirical phenomena.

16. A metaphysician may reject the decision theory paradigm for rational theory choice in metaphysics. Again, this should at least not remain unacknowledged. That paradigm, associated with probabilism in epistemology, is a rival to the traditional epistemologies that center on such ideas as induction, justification, and "proportioning one's belief to the evidence." To meet the present criticism, the metaphysician can alternatively try to demonstrate, within that sort of traditional approach, that metaphysical theory choice is likely or more likely than not to bring us true conclusions.

17. Indeed, the word "world" has very few uses as a mass noun, the only familiar one being perhaps the occurrence in Marvell's "Had we but world enough, and time."

18. C. S. Lewis explores the history of "world" and the relations between its various uses in chapter 9 of his *Studies in Words*. I thank Arnold Burms for this reference and for our illuminating conversations on this and other subjects.

19. Locke, *Human Understanding* IV, iii, 27.

20. I thank Michael Mahoney, whose translation I used, for drawing my attention to this work. Thanks as well to the students in my freshman seminar "The History, Philosophy, and Mythology of Light" for stimulating discussions.

21. The suggestion begins at the end of chapter 5, and the methodology is elaborated at length in chapter 6. My quotations are from Mahoney's translation.

22. For a more insightful treatment, I recommend Eleonore Stump's recent lectures (Stump 1999).

Lecture 2. What Is Empiricism and What Could It Be?

1. This will be brief; I will provide a slightly more detailed account in the appendix.

2. Bacon, *Novum Organum*, bk. 1, aph. 95, 64.

3. Mill, *A System of Logic*, bk. VI, x, 8; p. 930 (page references are to Mill, *Collected Works of John Stuart Mill*, vol. 8).

4. I'm not being original. See the views of Woolhouse and Loeb discussed in the appendix.

5. This may not be quite fair; in the appendix I'll be more even-handed on this. Specifically, Kant's use of the term "empiricist" in the last chapter of the First Critique (A854; B882) could be cited in favor of this "innate ideas" criterion. But Kant's own usage earlier in the book may not support that as the defining characteristic; for a further, more detailed discussion see the appendix on the history of "empiricism."

6. My views here are fashioned to some extent by a critique of ideas about scientific explanation (standard fare in philosophy of science textbooks and in the scientific realism debates); see my *Scientific Image*, ch. 2, sec. 4 and ch. 5.

7. A fourth example is the assertion: if mathematics is not the true description of a platonic realm of abstract entities, and also does not consist merely of logical tautologies, then you can't explain why it is useful for science.

8. See Reichenbach, "Rationalism and empiricism." In addition to the further discussion in the appendix, see my "False hopes of traditional epistemology."

9. We are here touching on various disputes in epistemology that I will take up further in the other lectures.

10. This point is effectively dramatized in William Golding's *Free Fall*, in the boy's relation to his classes on scripture and science.

11. Remember, the foundationalist epistemology associated with modern empiricism is just such a thesis!

12. I have clearly left out of account a third possibility: that the basis for empiricist critiques could be an a priori yet factual thesis, factual yet not admitting of rivals. I need hardly point out how long the denial of such an option has been part of the empiricist tradition. There are close neighbors of such an idea (pragmatic tautologies, of the order of Moore's paradox—see, e.g., my "Putnam's Paradox"), but they would not fit the bill here. For two different elaborations of the main argument in this section see my "Against Transcendental Empiricism" and "Against Naturalized Empiricism."

13. It is not always clear whether what is expressed is an attitude or a factual claim. Compare, for example, Wesley Salmon's characterization of empiricism in "Empiricism: The Key Question." Concept empiricism, he writes, is the view that "all of our ideas must originate in experience," which is close to the sort of candidate dogma for naïve empiricism that we have just seen self-destruct. Concerning statement empiricism he writes, "According to this doctrine, the sole basis on which we are justified in affirming or denying factual statements is observational evidence." It is not clear whether this doctrine is itself a factual statement, which would leave it vulnerable to an embarrassing question. If not,

it is presumably a value judgment or a commitment to a certain epistemic policy. (As will be seen in Lecture 3, this policy does not seem right for latter-day empiricists.)

14. Once this possibility occurs it is easily recognized in individual cases. For example, Arthur Fine turned the scientific realism debate in a new direction precisely by his depiction of what he called an "ontological attitude." See Fine, "The Natural Ontological Attitude" and especially Crasnow, "How Natural Can Ontology Be?" which has an extended discussion of philosophical attitudes. Also, I thank Arnold Burms for pointing out a similar distinction in ethics between the expression of attitudes characteristic of a position and endorsement of its general principles (for example, utilitarian attitudes as contrasted with endorsement of utilitarian principles).

15. Feyerabend, *Realism, Rationalism, and Scientific Method,* p. 199.

16. See, e.g., Richardson, "Philosophy as Science."

17. I will focus on a distinctly old-fashioned but straightforward sort of materialism. The argument seems to me not affected by such questions as whether the psychological reduces to or is merely supervenient on the physical. It also seems rather amusing to me that lately materialism has gone to formulations that presuppose just the sort of metaphysics that earlier materialists classed with the occult, such as realism about modalities. For a relevant critique of how contemporary materialists think to help themselves to bits of metaphysics, see Putnam, "After Empiricism" (a review of Ayer's *Philosophy in the Twentieth Century*), especially pp. 26–28. For a critical look at "supervenience" and the body-mind problem in the late twentieth century, with strong arguments against "token-identity" theories of mind, see Kim, *Mind in a Physical World.* But see also Clark Glymour's review of Kim's book, with its reflections on the ingression of analytic metaphysics into questions that properly belong to the empirical sciences.

18. Thus Galen Strawson's "Real Materialism" begins with "Materialism is the view that every thing and event in the universe is physical in every respect, that 'physical phenomenon' is coextensive with 'real phenomenon' or at least with 'real, concrete phenomenon.'"

19. Eleonore Stump's paper on Aquinas ("Non-Cartesian Substance Dualism and Materialism Without Reductionism") is very instructive here. If Aquinas's doctrine on souls is coherent it is at least not a mind-body dualism.

20. Davies, "Particles Do Not Exist."

21. Place, "Is Consciousness a Brain Process?"

22. Smart, "Sensations and Brain Processes"; Place, "Materialism as a Scientific Hypothesis." Place agreed in response to Smart that the conditions required for the assertability of such a hypothesis—conditions under which alone such an identity statement can be true—are subject to philosophical debate rather than empirical testing. But once such conditions are specified, the remaining question is empirical.

23. See, e.g., Armstrong's half of Armstrong and Malcolm, *Consciousness and Causality*, and his *Materialist Theory of Mind*.

24. Not to be forgotten in this connection is eliminative materialism, which is an option even if the logical structures of psychological and physicalist discourse are so mismatched as to preclude any form of reduction or supervenience. That was a great insight of Feyerabend, Sellars, Rorty, and Churchland, who did not care to play for such "small" stakes as Place did. Armstrong, however, says that if he were to be convinced of the irreducibility he would reluctantly become a dualist. I wonder if this means that he knows of a coherent and at least minimally adequate mind-body dualism? (For a critique of eliminative materialism, see Philipse, "Absolute Network Theory of Language and Traditional Epistemology.")

25. "Materialism," ch. 16 of his *Essays Metaphysical and Moral;* the paper was originally published in 1963. The passage quoted could be, for greater clarity, followed by David Lewis's acknowledgment that as physics changes, so must any such thesis: "[Materialism] was so named when the best physics of the day was the physics of matter alone. Now our best physics acknowledges other bearers of fundamental properties. . . . But it would be pedantry to change the name on that account" ("Reduction of Mind," p. 413). This is at the same time the continuation of Lewis's "Argument for the Identity Theory," which clearly belongs to the tradition of "Australian materialism" we are here examining.

26. A robust materialism may of course include a whole-hearted endorsement of the current physics as correct or essentially so. Thus David Lewis characterizes the materialism to which he subscribes as "metaphysics built to endorse the truth and descriptive completeness of physics more or less as we know it" (*Philosophical Papers* 2:x, n.). Galen Strawson cites this in his "Real Materialism" and disputes it, not wishing materialism to be saddled with so much faith in physics as it presently stands, but does not provide an alternative way to demarcate the physical from the nonphysical.

27. A century later Ludwig Buechner's *Force and Matter* compares very favorably with d'Holbach's work as far as knowledge of the sciences of the day was concerned. But Buechner belonged to that triumphal, scientifically enlightened part of the nineteenth century that was just about to see its most fundamental views of nature abandoned in the physical sciences. Again, in Buechner's writings, the position was presented as a view of what there is in the universe, oblivious to such possibilities of change in science.

28. The attitudes described here contrast with those I take to be typical of empiricism, of deference to or admiration for science as a paradigm of rational inquiry, characterized by mutual and self-criticism. The empiricist attitude does not imply deference to science in matters of opinion but rather a certain epistemic detachment with respect to the content of current or even ideal science. I will return to this below.

29. What exactly is the spirit of materialism? I will try to say a little more

later on. The making explicit of materialism, however, in the sense of a perennial philosophy, or support for the conclusion that it can exist without false consciousness, is properly a task for the materialists themselves. I would ask the reader to compare here two instances of recent work, both historically conscious and well-informed, but one of them naïve (in the sense of being directly vulnerable to the above sort of critique) and the other more sophisticated. The first is Vitzthum's *Materialism: An Affirmative History and Definition*. To see quite clearly how his view is posed on the edge between a strong commitment and a factual thesis about nature, turn first to chapter 6, "A Summary Definition of Materialism." The second is Jean Bricmont's reply, "Qu'est-ce que le matérialisme scientifique?," to a review of his joint book with Sokal. Read this in conjunction with his "Comment peut-on être 'positiviste'?" to see how a large part of his position allies closely with what I characterize as empiricism, while not leaving the materialist tradition as I view it here.

30. As final sidelight on this I would refer to Paul Feyerabend's early essay on materialism (1963, with 1980 postscript, in *Realism, Rationalism, and Scientific Method*). At the outset he specifies that the argument might as well focus on ancient atomism as on contemporary science, and his phrasing suggests that any materialist thesis takes the form of a completeness claim for a certain scientific description of the world. It also suggests that philosophical disputes concerning materialism are entirely independent of the content of the thesis in question. If both suggestions are correct, there is already a serious question whether there is any such thing as the philosophical thesis that materialism purports to be. In the note added in 1980 he arrives at something like the conception of materialism as stance: "It may well be that a materialistic language . . . is richer in cognitive content than commonsense. . . . But it will be much poorer in other respects. For example, it will lack the associations which now connect mental events with emotions, our relations to others, and which are the basis of the arts and the humanities." He adds, "The choice concerns the quality of our lives—it is a moral choice."

31. Both above and in the appendix I have indicated the sympathy found for this sort of view of philosophy among logical positivists and logical empiricists. But there is ample historical precedent for it elsewhere as well. Let me just mention one other example: the "historical" view associated in different forms with Dilthey and Collingwood. In the last chapter of his First Critique, "The History of Pure Reason," Kant briefly sketched a threefold typology of philosophical positions. This sketch was amended and amplified in Dilthey's "Types of World-view" (Dilthey, *Selected Writings*, pp. 133–54), in which each of three types is assigned three characteristic factors: a metaphysics, an epistemology, and a practical orientation. These worldviews have their basis in more fundamental attitudes toward life. ("They cannot owe their origin to any demonstration because they cannot be dissolved by any demonstration.") Collingwood's position was subtler and not as blatantly psychologizing as Dilthey's; he saw the

philosophical task as uncovering fundamental presuppositions that cannot ultimately be identified as factual beliefs or propositions.

32. One example is the scientific realism debate of the past few decades. This debate begins with apparently a factual disagreement about what science is, what its aims are, its criteria of success, and what is involved in accepting a scientific theory. But the debate hinges unmistakably on diverging value judgments, specifically on what is endorsed as rational. One side rejects inference to the best explanation, while the other exclaims, "If that is not rational, what is?" One side disdains the embrace of beliefs that can never face a true test in experience, while the other sees precisely in such beliefs the true appreciation of what reason and science have achieved for us.

33. Gordon Belot has an interesting relevant paper in progress on what it is to live with theories we know to be false, even ones at the very basis of our physics. This is certainly our situation as long as our most basic physical theories—general relativity and quantum theory—are not consistently combinable with each other.

34. These few remarks actually hide a whole budget of problems in epistemology; for at least some of them see my articles in the bibliography. For relativism specifically see my "From Vicious Circle to Infinite Regress."

Lecture 3. Scientific Revolution/Conversion as a Philosophical Problem

1. There is a great deal of literature on the revolutionary character of changes in science, of which I shall be able to cite only a small part. I owe personal debts to Catherine Chevalley for her work on Bohr and Heisenberg and to Adolf Grünbaum, who introduced me to the foundations of relativity as supervisor of my graduate studies.

2. Kuhn at least called successive theories in some cases "incommensurable" ("Reflection on My Critics," p. 267), while Davidson provided the central arguments against the possibility of that sort of incommensurability in his "Very Idea of a Conceptual Scheme." I think that Davidson mainly got the better of it. But there is one crucial place where I do think he went wrong in his exploration: the place signaled by his parenthetical remark "I shall neglect possible asymmetries." That the prior point of view can be reconstructed within the posterior view, in a way that is satisfactory by posterior lights, does not imply much about how the posterior looks from the prior point of view. Ignoring the asymmetry leaves us with a one-sided view.

3. For philosophy of science there is a quite specific problem, that of "royal succession" of theories in the historical development of the sciences. There too we walk a tightrope between denial of radical change and embrace of irrationalism. For a more technical discussion of the entire topic, see my "Structure: Its Shadow and Substance."

4. See Pais, *Niels Bohr's Times*, pp. 152–55.

5. I draw here on Vargish and Mook, *Inside Modernism*, ch. 2, "Epistemic Trauma"; the quotation is from W. F. Magie, "The Primary Concepts of Physics," *Science* 35 (1912): 290.

6. Reichenbach wrote this in an article published in 1921, "The present state of the discussion of relativity." I quote from Maria Reichenbach's translation in Reichenbach, *Modern Philosophy of Science*, pp. 1–2.

7. In logic and metamathematics the notions of stronger and richer theories and languages can be made precise, so as to furnish very clear examples, but to the nonlogician these are often too artificial to carry equal conviction. Still, we must keep those in mind to defuse the suspicion that things are not so bad after all and that the very idea of a real conceptual revolutions is somehow mistaken in intent.

8. I thank Bruce Pourciau ("Intuitionism as a [Failed] Kuhnian Revolution in Mathematics") for drawing my attention to the "Crowe-Dauben debate" over whether there can be conceptual revolutions in mathematics—see Gillies, *Revolutions in Mathematics*. As Pourciau points out in his valuable study, both sides agreed (to his mind, mistakenly) that changes in the history of mathematics cannot have the first characteristic I list (that some previously accepted notion is overthrown, discarded, seen as unintelligible or fundamentally defective).

9. Kuhn, *Structure of Scientific Revolutions*, p. 97.

10. One of the major credentials for a new theory offered as rival to an old one is that it be able to explain and preserve the successes of the old theory. For example, the special theory of relativity entails that Newton's laws of motion are approximately correct for phenomena with velocities that are small in comparison with the speed of light, and the quantum theory entails that for contexts in which Planck's quantum of action can be regarded as negligibly small. This does not, of course, qualify the point that the new theory, taken as a whole, contradicts the old theory, taken as a whole. I will return to this in the next lecture, but see further my "Structure: Its Shadow and Substance."

11. Let me show the philosophical character of this question by drawing an analogy (which I adapt from my teacher Wilfrid Sellars). Imagine you have been studying twentieth-century ethics and convinced yourself of one of the emotivist or "Cosa Nostra" relativist (quasi-objectivist) views: what is good (moral) is what meets our (moral) standards. Suppose you add, quite consistently, that the Roman values that justified slavery were mistaken and the practice immoral: that there were moral insights they did not yet have. A sufficiently sophisticated relativist position will allow you to assert that. But then suppose you suddenly reflect: we are not so different from the Romans; there may be moral insights that we have not yet attained. Now you find yourself in a philosophical crisis, for that assertion is self-contradictory by your newfound understanding of good.

12. Quine's argument in that paper looks historical, beginning with a sketch of a certain program pursued by philosophers from Hume through Carnap to elaborate and defend two major theses, which have turned out to be

untenable; what remains is to construct a theory of human cognitive functioning. (I won't query the historical accuracy.) The program had two parts: doctrinal and conceptual. The doctrinal part was the thesis that all our warranted beliefs, including the science we accept, can be inferred from the observational base. What exactly is that? Sometimes Quine says "sensations" or "sense data," but deduction can only be from statements, not from things or events or momentary states. Sometimes he speaks of "observation statements," variously described as reports of what sensations were had or as conditional responses to stimuli made by specific people but uniform across a certain range of stimulation for a whole cluster or community of people. The doctrinal part was in any case bankrupt after Hume's critique of induction.

The conceptual part was the thesis that all concepts utilized in framing our warranted beliefs (and most especially our accepted scientific theories) can be explicated as constructible from concepts pertaining directly to sensations. Presumably these "basic" concepts are the ones mobilized in the observation statements, or at least sufficiently rich so that all observation statements needed for the doctrinal part can be couched in them. But the doctrinal part being defunct, how do we identify these basic concepts? The most successful attempt at this conceptual reconstruction, according to Quine, was Carnap's *Aufbau*. If it had succeeded, each scientific statement would have been explicable or equivalent to a logical construction from observation statements. In order to assess that, we need an independent characterization of the observation base. We are again lost in the mists, since the doctrinal and conceptual theses appear to need each other to identify the "sufficient" or "adequate" observation base. But in any case, even with only some guesses about that, after the admission of defeat for the doctrinal part, Carnap's conceptual reconstruction failed. So both parts of the program failed.

13. To be quite candid, I share Quine's insistence that factual, descriptive theories should be allocated to the empirical sciences. Philosophers fall wrongly into the temptations of armchair science when they don't.

14. The strictest conception requires that the theories be in principle reducible to physics—if not physics today then physics later. Somewhat outside our present context but a striking example is Hartry Field's well-known article on truth: physicalism requires that the theory of reference and truth be in principle reducible to a description of physical properties and relations between utterances and environment.

15. See Giere, *Explaining Science and Science Without Laws*, and Laudan, "Normative Naturalism." (See further the note below on Giere's views.) The naturalism sometimes seems to be limited to the exclusion of point-wise identified instances of the supernatural. Moreover, the writer may or may not maintain that the having of values and goals in the community being described is reducible to its physical or biological characteristics, but that is not to the point here.

16. My reasons for the choice of this term will become clear in the last lecture. Here I should at least say that it is not meant to be derogatory, despite the fact that the objectifying epistemologies are precisely the ones I shall be criticizing.

17. In some contexts, "voluntarism" connotes such ancillary ideas as the supremacy of will and power and the absence of any higher values than self-interest to guide our choices. In my usage, no such ideas are associated.

18. In these recent cases the codes to look for are assertions to the effect that the position taken is "methodological" rather than "theoretical." The two sorts of views tend to be intertwined. For example, in Giere, *Explaining Science,* we find first the factual thesis: "Naturalism . . . is the view that theories come to be accepted (or not) through a natural process involving both individual judgment and social interaction. No appeal to supposed rational principles of theory choice is involved" (p. 7). But then we come to the methodological version: "the view that all human activities are to be understood as entirely natural phenomena, as are the activities of chemicals or animals" (p. 8). In Giere's more recent *Science Without Laws,* his naturalism is explicitly and emphatically methodological. Although still accompanied by certain (putatively) factual theses about human functioning, Giere has no sympathy for what he calls "metaphysical naturalism."

19. I should emphasize again that in this context "objectifying" is not a derogatory term; it is used here to indicate an important aspect of scientific inquiry.

20. These may not all be obvious examples of objectifying epistemologies in the sense defined. For example, I take reliabilism to include the theory that there is a certain psychological process that functions as an input-output device, taking in information and processing it in reliable ways to ways into appropriate propositional attitudes. But it may include more. (Thanks to Robert Adams and Keith DeRose for discussion on this subject.) As I will point out below, it is in any case not easy to find a pure example of such an epistemology, despite the rhetoric used in presentation.

21. Frege, review of Husserl's *Philosophy of Arithmetic.*

22. Kitcher, "The Naturalist's Return." It seems to me that Kitcher trades on a biased dichotomy (Frege/logicism vs. naturalism) but correctly points out how psychologism came back into vogue (as part of the reaction against positivism).

23. Leeds, "Constructive Empiricism," pp. 203–4.

24. Compare this with the reflection principle, which I do advocate (see my "Belief and the Will" and "Belief and the Problem of Ulysses and the Sirens"). To accord with that principle is to have one's present opinions in line with the disjunction (to put the matter briefly though imprecisely) of what one foresees as one's possible later opinions. This allows quite explicitly that we foresee ourselves as changing our opinion in unforeseen ways. The objectionable

feature I have here pointed out is that this stops at a certain level, namely, the scientific basis on which the naturalist erects a theory of cognition.

25. In his *Introduction to Metaphysics* (1953, late in his life), Heidegger described Europe as metaphysically caught between Russia and America; I see philosophy today just as uneasily situated between the metaphysician and the naturalist. Each says that what we can know depends on whether we are properly functioning and then adds a putative basis of fact on which to determine what functions properly. Thus all questions in epistemology are reduced to factual questions to be answered on the basis of what we take ourselves to know. As I see it, the central questions for epistemology are not of that sort— nor are they questions asking for value judgments in the sense of subjective preference.

26. I wish to thank Keith DeRose, Robert Adams, and Laurie Paul for an interesting correspondence on this and related questions after the Terry Lectures. DeRose wrote about the problem I raised for "objectifying" epistemologies—that "[t]he real problem is for any of us who would want a theory—the kind of theory that states how things are in the world—of how we cognitively interact with the world—and that should be all of us. . . . And the problem is that any such theory will include some current science that is subject to revision/revolution and so, according to any such theory, any such future revisions that might take place would be mistakes. If I've got the problem right, then the solution would seem to be to develop a stance toward our theories that would allow us to revise them." About the first part I answered that we want empirical science to study everything, including cognition, but that I do not think that we should want such theories in epistemology. Obviously I applaud all of empirical science; and people can wear many hats; but I don't applaud philosophical activity that has the form of scientific theorizing but is not at all part of genuine empirical science. (For actual attempts at such naturalized epistemology I have further arguments to the effect that real science does not support the assumptions behind them; see my "False Hopes of Traditional Epistemology"). Second, the point about revisability, the fragility of our opinions and theories, and the likelihood that we will need to revise them does indeed extend to all factual opinion and all scientific theories. Many philosophers and scientists too have written about how scientists are meant to hold their theories "nondogmatically"—and of course that is part of what empiricists point to when they want to encourage people to learn a lesson from science. I agree, but I think that we don't understand very well what it means. In fact, I think that the descriptive part of epistemology, even after so many centuries, is woefully and shamefully inadequate. We should have useful and quite nontheoretical descriptions of most of our common epistemic attitudes—let alone of those that are propositional attitudes. These include the many varieties of belief: conditional belief, supposition, degrees of belief, full and partial belief, and certainly "undogmatic belief." Just to show how puzzling it seems to me, let's imagine Carl Hempel

talking about one of his favorite examples. He says: "(1) I fully believe that all crows are black. (2) Of course I will give up that belief if I ever encounter a white crow." Now, it does not matter whether you construe (2) as a promise or as a prediction; it is clearly vacuous in the mouth of someone who truthfully asserts (1). It is like saying to a child that you will persuade Santa Claus to bring a bicycle if you meet him—or that you will build her a tree house if you get a Nobel Prize in architecture. Well, of course, it is really not like that, but who has an account of how it is different? I can raise similar problems for conditional probability. In fact, the whole subject of how to express opinions about your own future opinions, without falling into contradiction or incoherence, is a very difficult one. There is literature on that too, but it does not go very far yet (see further my "Belief and the will" and "Belief and the Problem of Ulysses and the Sirens"). So, to sum up, I do think there should be genuine scientific theories about cognition, as about everything else. I also think that there are really interesting problems about the epistemic attitudes we properly take toward scientific theories (about any subject whatever) and that those problems are something epistemologists should be working on. But I do not think that it is a fruitful enterprise in epistemology to be writing factual theories about cognition.

27. This is Isaac Levi's term, serving as the title of one of his books. The book is important in this context as a pointer to the continuing traditions of pragmatism in philosophy but also for alerting us to an example of someone pursuing this epistemology while placing subjective probability (rather than knowledge in a traditional sense) at the heart of epistemic description.

28. It also embodies that of the existentialists, to the extent that they address these sorts of problems. Recall Sartre's Kierkegaardian example of Abraham spoken to by the angel.

29. Compare my "Values and the Heart's Command."

30. For that reason Sellars's answer is not so much a direct answer as a schema, a schematic answer, so to speak. The underdetermined parameters, relating to what we and our community will take as satisfactory by way of explanation, are crucial to the content of Sellars's view. We are therefore left a bit dissatisfied, but his schematic generality may after all be proper to philosophical epistemology.

31. This is a main theme common to the three commentaries on Larry Laudan's normative naturalism by Doppelt, Leplin, and Rosenberg, and to Laudan's reply.

32. Sellars's view of the telos of belief and opinion reappears in more general, and to my mind much more tenable even if not less controversial, form in Catherine Elgin's *Considered Judgment.*

33. James, "The Will to Believe."

34. James, "The Sentiment of Rationality."

35. This point remains correct if we describe opinion in gradations of belief: the more probable is the less informative, and vice versa.

36. I owe the term "information economy" to Jeffrey Foss's insightful "Materialism, Reduction, Replacement, and the Place of Consciousness in Science."

37. What about that vaunted inference to the best explanation? Such an inference will increase the informational content of our opinion. But this virtue will be balanced against the likelihood of preserving truth. As for any putative rule, any nontrivial inductive tactic, we'll have a serious coherence constraint. If we are going to follow any such rule, we had better be of the opinion that its product is more likely to be true, or to eliminate error, than any of its rivals. The shortest route to that conclusion is some general view to the effect that explanatoriness—or whatever the given rule trades on—is a sign of truth. At this point the plausibility begins to fade. To this day no one has been able to make such a case for explanation, despite the prominence it has enjoyed in philosophical thinking. See further my *Laws and Symmetry*, ch. 6, secs. 4 and 5; ch. 7, sec. 4.

38. See further my "False Hopes of Traditional Epistemology."

39. But thanks to Paul Teller for forcefully pointing out that I need at least to touch on it.

40. See Suppe, "Credentialling Scientific Claims."

41. I am expressing part of the constructive empiricist story about science, a part that has certainly been contested as well. See my *Scientific Image*, pp. 12–13, "Empiricism in the Philosophy of Science," sec. 6 (pp. 276–81) and *Laws and Symmetry*, p. 150 and ch. 8, sec. 4.

42. There is another challenge that may well come right on the heels of my critique of objectifying epistemologies. Those, I argued, are themselves too vulnerable to scientific revolution, in that their picture of our epistemic progress itself threatens to dissolve during relevantly radical revolutionary change. Is this true also of the voluntarist epistemologies? In principle yes, but not in the same way. Such a voluntarist position is not a theory of how we function in nature. The epistemic enterprise cannot be naturalized. The voluntarist terms of assessment are evaluative and applicable only when certain commitments and goals are avowed as our own. But the elements of a stance other than belief are of course indirectly vulnerable to changes in belief. Suppose for example that Paul Churchland convinced us to see such terms as "belief," "intention," and "commitment" as theoretical terms in a discredited folk psychology. (Churchland assigns these roughly the same status that we now give to such terms as "phlogiston," "entelechy" or "caloric fluid.") Then we could no longer conceive of ourselves in terms crucial to a voluntarist epistemology. But this specter is a far cry from the sorts of changes that would nullify objectifying epistemologies grounded in current cognitive science, physiology, biology, chemistry, or physics. Almost nothing in these lectures will still be relevant or even intelligible once our view of ourselves as intentioning deliberative agents and subjects bites the dust. The possible coherence of this skeptical doubt I am content to leave aside.

43. I've advocated this view of rationality in several contexts; see my "Sulla

realtà degli enti matematici," *Scientific Image* (ch. 4, sec. 1, specifically its last paragraph), "Empiricism in Philosophy of Science" (specifically p. 248), and *Laws and Symmetry,* pp. 171–76.

44. Possibly apocryphal; always attributed, among climbers, to their favorite climbing hero of the moment.

45. The wager is found in Pascal's *Pensées* 418 (pp. 149–53 in the Penguin edition). Academic writing about it tends to fill me with such dismay that I can't bear to mention most of it. One wonderful exception is provided by Catherine Chevalley, to whom I am greatly indebted, in her *Pascal: Contingence et Probabilité.* In what follows I characterize Pascal's thought here with some hesitation as a departure from the decision paradigm that he introduced. Perhaps I should say: it is a departure from the more familiar "Bayesian" understanding in which we now normally first encounter that decision formula. There the formula is presented as providing the uniquely rational decision to be made, given the individual's input of utilities and probabilities. But that Bayesian understanding I take to be mistaken, a miscreant born of the uneasy marriage of probabilism with an incorrect or at least inappropriate traditional notion of rationality. The Bayesian says: it is irrational not to act so as to maximize your expected utility; reason dictates acting so as to maximize expected utility; to maximize expected utility is the rationally compelled decision. This is a sentiment entirely inconsistent, as I understand it, with Pascal's text.

46. This correspondence (1654) is often, only a little arbitrarily, designated as the first modern text on the subject (the first monograph being that of Huygens (1656–57), written with partial knowledge of this correspondence).

47. Arnauld, *Logic, or the Art of Thinking.*

48. There is perhaps a certain echo of Saint Paul here (faith: the sum of our hopes and the evidence of things unseen).

49. This is a modification of Pascal's decision formula if that formula was meant to apply universally to all conceivable options. There is no reason to take that to have been Pascal's intent. Bayesian decision theory so formulated is certainly not tenable.

50. Tossing a coin is fine when we are indifferent between the options—but only if we are truly indifferent, and not just in the technical sense that the reasons for neither side outweigh those for the other. The telling example is William Styron's *Sophie's Choice.*

51. A Dutch Book is a (compound) gamble that leads to a loss under all possible conditions. Whether or not a given gamble is thus seems to be largely a matter of interpretation, however. If I buy medical insurance that pays 85 percent of my medical costs, then I clearly lose money whether I get sick or not, namely the cost of the insurance plus 15 percent of the medical costs. But if I figure in my sense of security, risk aversion, or love of danger, the assessment may change.

52. Decision theory is of course applicable if the parameters are already

fixed, that is, if we lay out our values and probabilities beforehand. Once we do that, our reasoning with them is constrained by coherence conditions. See further my *Laws and Symmetry*, ch. 13, secs. 1 and 2.

53. Sartre, *Emotions*.

54. That is no longer an egregious position; see Neu, *A Tear Is an Intellectual Thing*.

55. I want to thank Pierre Livet for illuminating conversations on the subject of emotion, including his sharply critical view of Sartre's theory.

56. Arnold Burms pointed out to me that Sartre apparently noticed this difficulty, for he introduced a distinction in that passage on joy: "il faut distinguer entre la joie—sentiment, qui représente un équilibre, un état adapté, et la joie—émotion." But the distinction is not further elucidated there.

57. Jerry Neu pointed out that shaking a fist while angry may not be voodoo behavior at all but "venting" of emotion, or alternatively threatening to the target. What I have in mind here is fuming, raging, fist-shaking in the absence of the target. In such a case one might say, "I understand why you are angry, but this [behavior] is not doing you any good at all, it won't change anything, it does not help anything, you are just getting yourself more upset to no good purpose." These words presuppose that the behavior is vestigial aggressive action, that its point if any is to be effective, although it clearly is not: precisely what one would say of a superstitious recourse to magic.

Lecture 4. Experience: (Epistemic) Life Without Foundations

1. With reference to our earlier religious parallel we can recall here the early Christians' portrayal of themselves as fulfilling the Jewish sacred scriptures. The New Testament depicts a sustained act of (re)interpretation of those scriptures so as to allow this portrayal. Similarities to how contemporary science relates itself to "classical" modern science will spring to the eye below.

2. Although scientific revolutions provide our proximate topic of concern, my underlying aim is of course to explore prospects for an empiricist epistemology. The last lecture introduced the elements of will, choice, and emotion; this one will explore the delicate issues of ambiguity and "rule following," with tolerance for ambiguity. An abbreviated version of this lecture, delivered as part of the Chaire Cardinal Mercier Lectures at the Université Catholique de Louvain-la-Neuve in December 1999, has appeared in the *Revue Philosophique de Louvain* as "La fin de l'empirisme?"

3. I realize that I'm oversimplifying. How light could have the same velocity, a universal constant, in all frames of references was no less puzzling or incomprehensible to the Newtonian. So we know very well where his next stumbling block would have come. Einstein's searching critique of Newtonian terms had to go deeper. What precisely do the terms "length" and "simultaneous" carry by way of hidden assumptions? Find some, and again a hidden

collapse of possible distinctions, once uncovered, allows for radical innovation. These moves are not lapses of sense or violations of reason, although they violate the hidden theoretical assumptions that structured the old language.

4. Feyerabend, *Conquest of Abundance,* pp. 32–33. See further my review, "Sham Victory of Abstraction."

5. See Reichenbach, "Rationalism and Empiricism," and my "False Hopes of Traditional Epistemology."

6. Feyerabend, "Classical empiricism." Feyerabend draws on the account of Popkin, *History of Skepticism,* pp. 70–82. I shall discuss Feyerabend's construal of Veron's argument, with no presumption that it is historically accurate, nor even that it matches Popkin's understanding of the same material. My interest is in how Feyerabend's argument bears on the possibility of empiricist positions in epistemology.

7. A note about philosophical terminology: In epistemology , as in ethics, we should distinguish between positions and policies on one hand and ("meta-") views concerning such positions and policies on the other. Most philosophical discussion proceeds on the latter level of course. "Foundationalism" sometimes denotes just the metaview that foundationalist positions are the only viable epistemic positions. But that is not the sense in which I use it here.

8. The phrase "proportion belief to the evidence" occurs in Hume's "Of Miracles" and near enough in Locke, *Essay Concerning Human Understanding* (4. 15. 5), as well as in Russell's discussion of William James in his *History of Western Philosophy* (p. 770). The phrase has packed into it a traditional epistemological assumption about there being a natural, objective scale for the weighing of evidence and the proportioning of belief, which should not be allowed uncritical play in our discussion, of course. Thanks to Gideon Rosen for the references.

9. Interestingly, Lewis's remark illustrated a difficulty in contemporary epistemology. Suppose that we try to characterize an ideal rational agent (as in Bayesian epistemology or decision theory), and then ask for the criteria of rationality applicable to us non-ideal agents. The injunction to learn from how the ideal rational agent would proceed also has its difficulties of interpretation, in much the same way.

10. Newton, *Principles,* II, 160 ff., p. 400.

11. See Laudan, *Science and Hypothesis.*

12. Descartes (who may have heard the argument at La Flêche, where he was a student) had seen a third possibility: a foundation, but one that can be demonstrated a priori, admitting of no logical alternative. Catherine Chevalley aptly points out that Descartes and Pascal both saw, in the mid-seventeenth century, that if we conceive of science more geometrico, as in principle an axiomatic system, then science as a whole rests on nothing at all. Descartes concluded that in order for there to be knowledge, therefore, the axioms must be a priori, whereas Pascal concluded that knowledge can have no foundation.

Pascal, though in existential despair, was not driven to skeptical despair. In this prelude, too much ignored in the history of philosophy, our entire *problématique* is already foreshadowed.

13. I can certainly understand the reasons why Kant's critical philosophy could present itself as solution at the time. But from our present vantage point, we must see that solution through the eyes, at best, of the neo-Kantians, reconsidering it in the light of the new geometry and physics that appeared after the mid-nineteenth century—and furthermore, in the light of the Wittgensteinian critique of modern philosophy's conception of the mind and its "faculties."

14. The idea is not peculiarly Bacon's; the more famous injunction is Galileo's in *Il Saggiatore:* "The true philosophy is written in that great book of nature (questo grandissimo libro, io dico l'universo) which lies ever open before our eyes but which no one can read unless he has first learned to understand the language and to know the characters in which it is written. It is written in mathematical language, and the characters are triangles, circles, and other geometric figures" (translated in Drake, pp. 237–38).

15. For a lengthier exploration of this topic, see my "Literate Experience."

16. This is an old point, a staple of the idealist tradition's critique of the older empiricism. It needed to be made again in the twentieth century, after rather naïve attempts to reinstate a sort of "experience fundamentalism," and was made, brilliantly, by, e.g., Wilfrid Sellars and Donald Davidson. (See, e.g., Davidson, "Very Idea of a Conceptual Scheme.")

17. There are at least these two reasons; I make no pretense of an exhaustive analysis.

18. I want to acknowledge here my debt to Filip Buekens, "Observing in a Space of Reasons."

19. See further my "Literate Experience" and "From Vicious Circle to Infinite Regress."

20. For the logic and semantics of self-attribution see David Lewis, "Attitudes de dicto and de se" and Perry, *Problem of the Essential Indexical.*

21. There is a third important point. The event, his experience of winning a million dollars, is entirely public. It is not a private drama on a mental stage, accessible only to Ric O. Certainly, we can't conclude that he had the experience in question unless we know the form of his response (first-person judgment? self-attribution? self-location?) But what happened to him is a publicly observable event. The judgment may be made either out loud or *sotto voce* (as all reading can be done either way), but that is hardly crucial to the question whether he had the experience.

I say there are no private dramas enacted on mental stages, somewhere between me and the publicly accessible world. You may reply that then it is fine to stick me with a pin, because obviously I never have pain or pleasure. Such a reply would be predicated on the philosophical view I oppose. The pin would hurt, and I would feel pain. But feeling pain is only verbally like feeling a toe in my sock. The denial of some separate domain of entities only contradicts a philosophical theory, a particular philosophical account of what we all agree on. Similarly, in the flower example above, I would not deny that (quite possibly) I will be the only person who will ever know that I initially took the candy wrapper to be a flower. That really happened; I remember it, and perhaps I never told anyone. It does not follow that there is a mental entity whose image resides in my memory—except metaphorically speaking. On the other hand, my denial of a realm of mental entities does not imply advocacy of materialism, at least not in any worthwhile sense. What I advocate here is philosophical hygiene, not revisionary metaphysics of any sort.

Nowhere in the story do we see allusion to some further event, an "illiterate" experience that is distinct from (in between?) what happened to Ric O. and his literate response. A psychologist might wish to postulate such an intermediate event or construct a model with many hidden parameters. Philosophers have no business doing so; philosophers should not be armchair scientists. If they are, their every hidden variable is a red herring, a snare, and a deception.

22. See further the last sections of my "Putnam's Paradox" and "Elgin on Lewis's Putnam's Paradox." Coherence is a large and increasingly important topic for the present approach to epistemology. See further my "Belief and the Will" and "Belief and the Problem of Ulysses and the Sirens."

23. One suddenly feels the nineteenth-century idealist temptation to declare the contradiction real, and thus the demonstration that we live solely in Appearance, in Maya, in Illusion, and not in Reality at all. Shades of Bradley and McTaggart!

24. Although "Classical Empiricism" was one of Feyerabend's early papers, this theme (how the problem of incommensurability is, as it were, generated by a blindness to or intolerance for ambiguity) is developed in his later work, most fully in his posthumous *Conquest of Abundance*. See further my review, "Sham Victory of Abstraction."

25. I am still calling it a rule, but of course this requires a much broader sense of "rule" than that of recipe-like rules mobilized in deductive or algorithmic reasoning, which is meant when we deny that rationality is a matter of rule-following. As Paul Teller emphasized to me, we need a more general notion of rule to characterize this aspect of practice, which is quite unlike philosophers' standard examples of rules of chess or football.

26. See Cushing, *Quantum Mechanics*, as well as David Albert, "Bohm's Alternative to Quantum Theory" or ch. 7 of his *Quantum Mechanics and Experience* for exposition of the theory. I emphasize that I am not an advocate of Bohm's alternative.

27. Feyerabend discusses this only briefly, cryptically, ironically. If the rule of faith is actually empty but available for polemical use, we gain a terrible new freedom. Social factors, party lines, will drive debate when rationally compelling grounds are missing. But: "Party lines are not the problem. Problems arise

only when an attempt is made to turn the subjective conviction that makes a certain party line stand out into an infallible objective judge who withstands criticism. . . . [T]he democratic way in which praise, blame, and dogmatism are now distributed and the humanitarian way in which the word of a clever man is taken seriously, even too seriously, allow us to greet [this "Protestant" or "empiricist" practice] as the dawn of an even more enlightened future" (*Problem of Empiricism*, p. 51) This is still Feyerabend at least halfway into ironic mode, but there is a serious conviction at the core of his irony. In his own work, going forward from this critique of bygone epistemologies, we see him struggling with this task. The task not yet understood in the seventeenth century is as yet unfinished in the twentieth. Feyerabend put his shoulder to the wheel with the rest of us, even if he liked to chastise us scathingly from time to time for our laggard ways.

28. See my "Manifest Image" for the vagueness and ambiguity in mathematics and natural science, a theme more recently pursued by Paul Teller in forthcoming work.

29. See further my "The World We Speak Of."

30. See further van Fraassen and Sigman, "Interpretation in Science and in the Arts," on which I draw for this part.

31. I am omitting here a much-needed discussion of the distinctions to be drawn between vagueness and ambiguity; see the sources cited in the last few notes. The classic source on vagueness and ambiguity in literary criticism is Empson, *Seven Types of Ambiguity;* for a more theoretical treatment see Soames, *Understanding Truth,* chs. 6 and 7.

32. William Whewell, "On the Nature and Conditions of Inductive Science," p. 51.

33. Leplin, *Scientific Realism,* p. 2.

34. See Earman, *Primer on Determinism,* ch. 3 (especially sec. 8) and my *Laws and Symmetry,* ch. 10, sec. 4.

35. "Seemed," because the remaining incompleteness in the interpretation was of course not perceived. We should also add that the incompleteness is different at different historical stages. Perhaps after the addition of the conservation laws, mechanics as officially codified (say, around 1890) was deterministic. The diverging axiomatizations of classical mechanics that appeared over the next hundred years show, however, that the treatment of mass had still been left ambiguous. Those who took Mach's and Hertz's monographs on mechanics seriously could have perceived this then, but this sort of awareness grows slowly.

36. This parallels of course how Feyerabend sees the rule of *Sola Scriptura* functioning in the Protestant community; see further the next lecture. We may be able to discern other parallels to religious and ideological conversion. The general picture of Saint Paul's conversion seems similar to what I described here. From his prior point of view the new gospel made literally no sense; from

his later perspective its elements can actually be discerned in (the parts he then still values of) what he had accepted beforehand.

Lecture 5. What Is Science—and What Is It to Be Secular?

1. Let me explain one reason why it seemed so much better to ask what is it to be secular rather than what is it to be religious. In order to be understood by both sides, one can only focus on what the religious see as but one side of the equation, the human side. Philosophers of religion tend to focus for that reason on the inner and external changes that come with conversion, the hallmarks of a believing life, the criteria for backsliding, the place of rituals and myth in shaping intentions and behavior, and so forth. The religious are right to complain that from their point of view, this misses the point of what is studied, but that complaint has no right of entry here. For the religious, even while seeing themselves as falling far short, in the end the only true religion is mystical religion, and the only true experience that of being face to face with something or someone wholly Other, though manifest in the same world that we also know in other ways. To be satisfied with an account of the human side is all very well only for someone who feels quite certain of knowing pretty well what there is in the universe and what that universe is like. I have no such certainty. By choosing to focus on what it is to be secular I hope to avoid some of these pitfalls. At least the secular will not complain that I have narrowly focused on just the human side alone.

2. See my "Theory of Tragedy and of Science." In the question "What is science?" I focus there on the aim component as most important, in part because that is so much at issue between scientific realists and empiricists. Here my concern is different, namely, with the manner and form of scientific inquiry.

3. I am taking my cue here from an area and epoch of philosophy distinctly unfashionable today: the existentialism and existential phenomenology that flourished just after the Second World War. On this topic those philosophers continue a tradition begun by Kant (see the quotation below) and continued by Edmund Husserl's discussion of the character of the Galilean and Cartesian demarcation of scientific theorizing in *Crisis of European Sciences*, pt. 3A, secs. 34–35. Below I will also bring into this the thought of another currently unpopular figure, the existentialist theologian Rudolf Bultmann, who drew heavily on the philosophy of Sartre and Heidegger. Bultmann broaches the question of what science is in the context of the further questions whether theology is or can be a science, how history differs from natural science, and how scientific questions differ from historical questions. The origin of his ideas is fairly clear in preceding European thought, especially Husserl's description of what he calls the natural attitude or natural orientation. The contrasts drawn, however, are not the same. Bultmann is more directly indebted to Heidegger,

Being and Time, pp. 413–15, Heidegger's essay "Die Zeit des Weltbildes," and Merleau-Ponty, *Phenomenology of Perception,* pp. 241–42, 300–3.

4. Bultmann, *New Testament and Mythology,* p. 46: "To speak of a field of objects is to indicate that the researcher stands over against the subject matter; it is given precisely as an object."

5. These negative connotations are undoubtedly allied to the reasons why objectivity in certain contexts tends to strike us as failing in respect, even as impious, blasphemous, or dehumanizing. Although I will suggest that academic theologians can also engage in objectifying inquiry, they are of course not to be thought of as oblivious to such concerns. (Alvin Plantinga referred me here to Calvin's *Institutes of the Christian Religion,* bk. 3, ch. 2, 16. See also ch. 9, "Sealed in Our Hearts," in Plantinga, *Warranted Christian Belief.*) It is important, however, to distinguish what it is in itself from the ways in which such distancing may operate in some contexts.

6. I learned this way of putting it, as well as gaining other insight into the process, from Steven Tainer.

7. I've benefited much at this point and below from discussions and correspondence with Alvin Plantinga and also with Eleonore Stump. Although I realize that some of what I am writing here may seem to be indicting academic philosophical theology and philosophy of religion, I'll readily except both these friends' writings. I would like to mention especially Eleonore Stump's Stob Lectures at Calvin College (issued as a booklet by Calvin College Press) as realizing some of my ideals for such philosophical engagement.

8. "Quantities" is the more inclusive term, since we can think of properties as two-valued quantities. I am following the common practice in foundational studies of physics. There is a more traditional terminology, which I am at pains to avoid. I am thinking of such phrases as "the frog qua amphibious organism," "the environment insofar as it provides a habitat for frogs," "the frog as electro-mechanical system," and so forth. These peculiarly philosophical terms are hyperintensional, and although we have come quite far in our grasp of intensional logic, I continue to be deeply skeptical of our presumed understanding of the hyperintensional. Such phrases tend to breed metaphysics. In any case, with the understanding gained in foundational studies of science in our century there is no excuse for a discussion framed in this obscure scholastic fashion.

9. There is a good deal more to be said about the "manner" of scientific inquiry at this level. A philosopher must puzzle over the curious epistemic status of data as simultaneously assumed to be reliable and regarded as defeasible. (See further my "Against Naturalized Epistemology.") The data model too is a created object, although definitely a function of the input from nature—it is, as it were, a secondary phenomenon created in the laboratory that becomes the primary phenomenon to be saved by the theory. See further Teller, "Whither Constructive Empiricism?"

10. To my mind the best study of this aspect, though not perfect, is Clark Glymour's *Theory and Evidence* (the "bootstrap method"). In different ways both Poincaré and Joseph Sneed had drawn attention to the crucial point: some quantities, introduced in these hypotheses, are truly theoretical, since they can be measured only on the assumption that the system investigated satisfies those hypotheses. There is no vicious circularity here. A favorable outcome is by no means guaranteed, for the various thus measured values are new answers nature gives us, and they may or may not conform to that assumption.

11. The above is not meant as a chronological description. Experimentation and observation occur as part of three activities: exploration, testing, and writing theory by other means. In the above I followed the exploration format, which we do see, though rarely in pure form: the entire inquiry is typically guided by both previous theory and ideas for new hypotheses. For writing theory by other means see my *Scientific Image*, ch. 4, sec. 2, and for exploratory (as opposed to theory-driven) experimentation see Scheinle, "Entering New Fields." A look at the examples will show that these all fit into the pattern described as objectifying inquiry.

12. Typically the new parameters derive from some extant scientific discipline of wider scope (think of the introduction of electric charge into the study of frog physiology). See further my "Science, materialism, and false consciousness."

13. Bultmann, *New Testament and Mythology*, p. 142. Further references appear in the text.

14. Bultmann is remarkably insightful, well before Thomas Kuhn's discussion in *The Structure of Scientific Revolutions* educated us about this topic. Bultmann's background source for this insight is undoubtedly Husserl's *Crisis of European Sciences* (Husserl also included in his discussion of Galileo the demarcation of domains by means of "relevant" quantities).

15. Are any of the above aspects peculiar to empirical science? In a strict sense, only aspect 2, "putting nature to the question"; but even for that aspect we can see a corresponding general feature. For whatever the domain of inquiry is, the account or representation constructed as its product needs to be constantly accountable to that domain.

16. Bultmann (*New Testament*, pp. 140–41) gives other examples of cognition that are not objectifying, but they are not examples of forms of inquiry.

17. I am drawing here on Edgerton, *Heritage of Giotto's Geometry*, ch. 6. See also his illuminating discussion in ch. 3 of Fra Lippi's *Annunciation*, wherein the miraculous conception is rendered in the terms of Roger Bacon's geometric optics. I thank the students in my freshmen seminar (The History, Philosophy, and Mythology of Light, 1998) for discussion of this development.

18. See Chadwick, *Secularization of the European Mind*, pp. 90–91. See also his note to this remark with G. J. Holyoake's own account of the coining of "secularism" and "secularist": "The term 'Secularism' has been chosen . . . as expressing a certain positive and ethical element, which the terms 'Infidel',

'Sceptic', 'Atheist' do not express" (ibid., 271; see also n. 4). Holyoake was editor of the *Present,* a secular review, and active in the so-called secular societies formed in various English towns from 1852 onward to promote the spread of secularist opinions. These included the doctrine that morality should be based solely on regard to the well-being of mankind in the present life, to the exclusion of considerations that might be drawn from belief in God or in a future state, as well as the view that education, or the education provided at the public cost, should be purely secular.

19. Goethe, *From My Life,* pt. 3, bk. 11; pp. 363–64. Speaking of d'Holbach's *Système de la Nature,* Goethe writes, "To us it seemed so gray, so Cimmerian, so deathly that we could scarcely bear the sight of it." Thanks to Arthur Zajonc for the reference.

20. This lecture was delivered in New York in 1968 and published in *God's Presence in History.*

21. Ibid., p. 47. Further references appear in the text. The terms of the last clause are imported from Buber's discussion, of which more below.

22. See, e.g., Osler, *Divine Will and the Mechanical Philosophy,* p. 235 and references therein.

23. See Kuhn, *Copernican Revolution,* p. 111 for Aquinas's difficulties with, e.g., the New Testament descriptions of Jesus' ascension into heaven, in the last stages of the Christian assimilation of Aristotle's *De Caelo.*

24. See Kuhn, *Copernican Revolution,* p. 191–199 for a historical sketch. C. S. Lewis's *Discarded Image* gives a more nostalgic account of what we lost in this transition.

25. "It is entirely possible that in a past mythical world picture truths may be rediscovered that were lost during a period of enlightenment; and theology has every reason to ask whether this may be possible in the case of the world picture of the New Testament. But it is impossible to re-pristinate a past world picture by sheer resolve, especially a mythical world picture, now that all of our thinking is irrevocably formed by science.... [O]ne can [change in this respect] only insofar as, on the basis of certain facts that impress one as real, one perceives the impossibility of the prevailing world picture and either modifies it or develops a new one . . . for example, as a result of Nicolaus Copernicus's discovery or as a result of atomic theory; or, again, because romanticism discovers that the human subject is richer and more complicated than the world view of the Enlightenment and of idealism allowed for." (*New Testamant,* p. 3). Bultmann wrote this a decade or so before Kuhn supported it through his studies in the history of science.

26. See further my "World of Empiricism" for a discussion of the debate with Karl Jaspers and the relation of this to certain issues about theoretical terms in the language of science.

27. Confusingly, he also writes there, "Scientific anthropologies always al-

ready presuppose a certain understanding of existence, which is—consciously or unconsciously—a matter of decision." This may be read as suggesting that there can be rival scientific anthropologies that presuppose different understandings of existence, so once again, secular and Christian scientific theories. But he certainly does not have in mind here differences in content of the hypotheses; it concerns, rather, his understanding of how the human sciences (of which the paradigm for him is history) differ from the natural sciences. He does quite clearly envisage the same scientific activity and the same scientific theories incorporated in different ways of being in the world through different understandings of existence. In this way it seems to me that Bultmann is in sharp disagreement with Plantinga in his understanding of science and its relation to secularism.

28. Chalmers, *Conscious Mind.*

29. There are many arguments in the literature against reductionism; see, e.g., the papers in Agazzi, *Problem of Reductionism,* and especially that by Suppes, "Can Psychological Software Be Reduced to Physiological Hardware?" But like the above remarks about mind-body dualism and qualia, I mean to note this only as background. The point I wish to make about the concept of a person and objectification is a different point.

30. The judgment that some being is a person can be true or false, it can enter as a component in complex statements constructed with sentential connectives and quantifiers, and so on. It does not follow from this that the standard truth-and-reference semantics dear to many philosophers is adequate to dealing with them. I accept that we have difficult tasks in philosophy of language but I don't think that we should hold up our thinking about objectivity until they are solved. What I say is in any case not provocative within analytic philosophy in the way it would have been a few decades ago; although I am grateful for this without being able to accept, say, Simon Blackburn's noncognitivist account or Michael Smith's cognitivist rival, both of which seem to me to be ensnared in the confusions of naturalism.

31. For a philosophically illuminating dramatization, see Peter Høeg's novel *The Woman and the Ape.*

32. I add this for the sake of argument. Unfortunately, it invites the hackneyed question of whether God exists or whether God is real, a question which it is impossible to hear today unburdened by the concepts in which philosophers have simulated religion. There is a real question: does it ever really happen that anyone anywhere encounters God? I will leave it as an exercise for the readers to amuse themselves by imagining how this could be chosen as subject for an objectifying inquiry and what could come of that.

33. See further the discussion of science and myth in my "World of Empiricism."

34. Theology today offers some surprising variants on such themes; cf.

Hardwick, *Events of Grace*. Since physicalism is mainstream opinion in analytic philosophy, Hardwick contends, there is a clear need for a theology compatible with physicalism.

35. This is not a direct quotation from Cratylus 438–39 but is close enough in our present context, if classicists will forgive me.

Appendixes

1. Whitrow, *Structure and Evolution of the Universe*, p. 98.

2. The caution that empirical adequacy is stronger than what counts as success in practice (similarity in some respects between real system and model being enough) is well taken but does not affect the argument here.

3. In fact, scientific realists have some leeway on this issue. There will actually always be aspects of models that everyone agrees are not independently significant but were introduced there for mathematical convenience only. Therefore no reason of principle dictates necessarily that its models taken as whole structures must stand for the world as a whole. Hence, there is no reason of principle for the scientific realist to say that cosmology implies that there is such a thing as the (whole) world. Success could consist in every real physical system being adequately represented in the model, without there being a single physical system that is composed of all the others.

4. See further Savitt, "Selective Scientific Realism, Constructive Empiricism" and "Critical Notice of John Earman" for discussion of both Friedman and Earman in the context of the realism-antirealism issue.

5. This is actually misleading. A specific space-time is not a diffeomorphism invariant object. So it too is a "discarded image," if we look deeper into contemporary physics.

6. Compare my *Scientific Image*, p. 72. Savitt, "Selective Scientific Realism, Constructive Empiricism," argues convincingly that this is also the pattern in Friedman's own main example of the kinetic theory of heat in relation to atomic theory.

7. If I read Stephen Priest correctly, he proceeds on this assumption in his preface to *British Empiricists*. He indicates that he will leave the general historical question of what empiricism is aside—which presupposes that this is a well-posed question.

8. Woolhouse, *Empiricists*, pp. 1–2. (See further section 4 below, with reference to Loeb's more extended suggestion along these lines.)

9. Since we have quite a way to go through the history of this term, it may be useful for me to indicate here at the beginning how I see it. When I use the term without qualification or comment it is of course to be understood in its current standard sense in the philosophical literature. I do think that the term has such a sense—something reasonably called its "current standard sense"—in Western philosophy today. The term's criteria of use are not very strict or

extensive. For that reason it is possible for this use to evolve further and for novel positions (not previously envisaged and possibly in disagreement with all previously extant members of the term's extension) to be called empiricist. I hope that this view of the matter will be evidently tenable and plausible by the end of this terminological and (meta)historical discussion.

10. Bacon, *Novum Organum*, bk. 1, aph. 95, para. 64.

11. The thesis I mean here is that our knowledge of nature can be demonstrative, deduced from first principles known a priori, as opposed to gathered by induction from observational evidence. Happily rejection of the possibility of substantive a priori knowledge (which certainly belongs to the cluster of empiricist characteristics, it seems to me) does not imply any such view of induction and evidence.

12. Leibniz, *New Essays on Human Understanding*, p. 50 (numbering in translations follows the pagination of the Akademie-Verlag edition of the French text). The new translation by Remnant and Bennett uses the old term "empiric"; Mary Morris's translation, *The Philosophical Writings of Leibniz*, had "empiricists," which could be misleading, given current usage. There is a parallel passage in Leibniz's *Monadology*: "Men act like brutes in so far as the association of their perceptions results from the principle of memory alone, resembling the empiricist physicians who practice without theory; and we are simple empirics in three-fourths of our actions" (*Monadology*, p. 28; p. 538 in *Leibniz: Selections*).

13. I have benefited greatly from my colleague Beatrice Longuenesse's very helpful comments on a draft of this section as well as from two of her seminars on the *Critique of Pure Reason*.

14. One reading, advanced by Al-Azm and endorsed by Walsh, aligns the positions and arguments given in the antinomies with the positions on the sides of Newton and Leibniz in the Leibniz-Clarke correspondence. Surprisingly, the alignment has the theses on Newton's side and the antitheses (which Kant labels as "empiricist") on Leibniz's. (See Al-Azm, *Origins of Kant's Arguments;* Walsh, *Kant's Criticism of Metaphysics*, pp. 197–98.) As Longuenesse pointed out, Leibniz and Newton are not easily portrayed as pure cases of the two sides. Kant makes reference only to ancient philosophy, Epicureans and Platonists, but these are not easily seen as pure cases either, and he certainly does not mention Leibniz there by name. In the last chapter, where the empiricists are listed as those who hold that the origin of all knowledge is derived from experience (and even the origin of the modes of "knowledge through pure reason" is not independent of experience), Leibniz appears on the side opposed to the empiricists. Although I must agree that this constitutes prima facie evidence against the above interpretation, there were certainly also reasons to find Al-Azm's and Walsh's reasoning quite plausible. In any case I think that the point on divergent usage may stand: if a certain way of taking sides on the antinomies defines empiricism, then views on whether there are innate ideas do not, and vice versa.

15. The word "transcendental" in its various uses needs a little disentangling. Kant's transcendental idealism is not a doctrine consisting of transcendental assertions; on the contrary, the latter are the assertions involved in the sort of metaphysics that Kant is dismantling. In Kant's description (A466–A474; B497–502), empiricism means to allow of no such assertions. But when empiricism goes beyond this to a dogmatism of its own, it falls into the mistake of making contrary transcendental assertions. This remark initiates the critique of "transcendental empiricism" (as we should call it), the perennial reactionary pitfall for the empiricist rebellion.

16. The long speculative footnote about Epicurus appears to outline a sort of empiricism that would not be subject to this criticism, in which the antitheses are replaced by (not assertions but) "maxims for the speculative employment of reason."

17. Page references are to Robson and McRae, *Collected Works of John Stuart Mill*, vol. 8.

18. Mill, *Auguste Comte and Positivism*, p.121.

19. As pointed out by Anschutz, *Philosophy of J. S. Mill*, p. 74.

20. See, e.g., Mill's *Autobiography*, pp. 225–26.

21. Mill does assert explicitly that any claims we can make are in principle subject to revision. It is an open question for me just what the higher epistemic status is that he claims for the results of the methods of his *System of Logic*.

22. I think that this is his answer. I have never been able to assure myself that I have understood him on this score.

23. Loeb, *From Descartes to Hume*, pp. 25–36.

24. Copleston, *History of Philosophy*, vols. 4 and 5. T. H. Green's introduction to vol. 1 of Hume's *Treatise of Human Nature* (edited by him and T. H. Grose, London 1874) ran to 299 pages, presenting the Locke-Berkeley-Hume sequence from the British idealist point of view. The English translation of Kuno Fischer's history of philosophy appeared in 1887.

25. John Grier Hibben, *Problems of Philosophy*. Page references appear in the text.

26. Comte did not define his term "positive philosophy"; he makes it clear, however, that positive knowledge is restricted to knowledge of observed facts or their correlation and that such knowledge can be achieved only through the sciences, not through any extra- or meta-scientific inquiry. Only what admits of and can stand up to empirical testing counts as positive knowledge, and nothing else is knowledge.

27. Copleston refers to neopositivism as "the positivist mentality . . . becoming conscious of itself," 7:426–27. It seems to me that something like the view of Jaspers that he describes next could actually follow upon this, the dispute about philosophy as science being a mere quibble about words.

28. See further pp. 118 ff. in Delaney, *Science, Knowledge, and Mind*.

29. Bowne, *Immanence of God* (1905); see Copleston, vol. 8, ch. 13. In the title of my "Against Transcendental Empiricism," the term is used more broadly, not simply to refer to Bowne's position. I meant an empiricism that has fallen into the pitfall of making its own dogmatic transcendental assertions (in the above-noted sense established in Kant's *Critique*). The broad sense classifies the philosophical positions that include as their main thesis a claim about the way the world is, namely, that experience is our sole source of information, or something to that effect. Copleston also mentions that Dewey's teacher G. S. Morris called Hegel's philosophy "objective empiricism."

30. Comte's view of these matters is part of his view of human history, ahich he sees as parallel to the psychological development of the rational individual. This development has three stages: theological (infancy), metaphysical (youth), and positive (maturity). In the first, explanation is sought and provided in terms of personal agency by supernatural personal agents. In the second, personal agency is replaced (both in the request for explanation and in the answer supplied) by metaphysical abstractions, that is, experience-transcendent entities such as forces, nature or natures, essences, and causal powers. The positive stage is that of the mature scientific outlook, in which there is no such search for explanation. The mind concerns itself with empirical science, which is the systematic description of facts and correlations among them. From Comte's point of view, therefore, Bowne understood the critique of metaphysics but had regressed to infancy.

31. William James, *The Will to Believe*, p. vii. Further references appear in the text.

32. The preface does not include a statement of what monism is. One is tempted to think that it is presumably the neutral monism that Russell later came to maintain as well. I do not think that I can state its exact content, but it is to be contrasted with, for example, mind-body dualism. However, the pluralism that is its rival is explained at length and does not seem to be contrary merely to substance monism. Its most striking sentence is "There is no possible point of view from which the world can appear an absolutely single fact," which might codify what is now often called relativism or perspectivalism.

33. "Monism" is still in use, of course. One popular position in the philosophy of mind among analytic philosophers today is "substance monism/concept dualism." The option presupposes that one has made sense of the notion of substance sufficiently to understand the question whether there are more than one or only one (kind of) substance, in the relevant sense (not in the sense that monism is false because the world has toothpaste as well as marshmallow fluff).

34. That relations are real, and that there is direct perception of singular causal connections, are assertions that I can only classify as metaphysical. If James's radical empiricism is indeed a form of empiricism (and not related to empiricism as paste diamond is to diamond) then some metaphysical positions

fall under the classification of empiricism. But this is not a question of fact. It is a question of whether we will let James's use of the term "empiricism" figure thus in settling its eventual sense.

35. James, *Pragmatism*, p. 54.

36. Husserl, *Ideas*, First section, ch. 2, subsec. 19.

37. Ibid., subsec. 20.

38. John Dewey, "An Empirical Survey of Empiricisms," p. 4. Further references appear in the text.

39. His discussion of Locke and Hume later in the chapter makes clear that in "sense observation" (p. 75) he includes what used to be called "inner sense," i.e., observation of thoughts, perceptions, feelings, and the like. In this popular book the terminology appears to presuppose a given psychological classification of experiences. The discussion in *Experience and Prediction* should be the preferred source here.

40. Wesley Salmon, who was Reichenbach's student, has a different view of Reichenbach's philosophical position and development that should be noted here. In his "Empiricism: The Key Question," Salmon sees Reichenbach's *Experience and Prediction* not only as a rejection of foundationalism in epistemology (which it certainly is) but as defending scientific realism, mainly by means of a "common cause" argument. This requires a status for such arguments incompatible with the view that the principle of causality has been demoted to methodological rule or mere tactic for scientific theorizing. But Salmon himself comments that "one might wonder, in the light of [some of Reichenbach's remarks in 1951] whether his realism had not by that time been completely eviscerated" (p. 2).

41. I am thinking of his 1948 article on interpretation of quantum mechanics, "The Principle of Anomaly in Quantum Mechanics." See further my *Quantum Mechanics*, ch. 7, sec. 3.

42. See further my "World of Empiricism" on the relations between science and myth.

43. *New Testament and Mythology*, pp. 98–99. Bultmann adds, "Demythologizing seeks to bring out the real intention of myth, namely, its intention to talk about human existence as grounded in and limited by a transcendent, unworldly power, which is not visible to objectifying thinking." This refers to his project to woo theology away from objectifying inquiry.

Bibliography

Aerts, D., ed. *The White Book of "Einstein Meets Magritte."* Dordrecht: Kluwer, 1999.

Agazzi, E., ed. *The Problem of Reductionism in Science.* Dordrecht: Kluwer, 1991.

Al-Azm, S. *The Origins of Kant's Arguments in the Antinomies.* Oxford: Clarendon, 1972.

Albert, David. "Bohm's Alternative to Quantum Mechanics," *Scientific American,* May 1994.

——. *Quantum Mechanics and Experience.* Cambridge: Harvard University Press, 1992.

Anschutz, R. P. *The Philosophy of J. S. Mill.* Oxford: Clarendon, 1963.

Armstrong, David M. *What Is a Law of Nature?* Cambridge: Cambridge University Press, 1983.

——. *A Materialist Theory of Mind.* London: Routledge and Kegan Paul, 1968.

Armstrong, David M., and Norman Malcolm. *Consciousness and Causality.* Oxford: Blackwell, 1984.

Arnauld, Antoine, and Pierre Nicole. *Logic, or the Art of Thinking.* [Port Royal Logic] 5th ed. Ed. Jill V. Buroker. Cambridge: Cambridge University Press, 1996.

Ayer, Alfred J. *Philosophy in the Twentieth Century.* New York: Vintage, 1984.

Bacon, Francis. *Novum Organum, With Other Parts of the Great Instauration*. Trans. and ed. P. Urbach and J. Gibson. Chicago: Open Court, 1994.

——. *The Physical and Metaphysical Works of Lord Bacon*. Trans. and ed. J. Devey. London: Henry G. Bohn, 1856.

——. *The Works of Francis Bacon*. Ed. J. Spedding, R. E. Ellis, and D. D. Heath. London: Longman, 1857–74, in 14 vols. Reprint, Stutgart: Frommann-Holzboog, 1986.

Beck, Lewis White. *Kant's Latin Writings*. New York: Peter Lang, 1992.

Beckermann, Ansgar, Hans Flor, and Jaegwon Kim, eds.*Emergence or Reduction? Essays on the Prospects of Non-Reductive Physicalism*. Berlin: de Gruyter, 1992.

Bohr, Niels. *Physique Atomique et Connaissance Humaine*. Ed. and intro. Catherine Chevalley. Paris: Gallimard, 1991.

Bricmont, Jean. "Comment peut-on être 'positiviste'?" pp. 71–90 in Martens.

——. "Qu'est-ce que le matérialisme scientifique?" pt. 1, *La Raison* 441 (May 1999): 19–20; pt. 2, *La Raison* 442 (June 1999): 20–21.

Buber, Martin. *Eclipse of God*. Republished with new introduction. Atlantic Highlands, N.J.: Humanities, 1988.

Buekens, Filip. "Observing in a Space of Reasons." Typescript. 1996.

Bultmann, Rudolf. *Jesus Christ and Mythology*. New York: Charles Scribner's Sons, 1958.

——. *New Testament and Mythology and Other Basic Writings*. Ed. S. M Ogden. Philadelphia: Fortress, 1984.

Butts, R. E., and J. W. Davis. *The Methodological Heritage of Newton*. Oxford: Blackwell 1970.

Calvin, John. *The Institutes of Christian Religion*. Ed. T. Lane and H. Osborne. Grand Rapids, Mich.: Baker, 1996.

Carnap, Rudolf. [Aufbau] *The Logical Structure of the World and Pseudo-Problems in Philosophy*. Trans. Rolf A. George. Berkeley: University of California Press, 1967.

Chadwick, Owen. *The Secularization of the European Mind in the 19th Century*. Cambridge: Cambridge University Press, 1993.

Chalmers, David. *The Conscious Mind*. Oxford: Oxford University Press, 1996.

Chevalley, Catherine. Introduction to Bohr, *Physique Atomique.*

——. Introduction to van Fraassen, *Lois et Symétrie.* Paris: Vrin, 1994.

——. *Pascal: Contingence et Probabilité.* Paris: Presses Universitaires de France, 1995.

Christensen, S., ed. *Quantum Theory of Gravity.* Bristol: Hilger, 1984.

Churchland, Paul M., and Clifford A. Hooker, eds. *Images of Science: Essays on Realism and Empiricism, with a Reply by Bas C. van Fraassen.* Chicago: University of Chicago Press, 1985.

Copleston, Frederick. *A History of Philosophy.* New York: Doubleday, 1985.

Crasnow, Sharon L. "How Natural Can Ontology Be?" *Philosophy of Science* 67 (2000): 114–32.

Cushing, James T. *Quantum Mechanics: Historical Contingency and the Copenhagen Hegemony.* Chicago: University of Chicago Press, 1994.

Davidson, Donald. "The Very Idea of a Conceptual Scheme," *Proceedings and Addresses of the American Philosophical Association* 47 (1974): 5–20.

Davies, P. C. W. "Particles Do Not Exist," pp. 66–77 in Christensen, *Quantum Theory of Gravity.*

Delaney, C. F. *Science, Knowledge, and Mind: A Study in the Philosophy of C. S. Peirce.* Notre Dame, Ind.: University of Notre Dame Press, 1993.

Descartes, René. *Le Monde, ou, Traité de la Lumière.* Trans. and intro. Michael Sean Mahoney. New York: Abaris, 1979.

Dewey, John. "An Empirical Survey of Empiricisms," *Studies in the History of Ideas* 3 (1935): 3–22.

Dilthey, Wilhelm. *Selected Writings.* Ed. and trans. H. P. Rickman. Cambridge: Cambridge University Press, 1976.

Doppelt, Gerald. "The Naturalist Conception of Methodological Standards in Science," *Philosophy of Science* 57 (1990): 1–19.

Drake, Stillman. *Discoveries and Opinions of Galileo.* New York: Doubleday Anchor, 1957.

Earman, John. *A Primer on Determinism.* Dordrecht: Reidel, 1986.

——. *World Enough and Space-Time.* Cambridge: MIT Press, 1989.

Eco, Umberto. *The Name of the Rose*. Trans. W. Weaver. New York: Harcourt, Brace, Jovanovich, 1983.

Edgerton, S. Y. *The Heritage of Giotto's Geometry: Art and Science on the Eve of the Scientific Revolution*. Ithaca: Cornell University Press, 1991.

Elgin, Catherine Z. *Considered Judgment*. Princeton: Princeton University Press, 1996.

Empson, William. *Seven Types of Ambiguity*. London, 1930; reprint, New York: W. W. Norton, 1966.

Fackenheim, Emil L. *God's Presence in History: Jewish Affirmations and Philosophical Reflections*. New York: New York University Press, 1970.

Farber, M., ed. *Philosophical Essays in Honor of Edmund Husserl*. Cambridge: Harvard University Press, 1940.

Feyerabend, Paul K. "Classical empiricism," Feyerabend, *Problems of Empiricism*, pp. 34–51.

——.*Conquest of Abundance: A Tale of Abstraction Versus the Richness of Being*. Chicago: University of Chicago Press, 1999.

——. *Problems of Empiricism*. Philosophical Papers, vol. 2. Cambridge: Cambridge University Press, 1981.

——. *Realism, Rationalism, and Scientific Method*. Philosophical Papers, vol. 1. Cambridge: Cambridge University Press, 1981.

Fine, Arthur. "The Natural Ontological Attitude," pp. 83–107 in Leplin, *Scientific Realism*.

Foss, Jeffrey. "Materialism, Reduction, Replacement, and the Place of Consciousness in Science," *Journal of Philosophy* 92 (1995): 401–29.

Frege, Gottlob. *Collected Papers on Mathematics, Logic, and Philosophy*. Ed. Brian McGuinness Oxford: Blackwell, 1984.

——. Review of *Philosophie der Arithmetik*, by Edmund Husserl. *Zeitschrift fuer Philosophie und philosophische Kritik* (1894). Reprinted in his *Collected Papers*, pp. 195–209.

Friedman, Michael. *Foundations of Space-Time Theories*. Princeton: Princeton University Press, 1983.

——. *Kant and the Exact Sciences*. Cambridge: Harvard University Press, 1992.

Giere, Ronald. *Explaining Science: A Cognitive Approach*. Chicago: University of Chicago Press, 1988.

——. *Science Without Laws.* Chicago: University of Chicago Press, 1999.

Gillies, D. *Revolutions in Mathematics.* Oxford: Oxford University Press, 1992.

Glymour, Clark. "A Mind Is a Terrible Thing to Waste." Review of *Mind in a Physical World,* by Jaegwon Kim. *Philosophy of Science* 66 (1999): 455–71.

Goethe, Johann W. von. *From My Life: Poetry and Truth.* Trans. R. R. Heitner. Princeton: Princeton University Press, 1994.

Golding, William. *Free Fall.* New York: Harcourt, Brace, Jovanovich, 1959.

Guttenplan, S., ed. *A Companion to the Philosophy of Mind.* Oxford: Blackwell, 1994.

Hardwick, Charley D. *Events of Grace: Naturalism, Existentialism, and Theology.* Cambridge: Cambridge University Press, 1996.

Heidegger, Martin. *Being and Time.* Trans. J. Macquarrie and E. Robinson. New York: Harper and Row, 1962.

——. *An Introduction to Metaphysics.* Trans. R. Manheim. New York: Doubleday, 1961.

Hibben, John Grier. *The Problems of Philosophy.* New York: Charles Scribner's Sons, 1898.

Hilgevoort, Jan, ed. *Physics and Our View of the World.* Cambridge: Cambridge University Press, 1994.

Høeg, Peter. *The Woman and the Ape.* New York: Penguin, 1997.

Hull, D., M. Forbes, and K. Ohkruhlik, eds. *PSA 1992,* vol. 2. Evanston, Ill.: Northwestern University Press, 1993.

Hume, David. *A Treatise of Human Nature.* Ed. T. H. Green and T. H. Grose. London: Longmans, Green, 1874.

Husserl, Edmund. *The Crisis of European Sciences and Transcendental Phenomenology.* Trans. D. Carr. Evanston, Ill.: Northwestern University Press, 1970.

——. *Ideas: General Introduction to Pure Phenomenology.* Trans. W. R. Boyce Gibson. London: George Allen and Unwin, 1931.

——. *Philosophie der Arithmetik.* Halle: C. Pfeffer, 1891.

James, William. *The Meaning of Truth.* New York: Longmans, Green, 1909.

——. *Pragmatism.* Ed. B. Kuklick. Indianapolis: Hacket, 1981.

——. "The Sentiment of Rationality," pp. 63–110 in his *Will to Believe.*

——. "The Will to Believe," pp. 1–31 in his *Will to Believe.*

——. *The Will to Believe and Human Immortality.* New York: Dover Publications, 1956.

Jammer, Max. *The Concept of Mass.* Cambridge: Harvard University Press, 1961; reprint, New York: Harper and Row, 1964.

Kant, Immanuel. *Critique of Pure Reason.* Trans. N. K. Smith. New York: St. Martin's Press, 1965.

——. "On the Form and Principles of the Sensible and the Intelligible World [Inaugural Dissertation]," pp. 109–60 in Beck, *Kant's Latin Writings.*

Kim, Jaegwon. *Mind in a Physical World.* Cambridge: MIT Press, 1998.

Kitcher, Philip. "The Naturalist's Return," *Philosophical Review* 101 (1992): 53–114.

Kockelmans, J. J., ed. *Philosophy of Science—The Historical Background.* New York: Free Press, 1968.

Kuhn, Thomas. *The Copernican Revolution.* Cambridge: Harvard University Press, 1985.

——. "Reflections on My Critics," pp. 231–78 in Lakatos and Musgrave, *Criticism and the Growth of Knowledge.*

——. *The Structure of Scientific Revolutions.* 2d ed. Chicago: University of Chicago Press, 1970.

Lakatos, Imre, and Alan Musgrave, eds. *Criticism and the Growth of Knowledge.* Cambridge: Cambridge University Press, 1970.

Laudan, Larry. "Normative Naturalism," *Philosophy of Science* 57 (1990): 44–59.

——. *Science and Hypothesis.* Dordrecht: Reidel, 1981.

Leeds, Stephen. "Constructive Empiricism," *Synthèse* 101 (1994): 187–221.

Leibniz, G. W. *Leibniz: Selections.* Ed. P. P. Wiener. New York: Charles Scribner's Sons, 1951.

——. *New Essays on Human Understanding.* Trans. Peter Remnant and Jonathan Bennett. Cambridge: Cambridge University Press, 1982.

——. *The Philosophical Writings of Leibniz.* Ed. Mary Morris. London: J. Dent, 1934.

Leonardi, P., and M. Santambrogio, eds. *On Quine.* Cambridge University Press, 1995.

Leplin, Jarrett. "Renormalizing Naturalism," *Philosophy of Science* 57 (1990): 20–33.

——, ed. *Scientific Realism.* Berkeley: University of California Press, 1984.

Levi, Isaac. *The Enterprise of Knowledge.* Cambridge: MIT Press, 1980.

Levine, G., ed. *Realism and Representation.* Madison: University of Wisconsin Press, 1993.

Lewis, C. S. *The Discarded Image.* Cambridge: Cambridge University Press, 1964.

——. *Studies in Words.* Cambridge: Cambridge University Press, 1960.

Lewis, David K. "An Argument for the Identity Theory," *Journal of Philosophy* 63 (1966): 17–25; reprinted with additions in his *Philosophical Papers,* vol. 1.

——. "Attitudes de dicto and de se," *Philosophical Review* 88 (1979): 513–43.

——. *On the Plurality of Worlds.* Oxford: Blackwell, 1986.

——. *Parts of Classes.* Oxford: Blackwell, 1991.

——. *Philosophical Papers,* vols. 1 and 2. Oxford: Oxford University Press, 1983, 1986.

——. "Reduction of Mind," pp. 412–31 in Guttenplan, *Companion to the Philosophy of Mind.*

Locke, John. *An Essay Concering Human Understanding.* London: T. Longman, 1796.

Loeb, L. E. *From Descartes to Hume.* Ithaca: Cornell University Press, 1981.

Martens, Francis, ed. *Psychanalyse, que reste-t-il de nos amours?* Brussels: Revue de l'Université de Bruxelles, Editions Complexe, 2000.

Merleau-Ponty, Maurice. *Phenomenology of Perception.* Trans. C. Smith. London: Routledge and Kegan Paul, 1962.

Mill, John Stuart. *Auguste Comte and Positivism.* 2d ed. London: Traubner, 1866.

——. *Autobiography.* London: Longmans, Green, Reader, and Dyer, 1873.

——. *Collected Works of John Stuart Mill.* Ed. J. M. Robson and R. F. McRae. London: Routledge and Kegan Paul, 1974.

——. *A System of Logic Ratiocinative and Inductive.* 1843. Reprinted in Mill, *Collected Works.*

Neu, Jerome. *A Tear Is an Intellectual Thing: The Meanings of Emotion.* Oxford: Oxford University Press, 2000.

Newton, Isaac. *Principia: Mathematical Principles of Natural Philosophy and His System of the World.* Trans. Andrew Motte, ed. Florian Cajori. Berkeley: University of California Press, 1966.

Osler, M. J. *Divine Will and the Mechanical Philosophy.* Cambridge: Cambridge University Press, 1994.

Pais, A. *Niels Bohr's Times, in Physics, Philosophy, and Polity.* Oxford: Clarendon Press, 1991.

Pascal, Blaise. *Pensées.* Trans. A. J. Krailsheimer. Hammondsworth: Penguin, 1966.

Peirce, Charles Sanders. *Collected Papers,* vols. 5 and 6. Cambridge: Harvard University Press, 1972.

Perry, John. *The Problem of the Essential Indexical and Other Essays.* Oxford: Oxford University Press, 1993.

Philipse, Herman. "The Absolute Network Theory of Language and Traditional Epistemology," *Inquiry* 33 (1990): 127–78.

Piatelli-Palmerini, M., ed. *Livelli di Realtà.* Milan: Feltrinelli, 1984

Place, U. T. "Is Consciousness a Brain Process?" *British Journal of Psychology* 47 (1956): 44–50.

——. "Materialism as a scientific hypothesis," *Philosophical Review* 69 (1960): 101–4.

Plantinga, Alvin. *Warrant: The Current Debate.* Oxford: Oxford University Press, 1993.

——. *Warrant and Proper Function.* Oxford: Oxford University Press, 1993.

——. *Warranted Christian Belief.* Oxford: Oxford University Press, 1999.

Popkin, R. H. *The History of Skepticism from Erasmus to Spinoza.* Berkeley: University of California Press, 1979.

Pourciau, Bruce. "Intuitionism as a (Failed) Kuhnian Revolution in Mathematics." *Studies in the History and Philosophy of Science* 31 (2000): 297–329.

Priest, Stephen. *The British Empiricists: Hobbes to Ayer.* London: Penguin, 1990.

Putnam, Hilary. "After Empiricism," pp. 20–30 in Rajchman and West, *Post-Analytic Philosophy.*

——. *Renewing Philosophy.* Cambridge: Harvard University Press, 1992.

Quine, Willard V. "Epistemology Naturalized," pp. 69–89 in his *Ontological Relativity and Other Essays.*

——. *Ontological Relativity and Other Essays.* New York: Columbia University Press, 1969.

——. *Pursuit of Truth.* Cambridge: Harvard University Press, 1990.

Rajchman, John, and Cornell West, eds. *Post-Analytic Philosophy.* New York: Columbia University Press, 1985.

Reichenbach, Hans. *Experience and Prediction.* Chicago: University of Chicago Press, 1938.

——. *Modern Philosophy of Science.* Trans. and ed. Maria Reichenbach. London: Routledge and Kegan Paul, 1959.

——. "The Principle of Anomaly in Quantum Mechanics," *Dialectica* 2 (1948): 337–50.

——. "Rationalism and Empiricism: An Inquiry into the Roots of Philosophical Error," in his *Modern Philosophy of Science.*

——. *The Rise of Scientific Philosophy.* Berkeley: University of California Press, 1951.

Rescher, Nicholas. *The Heritage of Logical Positivism.* New York: University Press of America, 1985.

Richardson, Alan. "Philosophy as Science: The Modernist Agenda of Philosophy of Science, 1900–1950," forthcoming.

Rorty, Amelie, and Brian McLaughlin, eds. *Perspectives on Self-Deception.* Berkeley: University of California Press, 1988.

Rosenberg, A. "Normative Naturalism and the Role of Philosophy," *Philosophy of Science* 57 (1990): 34–43.

Russell, Bertrand. *A History of Western Philosophy.* New York : Simon and Schuster, 1972.

Salmon, Wesley. "Empiricism: The Key Question," pp. 1–21 in Rescher, *Heritage of Logical Positivism.*

Sanford, David. "The Problem of the Many, Many Composition Questions, and Naïve Mereology," *Nous* 27 (1993): 219–20.

Sartre, Jean-Paul. *The Emotions: Outline of a Theory.* Trans. B. Frechtman. New York: Philosophical Library, 1948.

Savitt, Steven. "Critical Notice of John Earman, *World Enough and Space-Time,*" *Dialogue* 31 (1992): 701–6.

———. "Selective Scientific Realism, Constructive Empiricism, and the Unification of Theories," *Midwest Studies in Philosophy* 18 (1993): 154–65.

Schaffner, Kenneth F., and Robert S. Cohen, eds. *PSA 1972.* Dordrecht: Reidel, 1974.

Scheinle, Friedrich. "Entering New Fields: Exploratory Uses of Experimentation," *Philosophy of Science* 64 (1997), S65–S74.

Sfendoni-Mentzou, Demetra, ed. *Aristotle and Contemporary Science,* vol 1. New York: Peter Lang, 2000.

Smart, J. J. C. *Essays Metaphysical and Moral.* Oxford: Blackwell, 1987.

———. "Materialism," pp. 203–214 of his *Essays Metaphysical and Moral.*

———. "Sensations and Brain Processes," *Philosophical Review* 68 (1959): 141–56. Revised version in Smart, *Essays Metaphysical and Moral,* pp. 189– 202.

Soames, Scott. *Understanding Truth.* New York: Oxford University Press, 1999.

Stapledon, T. J., ed. *The Question of Hermeneutics.* Dordrecht: Kluwer, 1994.

Strawson, Galen. "Real Materialism," forthcoming.

Stump, Eleonore. "Faith and the Problem of Evil." The Stob Lectures, Calvin College. Grand Rapids, Mich.: Calvin College, 1999.

———. "Non-Cartesian Substance Dualism and Materialism Without Reductionism," *Faith and Philosophy* 12 (1995): 505–31.

Styron, William. *Sophie's Choice.* New York: Modern Library, 1999.

Suppe, Frederick. "Credentialling Scientific Claims," *Perspectives on Science* 1 (1993): 153–203.

Suppes, Patrick. "Can Psychological Software Be Reduced to Physiological Hardware?" pp. 183–98 in Agazzi, *The Problem of Reductionism.*

Teller, Paul. "A Contemporary Look at Emergence," pp. 139–53 in Beckermann et al., *Emergence or Reduction?*

——. "Subjectivity and Knowing What It's Like," pp. 180–200 in Beckermann et al., *Emergence or Reduction?*

——. "Whither Constructive Empiricism?" *Philosophical Studies*, forthcoming 2001.

van Fraassen, Bas C. "Against Naturalized Empiricism," pp. 68–88 in Leonardi and Santambrogio, *On Quine.*

——. "Against Transcendental Empiricism," in Stapledon, *Question of Hermeneutics.*

——. "Belief and the Problem of Ulysses and the Sirens," *Philosophical Studies* 77 (1995): 7–37.

——. "Belief and the Will," *Journal of Philosophy* 81 (1984): 235–56.

——. "Bressan and Suppes on Modality," pp. 323–330 in Schaffner and Cohen, *PSA 1972.*

——. "Conditionalization, A New Argument For," *Topoi* 18 (1999): 93–96.

——. "Elgin on Lewis Putnam's Paradox," *Journal of Philosophy* 94 (1997): 85–93.

——. "Empiricism in the Philosophy of Science," pp. 245–308 in Churchland and Hooker, *Images of Science.*

——. "The False Hopes of Traditional Epistemology," *Philosophy and Phenomenological Research* 60 (2000): 253–80.

——. "From Vicious Circle to Infinite Regress, and Back Again," pp. 6–29 in Hull et al., *PSA 1992*, vol. 2.

——. "La fin de l'empirisme?" *Revue Philosophique de Louvain* 98 (2000): 449–79.

——. *Laws and Symmetry.* Oxford: Oxford University Press, 1989.

——. "Literate Experience: The [De-, Re-] Interpretation of Nature," forthcoming.

——. "The Manifest Image and the Scientific Image," pp. 29–52 in Aerts, *Einstein Meets Magritte.*

——. "The Peculiar Effects of Love and Desire," pp. 123–156 in Rorty and McLaughlin, *Perspectives on Self-Deception.*

——. "Putnam's Paradox: Metaphysical Realism Revamped and Evaded," *Philosophical Perspectives* 11 (1997): 17–42.

——. *Quantum Mechanics: An Empiricist View.* Oxford: Oxford University Press, 1991.

——. Review of *Pursuit of Truth,* by W. V. O. Quine. *Times Literary Supplement,* 10–16 August 1990.

——. *The Scientific Image.* Oxford: Oxford University Press, 1980.

——. "The Sham Victory of Abstraction." Review of *Conquest of Abundance,* by Paul Feyerabend. *Times Literary Supplement,* 23 June 2000.

——. "Sola experientia? Feyerabend's Refutation of Classical Empiricism," *Philosophy of Science* 64 (1997): S385–S95.

——. "Structure: Its Shadow and Substance," forthcoming.

——. "Sulla realtà degli enti matematici," pp. 90–110 in Piatelli-Palmerini, *Livelli di Realtà.*

——. "The Theory of Tragedy and of Science: Does Nature Have Narrative Structure?" pp. 31–59 in Sfendoni-Mentzou, *Aristotle and Contemporary Science.*

——. "Values and the Heart's Command," *Journal of Philosophy* 70 (1973): 5–19.

——. "The World of Empiricism," pp. 114–34 in Hilgevoort, *Physics and Our View of the World.*

——. " 'World' Is Not a Count Noun," *Nous* 29 (1995): 139–57.

——. "The World We Speak Of, and the Language We Live In," pp. 213–21 in *Philosophy and Culture: Proceedings of the XVIIth World Congress of Philosophy* (Montreal, 1983). Montreal: Editions du Beffroi, 1986.

van Fraassen, Bas C., and Jill Sigman. "Interpretation in Science and in the Arts," pp. 73–99 in Levine, *Realism and Representation.*

van Inwagen, Peter. *Material Beings.* Ithaca: Cornell University Press, 1990.

——. *Metaphysics.* Oxford: Oxford University Press, 1993.

Vargish, Thomas, and Delo E. Mook. *Inside Modernism: Relativity Theory, Cubism, Narrative.* New Haven: Yale University Press, 1999.

Vitzthum, Richard C. *Materialism: An Affirmative History and Definition.* Amherst, N.Y.: Prometheus, 1995.

Walsh, W. H. *Kant's Criticism of Metaphysics*. Edinburgh: Edinburgh University Press, 1975.

Weinberg, Steven. "The Revolution That Didn't Happen." Review of *The Structure of Scientific Revolutions,* by Thomas Kuhn. *New York Review of Books,* 8 October 1998.

Weyl, Herman. "The Ghost of Modality," in Farber, *Philosophical Essays.*

Wheeler, John. "Assessment of Everett's 'Relative State' Formulation of Quantum Theory," *Review of Modern Physics* 29 (1957): 463–65.

Whewell, William. "On the Nature and Conditions of Inductive Science," pp. 51–79 in Kockelmans, *Philosophy of Science.*

Whitrow, G.J. *Structure and Evolution of the Universe*. New York: Harper, 1959.

Woolhouse, Roger. *The Empiricists*. Oxford: Oxford University Press, 1988.

Index

romain.loriol@ens-lsh.fr